T0386063

Praise for *Building Justice*

"A beautifully written book explaining how Frank Iacobucci's vision and humanity merged seamlessly with his brilliance to make him one of Canada's best judges."

Rosalie Silberman Abella, Justice of the Supreme Court of Canada and Samuel and Judith Pisar Visiting Professor of Law, Harvard Law School

"Through an innovative braiding of interviews, stories, scholarly analysis, poetry, myths, and metaphors, Shauna Van Praagh presents a compelling account of one of Canada's most distinguished and accomplished jurists and in so doing reveals the multiple ways in which it is possible (although sometimes difficult) to practice law in the public interest."

Richard Devlin, Professor of Law, Schulich School of Law, Dalhousie University

"This is a remarkable story about an amazing Canadian and best of all, it's told in an accessible and engaging style, and with deep intelligence. A book worthy of its subject, a vivid portrait of Frank Iacobucci and his unique contributions to the country."

Sean Fine, Justice Writer, *The Globe and Mail*

"Frank Iacobucci has been an inspirational teacher, public servant, scholar, mediator, and jurist. Shauna Van Praagh brings together the melody of his life's work in this fine book."

Bob Rae, Canadian Ambassador to the United Nations

Building Justice

FRANK IACOBUCCI
AND THE LIFE CYCLES OF LAW

Shauna Van Praagh

ÆVO UTP

Aevo UTP
An imprint of University of Toronto Press
Toronto Buffalo London
utorontopress.com

© University of Toronto Press 2022

Library and Archives Canada Cataloguing in Publication
Title: Building justice : Frank Iacobucci and the life cycles of law / Shauna Van Praagh.
Names: Van Praagh, Shauna, author.
Description: Includes bibliographical references and index.
  Identifiers: Canadiana (print) 20220241325 | Canadiana (ebook) 20220241376 |
  ISBN 9781487566289 (cloth) | ISBN 9781487570057 (EPUB) |
  ISBN 9781487567927 (PDF)
Subjects: LCSH: Iacobucci, Frank. | LCSH: Lawyers – Canada – Biography. |
  LCSH: Law teachers – Canada – Biography. | LCSH: Judges – Canada –
  Biography. | LCGFT: Biographies.
  Classification: LCC KE416.I23 V36 2022 | LCC KF345.Z9 I23 V36 2022 kfmod |
  DDC 340.092–dc23

ISBN 978-1-4875-6628-9 (cloth)   ISBN 978-1-4875-7005-7 (EPUB)
                                     ISBN 978-1-4875-6792-7 (PDF)
Printed in Canada

We wish to acknowledge the land on which the University of Toronto Press operates. This land is the traditional territory of the Wendat, the Anishnaabeg, the Haudenosaunee, the Métis, and the Mississaugas of the Credit First Nation.

University of Toronto Press acknowledges the financial support of the Government of Canada, the Canada Council for the Arts, and the Ontario Arts Council, an agency of the Government of Ontario, for its publishing activities.

 Canada Council for the Arts   Conseil des Arts du Canada

 ONTARIO ARTS COUNCIL CONSEIL DES ARTS DE L'ONTARIO an Ontario government agency un organisme du gouvernement de l'Ontario

 Funded by the Government of Canada   Financé par le gouvernement du Canada   Canada

 FSC MIX Paper from responsible sources FSC® C016245

For all my students

Contents

Prologue – Foot Fragments and the Cathedral

One wall of the Rodin Museum in Paris is covered in foot fragments – pieces of sculpted human feet, some in sandals, some unshod, each unique, each suggestive of a once-attached or intended body at rest or on the go. Auguste Rodin is known, of course, for his finished sculptures; most visitors to the museum spend their time in the garden admiring the compelling curves of the complete, awesome statues in their realistic and, at the same time, symbolic poses. The foot fragments are humble pieces of art, not particularly special on their own. But, gathered together on a wall, they are beautiful, evocative, compelling.

Each foot fragment is subjected to the imagination of each viewer. We are invited to create stories, to follow elusive footprints, to see the entire sandal or bare foot even if it isn't there before us and then to envisage its owner. It is as if the sculpted human beings to which they belong are both invisible and present through these small pieces of themselves placed in juxtaposition with other small pieces and their respective people. And each piece is distinctive; in their collectivity, the foot fragments remind us to recognize the importance of the individual and to notice the ways in which each is placed in relationship to the other.

It is possible to imagine a similar wall display of the fragments not of different feet but of one person – not the neat pieces of a jigsaw puzzle waiting to be put together within a frame, but a collection of bits resembling shards labelled and numbered by an archeologist. Indeed, viewers might wonder whether the human subjects of a sculptor's work can be represented realistically as fragments just as much as full head-to-toe sculptures. Alternatively, they might ask whether the foot fragments, like the hand fragments on the facing wall – these life-like pieces of other people – are perhaps an evocative composite of Rodin himself, placed together to illustrate the depth and breadth of the artist's work.

In June 2017, the Honourable Frank Iacobucci turned 80. On the occasion of his birthday, I organized a colloquium entitled "To Be Frank." The title of the colloquium suggested there could be a collective Frank, a way to play a part in what "being Frank" signifies, a way to step into Frank's shoes. The format of the colloquium was conceived as an effective laboratory for exploring the listening, imagination, collaboration, and exercise of responsibility that a career of engagement with Canadian law and society entails. Invited contributors to the colloquium came from all stages of Frank Iacobucci's life and career: from his childhood in Vancouver, his practice as a young lawyer, his time at the University of Toronto and with the Federal Department of Justice, his work as a judge at the highest level of court, and his post-retirement engagement with Canada's Indigenous peoples. They were all asked to write short reflections on his impact with respect to their own projects and paths.[1]

What do people talk about when they talk about Frank Iacobucci? They call him intuitive, authentic, generous, a chronic teacher, a mensch; they talk about his sense of humour, his ethical rigour, his empathy, and his ability to encourage others. They offer accounts of Frank as student and teacher, adviser and decision-maker, planner and policy designer, supporter and team player, parent and partner. They recount how they have worked for him, learned from him, laughed with him, and been inspired by him. Like Rodin's foot fragments, the reflections offer a glimpse of the individuals who provided them. And like the foot fragments, their co-existence conveys both humanity and humility.

In the words of David Johnston, Governor General of Canada in 2017 at the time of the "To Be Frank" colloquium:

> I've long been an admirer of Frank's many exceptional qualities. He is a true renaissance man, warm and wise in equal measure. His career in legal practice, in postsecondary education, in public service and in the judiciary demonstrates his belief that experience in each sphere can lead to and reinforce success in the others. It also reflects his commitment to the greater good. A generous teacher and mentor, Frank has helped foster a generation of Canadian leaders in law ...
>
> Fairness, hard work, resilience, civility, innovation, compromise, excellence, openness and the absence of rigid class or hierarchical structures: these are the Canadian values we most celebrate, and they are a constant presence in Frank's story ... Instructive lessons can be extrapolated from his decades of distinguished service to Canada. Underlying it all is his philosophy and practice of giving back to community and country, his deep and abiding passion for law and his lifelong pursuit of justice. It's an example that has inspired many, myself included.

Instead of gathering fragments, one could certainly imagine turning the career path of Frank Iacobucci into one larger-than-life sculpture of a person known for his contributions over more than five decades to Canadian law, legal practice, public policy, and governance: "Le Juriste" as a complement to Rodin's *Le Penseur*.

The broad lines of the sculpture would trace his impressive and multi-faceted trajectory. Frank Iacobucci, a graduate of the University of British Columbia in Commerce and in Law, completed his Master of Laws (LLM) degree at Cambridge University and then, after a brief period in corporate practice in New York, joined the Canadian academy as a law professor at the University of Toronto where he later served as dean of Law, as provost, and – much later – as interim president. He was deputy minister of Justice during Meech Lake negotiations regarding the structure of federalism in Canada; he served as chief justice of the Federal Court of Canada for three years prior to being appointed in 1991 to the Supreme Court of Canada. Post retirement in 2004 from the Supreme Court, the Honourable Frank Iacobucci is best known for representing the Canadian government in negotiations leading to the 2007 settlement for survivors of Indian residential schools and the creation of the Truth and Reconciliation Commission.

But if we did try to create a biographical sculpture – an image of "The Jurist" as illustrated by the Honourable Frank Iacobucci – it might be hard to figure out how to represent the special fact that the chief justice of Canada welcomed this son of semi-literate immigrants to the Supreme Court in Italian as well as in French and English. It wouldn't be obvious how to include Nancy – his spouse, life partner, and primary legal consultant – in the work of art. It would be difficult to show his equal comfort in tennis clothes, a soccer uniform, an unpretentious professor's suit, and judicial robes. It would be impossible to capture the multi-dimensional ripple effect of his work as a lawyer and leader.

I am not a museum curator. But my objectives in this work are shaped by some of the sensibilities and skills that I imagine are required in designing a meaningful exhibit. While I aim to offer a picture of a particular individual, I have chosen to do so through fragments collected in collage format, understood in different ways by different viewers. I focus on Frank Iacobucci's footprints – tracing paths in various directions, indicative of the distinctive and yet dispersed impact that we can have on others through our shared projects. It is through others in his life that we see what it means "to be Frank" – at each of his stages, playing each of his roles, carrying out each set of responsibilities. As I did with the colloquium that brought together a diverse group of people with a diverse set of stories, I try to make space for many voices, many ways of learning from Frank's particular *rayonnement*, his way of being a jurist in the world.[2]

As a professor of law, I understand legal education to be grounded in the study of human communities and the interactions, institutions, and governance that sustain them. In this project, I suggest that we think about legal education in a fresh and inspiring way by taking seriously the potential of the individual as law creator and the power of a life story as legal source. The choices, actions, interactions in one person's life carry value and guidance, and are basic elements of lawmaking. And narratives by and about the individual, told and retold, sharpen our appreciation of what it means to learn, practice, and live law.

The most striking impact of the "To Be Frank" colloquium was on young people – law students who were meeting Frank Iacobucci for the first time. This book extends that impact beyond a closed birthday celebration to wide-open exploration and reflection. It speaks to readers who think they might want to be lawyers and to readers who are interested in what lawyers do; it should be relevant to readers immersed in legal education and practice, but also to those simply curious about the contributions to Canada and Canadians that this one individual has made.

Frank Iacobucci likes to tell a story of three workers. Asked what they were doing, the first replied, "I'm cutting stone." The second said, "I'm making $5 a day." The third announced, "I'm building a cathedral." The fact that a number of participants in the colloquium recounted the same story suggests that it's one of the favourites in the Iacobucci repertoire. It also underscores the staying power of a simple parable. The listener is called upon to consider her attitude, to realize that she's a member of a team, to see her daily work as a crucial part of a shared and very large project.

It is also a story that paradoxically warns against turning Frank Iacobucci into a hero, even if it is told in tribute to him. The stone-cutter is doing the same job as the cathedral builder, and all of them take home $5 a day to support their families. There's humility in every job – and no one builds a cathedral alone. Others in Frank's life build alongside him; there is a constant back-and-forth of tools and knowledge and support. Instead of a hero, the better image for Frank

Iacobucci, as revealed through the fragments, is that of mentor – the person who encourages the stonecutter to look up from time to time, who models what can be done with a little investment, who appreciates the various skills needed to move the cathedral from blueprint to realized structure.

The three workers provide the scaffolding for what follows. The stonecutter comes first – illustrating the importance of learning, of developing life skills, of moving through the stages of apprenticeship, of developing identity. The wage earner comes second – showing the necessity and value of practice, of teaching others, of sustaining strong teams. The cathedral builder comes third – shifting us to the plane of participation in grand dreams and projects of symbolic significance and human congregation. Rather than selecting one version of the worker as the ideal, I suggest that all three co-exist and indeed depend on each other as different stages of self-realization and approach to the task at hand.

Part I is entitled "Cutting Stone – Welcome to Law." It asks the question of what prepares someone for legal education by tracing Frank Iacobucci's trajectory to, and through, the formal study of law. Part II is entitled "$5 a Day – Lawyering in the World"; it responds to the question of what you can do with a law degree by piecing together Frank Iacobucci's varied job descriptions and achievements. Part III is entitled "Building a Cathedral – Called to Action." It begins with Frank Iacobucci's retirement from the Supreme Court and explores the question of what it means to serve as a jurist and to infuse one's work for justice with wisdom, care, and compassion.

How do individuals come to law, engage with central and defining issues as part of their legal education, and then set off as lawyers? How are our connections to law shaped – through our everyday lives, our institutions, and our formal and informal relationships? What burden do jurists carry on our shoulders – as citizens with specialized capacities to listen and respond to human stories, and to dream of, advocate for, and accompany the collective building of communities and cathedrals? These are the central themes and lines of inquiry captured by the following fragments of, by, and about the Honourable Frank Iacobucci. While the selection of Frank Iacobucci is justifiable on many levels, it is not meant to suggest that his stories and path are the only or best source for observations and insights related to legal education and practice. But – as we will see – they're pretty good. In Frank's words, "*it is easy to underestimate one's impact, and dangerous to overestimate.*"[3]

PART I

Cutting Stone – Welcome to Law

1

The Dean's Speech

In the final book[1] of the *Harry Potter* series, the Minister of Magic – taken aback by Hermione's precise knowledge of applicable rules – asks the young witch, "Are you planning to follow a career in Magical Law, Miss Granger?" "No, I'm not," retorts Hermione. "I'm hoping to do some good in the world!"

At the beginning of every fall semester, new law students – most who, like Hermione, hope to do some good in the world – are introduced to their first year of legal education with a formal welcome from the dean. Ingredients of the speech typically include insights into the particular law school community to which the students now belong, a reminder of the diverse paths that individuals have taken to get here, encouragement to enjoy a mix of academic and extra-curricular pursuits, and some hints of what lies ahead in terms of substance and schedule. Inspired by the words they hear on their first day, the students feel wary, excited, and hesitantly confident about this new adventure.

Over three decades ago, I sat with my new classmates in the Moot Court of the University of Toronto's Faculty of Law to be welcomed by the dean. In most of the Septembers since, I have joined my teaching colleagues in the front row of McGill's Moot Court, listening to the dean speak to generation after generation of incoming law students. As both student and teacher, I would challenge Hermione's assumption that doing good and practising law can't or don't fit together. Choosing an education and career in law, "magical" or not, can indeed go hand in hand with planning to make a positive contribution to the world, even if it's not easy from the beginning to see exactly what shape that contribution will take.

Law students arrive at the start of each academic year with varied and distinctive backgrounds and baggage. There is no prescribed academic path to law; instead, admissions committees consider indications of intellectual curiosity, academic ability, capacity for logical argumentation, and openness to challenging ideas and experience. There's no expected or shared pre-law knowledge, no entrance exam or boxes to tick off. No one asks if you hope to do good in the world. But if you end up in the Moot Court, you're ready. And all jurists – people who have studied law whether or not they practise as professional lawyers – have individual stories that explain why and how they ended up listening to that speech on the first day of law school.

How did Frank Iacobucci get to his own first day as a law student? At the age of 12, Frank had already made up his mind he would be a lawyer, thanks to the suggestion of his elementary school principal who knew him to be a good talker and fair with his classmates. Frank had no clear idea about what it was that lawyers do, let alone what it meant to be one. For him, his principal's comment just convinced him that, at the right time, he would go to school to study law. A few years later, when he shared his plan with one of his undergraduate professors, his prof's advice was honest and direct. That would be a mistake, he said: "you don't have the right name." Frank insisted on going anyway.

Frank often tells this story, turning it into more than a story about the law's unwelcoming stance vis-à-vis Italian Canadians in the late 1950s. For him, it is a story about and for anyone with a *funny sounding name,* anyone whose identity might be perceived as problematic or challenging by others, anyone determined to challenge rigid rules and established expectations. It is a reason to encourage young people to study law, or whatever else they're interested in, never dissuaded by the assumptions of others. And it's a reminder to be proud of funny sounding names and everything that comes along with them.

The story is connected to my own reasons for selecting Frank Iacobucci as my central protagonist. He was never my teacher, he wasn't the judge I clerked for, he was never a colleague or a boss. Instead, he was an informal mentor, the person who, as a university administrator, suggested to a young student – me, in a previous incarnation – that I study law. Neither he nor I worried about my funny sounding name.

I started law school in the fall of 1986 with a very fuzzy idea of what it would mean or feel like to find myself transformed into a law student. The two concrete pieces of insight that I held onto as I joined my new colleagues for the traditional welcome speech by the dean came from Frank Iacobucci. He had told me, first, that legal education would hand me power whether I wanted it – or deserved it – or not. People are prepared to give lawyers a lot of power, he said: Whether that's right is another issue, but it's important to recognize and appreciate the weight and influence of a law degree. Second, he said, be careful. Some knight on a white horse might come along while you're a law student, and you just might be tempted to ride away. Don't, he urged – stay focused, stay independent, and make sure you choose your own path.

Together, they constituted simple and solid counsel, not surprising from someone who had taught many law students and watched them trace their varied trajectories as young lawyers. An awareness of the power that comes with fluency in the language and forms of law is crucial – particularly, perhaps, if we care about the empowerment of all human beings. As for the warning about potential knights in shining armour, Frank Iacobucci didn't mean to tell an aspiring law student never to fall in love. Instead, his message was more complex and more constructive. Beware of taking what you think is an easy way out, the way that appears safe but is also submissive and even suffocating, the way that promises perfection but might deliver a dead end. Don't fall for fairy tales – whether about personal lives or professional pathways.

It was a message markedly tailored to a 21-year-old young woman in the mid 1980s, about to join a law class in which only 30 per cent of the students were female. If you're going to do this, then give it your all and show you can succeed – not all on your own, but never overshadowed or relegated to companion princess. Don't let others define your gifts, your contributions, your direction. This is your time to learn, to figure out who you are as a young lawyer, to question myths rather than lose yourself in them, to assert your own qualities and develop your own capacities.

Advice that gets remembered for over 30 years links two people together. It is central to the meaning of mentoring – given with care and support and the weight of responsibility. Mentors take time to listen, to follow, to contribute to the flourishing of the people they encourage and inspire. They engage in intergenerational investment; they select words and actions that guide and bolster and often lead by example.

If I were to reconstruct the welcome speech that Frank sat through as a law student in 1959 or the one I vaguely remember from 1986, I would find a way to insert the following messages. You will hear the stories of real people in arguments, through judgments, and embedded in scholarship; learn to listen, translate, and advocate. You will become a decision-maker and a team player; learn to acknowledge the viewpoints of others. You will recognize the exercise of power and see the need for change; learn to interpret principles, analyze policy, and question practice. And finally, remember where you came from, what you've learned, and how to behave with the people around you. You just might do some good in the world.

2

Frank's Facts

Frank Iacobucci was born in East Vancouver on 29 June 1937, to Gabriel and Rosina, who had immigrated separately from Italy in the 1920s (Abruzzo and Calabria, respectively) and were married in 1929. He was the third of four children: Danny and Teresa were older, and John was the youngest brother. While his father worked in a steel foundry, his mother, Rose, directed home and family. Frank was eight years old at the end of the Second World War, marked in Vancouver by the return of Japanese-Canadian internees and, to a lesser extent, their Italian-Canadian counterparts.

Frank discovered his aptitude for school early on and recounts that it was at his graduation ceremony from Grade 6 at Hastings School that he decided he would study law. From Templeton Junior High for Grades 7–9, he headed to Britannia High School where he graduated in 1955 with the Bronze Medal. Frank was also gifted, and perhaps even more determined, as an athlete. His principal sport was soccer, although he also played base-ball and basketball. By age 17, Frank was called up to the semi-pro Pacific Coast Soccer League, and he was later a star player for UBC's varsity soccer team.

Frank didn't leave home in 1955 to go to university. He stayed in Vancouver for seven years as a student at the University of British Columbia. His first year of undergraduate study was a general arts program, followed by three years to obtain a bachelor of commerce (BComm) degree, graduating in 1959. In the fall of 1959, he started law school at UBC and, in 1962, graduated with an LLB (bachelor of laws), with the distinction of finishing second in his class. He had spent one summer travelling in Europe with his friends – an experience that made him keen to study abroad – so, in his third year in law, he applied to the Master of Laws program at Cambridge University and for scholarships that could get him there.

Frank left for England in the fall of 1962, with the support of a Newton W. Rowell Fellowship in International Law (awarded by Cambridge University to an incoming student) and a Mackenzie King Travelling Scholarship (awarded to a Canadian leaving the country to pursue graduate studies). He graduated from Cambridge in 1964 with an LLM degree and a Diploma in International Law. His thesis was entitled "The Proposed International Disarmament Organization: Some Legal Problems." While at Cambridge, he tutored at St. John's College and, early on, met his future wife, Nancy. Nancy Elizabeth Eastham (AB, Mt Holyoke; LLB, Harvard; Dip Int'l Law, Cambridge) was also a law graduate whose academic path had led her from Cambridge, Massachusetts, where she had studied at Harvard, to Cambridge, England, for a Diploma in International Law. Nancy and Frank were married in Andover, Massachusetts on 31 October 1964 – the Hallowe'en after their graduation.

3

Prelude to a Legal Education:
Frank's Stories

Messy Sandwiches

When I was growing up, my mother used to make my lunch and send it with me to school. Every day, I would open my lunchbox and find a big sandwich overflowing with tomatoes, eggs, peppers, cheese, prosciutto. Those sandwiches were so delicious and so messy – and so Italian! They were impossible to eat neatly, not like peanut butter or bologna on pre-sliced bread that all the other kids had. I felt like everyone was watching me at lunchtime. There was no way to hide the fact that I came from an Italian family.

This is one of Frank Iacobucci's stories. He tells it to describe what it was like growing up Italian in East Vancouver in the 1940s and 50s. He tells it to university students, reaching out to young people who have grown up in all kinds of families. I once listened to him tell it to a group of Asian Canadian lawyers, all of whom laughed and nodded their heads at what was obviously a widely shared if culturally modified experience. He tells it to share the mixed feelings of pride, resignation, discomfort, and developing confidence connected to coming of age with a particular community-based identity. Each time he tells it, he doesn't pretend he never coveted those peanut butter-on-sliced-bread sandwiches. And each time he tells it, he conjures up detailed memories that bring to life the look and taste and bittersweet delight of the lunches he carried to school and ate day after day.

Frank Iacobucci can't present himself without sharing his stories. Telling those around him about his mother and father, his brothers and sister, and the friends he grew up with is his way of underscoring the importance of where he comes from. Like anyone, Frank chooses the stories he tells and retells. Our stories situate us; they are somehow meant to explain the actions and decisions we've taken; they shape the relationships that stretch back to our childhood and forward to our own children and grandchildren. Indeed, as they get retold by the next generation, they serve as guideposts for its members. Frank's stories are borrowed and told by his children – Andrew, Edward, and Catherine – to their own children for whom their always-funny grandfather is simply "Bucci."

Frank's mother, Rosina, left her parents in Magone, Cosenza, in the Italian province of Calabria, to come to Canada at the age of 16 in the care of her uncles. Once there, settled in Vancouver, she refused to marry the much older man they had chosen for her. *I wish she had told me that story while she was still alive. I am so impressed with how much courage that must have taken. I would have liked to tell her that – that I thought she was really brave.*

Frank's father, Gabriel, arrived in Vancouver at the age of 19 from Cepagatti, Pescara, in the province of Abruzzo. Illiterate as a younger teenager in Italy, he had been absolutely overwhelmed one Sunday by the beauty of a girl he had spotted in church. He asked a friend to write a note on his behalf and, during Mass the following week, he passed the note along to the young woman. The note was crude, the girl and her mother were horrified. The result of the incident was that Gabriel became determined to read.

Without permission from his father, Gabriel sold some grain from the family farm in order to pay for evening lessons – an arrangement that was decisively ended by Gabriel's father when the teacher turned up at the house to suggest that his student be sent to school. Without any hope of changing or directing his own future, Gabriel left for Canada. *He never really learned to read … I think he ended up able to read a little English. I know he could write his name.*

At first Gabriel found work as a lumberjack (*at 5 feet 5 inches tall!*) in central British Columbia. Later, when he moved to Vancouver, he rented a small apartment from a fellow Italian. And there he met and fell in love with the landlord's niece. Gabriel and Rosina were married and moved to the east end of the city. He worked as a labourer in the steel foundry; she raised goats, rabbits, chickens, and four Canadian children.

There were no books in our house, other than a Bible in Italian. It had been a gift from the evangelical preacher who visited our house and convinced my parents to make the switch from the Catholic Church. My parents couldn't read it. Neither could I. People often think that I must have been baptized and raised a Catholic – but I wasn't. People also think I grew up speaking Italian – but I didn't. My parents insisted that we speak English at home. They wanted us to succeed, to fit in, not to stand out too much.

When Frank talks about his father, he focuses on how hard Gabriel worked. As recounted by Frank's own children when they share the family stories, Gabriel was the antithesis of a complainer. Andrew, the eldest, and Catherine, the youngest, together recall the tales they grew up with:

"The stories are legion, but one is particularly remarkable. Gabriel worked for many years in the steel foundry and was a formidable worker and a natural leader. As foreman, he would regularly work double shifts when less dependable workers failed to show. Not easy to do, given the incredible heat in the forge area where he worked. We are told he once worked 40 hours straight after successive no-shows, a feat we find hard to fathom.

"Many years later, Dad by utter coincidence met the owner of the foundry where Gabriel had worked. The erstwhile owner was in his 80s at the time and was reminiscing fondly about the work ethic of the men who had worked with him over the years. Unprovoked and without knowing who Dad was or realizing his relationship with Gabriel, he went on to single out our grandfather as the paragon. None of us was there at the time, but can only imagine how moved he must have been to hear this posthumous praise of his father!"

The pride and awe for Frank's father goes hand in hand with Frank's marked insistence that his own children would never even contemplate a similar path. I have talked with Frank about the sometimes trying experience of parenting a first son, something we share given my own three boys. He remembered a moment when Andrew encountered academic difficulty: *I was scared that he would end up in shirtsleeves.* The worst fate for the next generation of Italo-Canadians in the Iacobucci family would be to fail at school and to work in manual labour. Gabriel would probably agree.

"As Dad tells it," Andrew and Catherine continue, "Rose was in many ways the real brains of the family. The story he often tells is of Gabriel breaking the news to his wife that he had spent his last penny on his only daughter Teresa's wedding. Rose answered that, unbeknownst to her husband, she had stashed away many thousands of dollars in anticipation of this very eventuality. The news apparently reduced Gabriel to tears. She went on to buy and rent out a half dozen or some homes over the years (all paid with "cash money" of course) with the result that, despite their humble beginnings, the family never really had to worry about money."

Rose was also the one who loved to laugh. Andrew and Catherine recall: "Another favourite was when the youngest brother, John, had repeatedly refused to go to bed and had frustrated Rose to the point where she grabbed a nearby broom and thumped the body lying in bed that she assumed was John pretending to be asleep. It turns out that the person she was hitting (gently we hope) was Dad – he and John shared a bed – who had been fast asleep up to the moment he was bashed on the rear end with a broomstick! When she realized her mistake, she burst into gales of laughter. Dad was less amused – and John, of course, was in the closet giggling. Later, John would often quip that the name Iacobucci means "anything for a laugh' in Italian." (Andrew and Catherine Iacobucci)

One of the stories Frank most enjoys telling about his mother illustrates her good humour combined with canny intelligence. Mentored by Mrs. Brown across the street, Mrs. Iacobucci grew beautiful flowers in the front yard. But, when the family's nanny goat got loose and ate up Mrs. Brown's rose garden, it was just too much for an otherwise friendly neighbour.

Mrs. Brown called the police. One of the officers looked down at my mother, standing at 4 feet 10 inches tall, and asked with a Scottish burr whether she owned a goat. Yes, came the answer. Did the goat eat Mrs. Brown's roses? Yes again. And what is your name? Mrs. Mackenzie, replied my mother. The cops collapsed with laughter and left.

The story testifies to more than Rosina Iacobucci's quick wit and love of laughter. There she was, testing the rules by keeping the goat in the first place, able to figure out how to accept responsibility while at the same time avoiding embarrassment and even potential punishment. No doubt she still had to make amends to Mrs. Brown. But she held her own, turned what could have been a very unpleasant confrontation into a family story-telling treasure, and above all managed to protect the badly behaved goat!

Carolyn Tuohy, Professor Emerita at University of Toronto's School of Public Policy and Governance, writes about storytelling and the development of empathy through narrative. "Narratives may be organic or crafted, although this distinction is best thought of as a continuum rather than a dichotomy." She connects her reflections on the power of narrative to the stories told by her colleague, Frank Iacobucci:

"Frank loves stories. And that is more than a personality trait: it reveals a fundamental dimension of his character. Much has been said about Frank's capacity for consensus building. I suspect that is because he sees not only the principles in play in any given case (which he most surely does) but because he also sees the context, the lived experience of the people before him. In other words, he understands their stories. This is a human quality much needed in public policy.

"Narratives are ubiquitous in our lives. They are a distinctive form of discourse: a narrative takes the form of a story that engages the imagination by appealing to aspects of lived experience. It has a story-telling arc, which may or may not be chronological, in which tension builds, crests and subsides. It typically involves the personification of forces in characters who (individually or as groups) may be heroes, villains, or victims. By sharpening certain elements of reality and suppressing others, it can serve both as a means of communication (as a form of rhetoric) and as a method of cognitive organization in the face of ambiguity or complexity." (Carolyn Tuohy)

Identity, belonging to family, doing the right thing, finding joy in everyday encounters: all are captured by the sandwich story, the foundry, the roses. All underscore the importance of knowing your roots, your heritage, and the direction you're headed in.

None of Frank Iacobucci's three children, Andrew, Edward, and Catherine, took messy Italian sandwiches to school. None of them lived through the acute feelings of self-consciousness that accompanied lunchtime day after day. None was the first in their family to go to university. None grew up with a goat in the backyard. But all of them have absorbed the Iacobucci stories; all of them connect Frank's life narrative to the tales he tells of growing up; all of them are entrusted with passing them on and turning them into the family patrimony.

From their grandmother, Rose, comes the value of laughter and the central importance of education. From Gabriel, their Iacobucci grandfather, comes dedication to the task, anchored in honesty and ethical behaviour. And their father, Frank, manifests all of that in his easy warmth with other people, the way he invites others to tell their own stories, to reflect on how they grew up, to figure out how they situate themselves – whether in the school lunchroom or in working out differences or in articulating plans for the future.

Edward, the second of the three Iacobucci children – like Frank, neither the first nor last in the family but comfortably in the middle and, also like Frank, a law professor and dean – reflects on the way people talk about his father: "In the Canadian legal landscape, it turns out that Iacobucci is not a common surname. In Abruzzese law circles, it may be different, but in Canada, trust me, it is unusual. It therefore cannot be all that surprising that when I am introduced to a Canadian lawyer, he or she often asks whether I have some relationship with the professor/justice/lawyer of the same last name …

"This is all, to be clear, predictable, understandable, and entirely unobjectionable. Given our distinctive surname, and my lack of imagination in choosing a career path (lawyer, ok; law professor, perhaps; law professor at U of T, a bit much; Law dean at U of T, staggeringly uncreative …), it would be surprising if it were otherwise. Yes, at times, it would be nice to make a first impression that is less connected to my father, but I also recognize that I benefit from a favourable presumption. Because, to a person, the response to my Dad is not just favourable, but over the top admiring, warm, affectionate, slightly awed; pick a superlative …"

"What is striking is not just how many people like Dad, but how many people feel an important connection with him. He has played some significant part of countless lives of people that I've encountered. Here is my best guess as to why. Yes, he has many of the qualities that you would expect from popular people: a good sense of humour, good judgment, humility, etc. But the key to the esteem in which he is held is fundamentally straightforward: he likes people. He believes that they are good, and that they have something important to offer. He connects with people because he is genuinely interested in them and is happy to help them where he can." (Edward Iacobucci)

Don't Bring Shame

When Frank was born, he wasn't christened. His parents simply named him Francesco Iacobucci, ignoring warnings from two Catholic priests that their baby was destined to purgatory. By the time Frank, their third child, arrived on 29 June 1937, Rosina and Gabriel had turned their back on the Church, uninspired by the Latin Mass they couldn't understand.

They had been persuaded by Mr. Hall, a friendly evangelist preacher in their Vancouver neighbourhood, to join a newly created Baptist congregation of previously Catholic Italian Canadians.

The Italian Bible in their home was a special gift from Mr. Hall. Even if Frank remembers that it remained unread, it symbolized the enthusiasm with which the Iacobuccis welcomed a new form of joyous and fervent worship in their lives. And its very presence – literally on a shelf and metaphorically in family history – stood for right and wrong, for faith and the bonds of community, for adherence to strong and unshakeable values.

I got my values from my mother. There were three things that mattered, three things I knew I had to do. First, get an education; second, work hard; third, don't bring shame to the family. Don't bring shame to the family ... not "try to succeed" or "make sure you excel" or "bring honour to your family" ... just don't bring shame.

This is the foundation for Frank – the solid stone base for what his colleague Carolyn Tuohy might call the storytelling arc of his narrative. It's unlikely that his mother repeated the three things in a mantra-like list day in, day out. But, regardless of how they were articulated, they instilled themselves in Frank's consciousness; these are his pillars of character and vocation.

He often repeats them, and the people who hear them can often make connections to their own childhoods and upbringing. When I related Frank's listing of family values in a lecture at Hebrew University, one listener – Allen Zysblat, a retired Canadian law professor – remembered hearing precisely the same message as he grew up in a Polish Jewish immigrant family. Another – Diana Muntayer, a young Palestinian woman living in East Jerusalem – couldn't get over the fact that her parents said exactly the same thing over and over again to their children. You learn early on that you represent your family in the world, you understand from a young age that your family belongs to a community determined to thrive.

The first day I went to school, I got the strap. I was six, and I was very excited about starting grade one. We took out our brand new scribblers and opened them to the first clean page on top. The boy sitting next to me took his pencil and drew a big X on my page. So I bopped him one. The teacher, Miss Shaw, turned around just as I was bopping. I got called up to the front and was given the strap on my hand. I think I must have been crying when I sat down again. The teacher came and asked me why I had done what I did. So I showed her the X so she would understand. But I didn't think my mother would forgive me for getting into trouble on my very first day. I was scared I had brought shame to the family.

Frank received a reprimand, he learned how not to react too fast when others did the wrong thing, and, most importantly, he was forgiven and allowed to start again. He tells the story without any real regret at what he did, even as he accepts that growing up means figuring out more effective ways to point out what isn't right. And he tells the story without any ongoing resentment at what the teacher did, instead acknowledging her responsibility for implementing consequences.

The first day of school was, for Frank as for most of us, an introduction to life beyond family. His teacher now co-existed with his parents as the adults whose words and directives and example mattered, and who exercised considerable and concrete authority. In that very first interaction with his teacher, he probably realized that being a child subjected to an adult's power can feel unfair. But he also realized that Miss Shaw would listen to him and make sure he had a place in the classroom. When he recounts the trauma of day one, Frank adds: *I think my teachers turned into mentors for me from then on.*

My teachers were pretty special along the way. I had a lot of helping hands. For me, my inner desire to do well came from home. Encouragement and support came from school. I think my high school teachers were just the most outstanding teachers I had – those women were stars. I lived in an environment where kids got into trouble. There were people in my older brother's cohort who did time in jail. I think my teachers – along with sports – kept me on track.

As a law professor, I always made sure my students knew I was on their side. I was there for them. After my own family – and we are immensely proud of

our children – come my students. I take pride in being a supporter and par-
ticipant in their journeys. It's one of the great returns that come from teaching.

Get an education, work hard, and, above all, don't bring shame to the family. Along with parents, teachers are the primary individuals charged with bringing us up, providing life lessons, accompanying and guiding us, and exercising authority and responsibility. Frank discovered that he liked school and could excel, that he was willing to work hard at the things he cared about, and that his performance as a student made his parents proud. Much later, he realized how crucial his teachers had been in ensuring not only that he adhere to Iacobucci family dictates, but that he embark on his own journey.

Soccer and the Lemonade Stand

While the weekdays of Frank's existence as of age six were taken up with school, afternoons and weekends were primarily devoted to sports. For his parents, Sunday might have remained a day of rest and prayer; for him, it was spent ideally on the soccer pitch. He played baseball and basketball too, but the "beautiful game" – football, called soccer in North America – was where he excelled. *I was a good little soccer player – small and fast and a playmaker. That was my job – to make the plays.*

The playmaker has to be a talented player and a generous member of the group – willing to pass to teammates and, above all, trusted by the others. The goalkeeper might have the potential for stardom but carries a particular and lonely responsibility; the role of principal scorer comes with intense flashes of fame and accomplishment. It's the playmaker in the middle of the field who helps ensure the success of the whole team.

Quotes from individuals immersed in the game help convey the intensity of the world of soccer, in particular for young players like Frank. They capture the ways in which they grew up kicking a soccer ball, playing with others, and learning lessons with resonance on and off the pitch.

In his foreword to the book *A Beautiful Game*,[2] Arsène Wenger asserts: "[F]ootball is a common language and a culture shared: joy, passion, knowing what it is to be in a team; an escape, an inspiration, an affirmation of identity … The game is at the heart of growing up, at the heart of life itself, for millions of children all over the world."[3] Austrian footballer Emanuel Pogatetz agrees: "I don't ever want to lose that love I had for football when I first started to play, when I was a boy."[4]

One of the greatest Italian players, Fabio Cannavaro, describes growing up as a young footballer playing on the streets of Naples: "You get used to having to be alert to everything, to seeing things quickly, to being really tuned in. You never turn your back or look down at the ground … if you drop your guard someone will take advantage, take the ball from you. You have to make sure you're in control … We played because we enjoyed it, because we loved the feeling of winning. You know, we played for the chance to go home happy, thinking: 'I won' or 'I scored' or 'I played really well.'"[5]

Gilberto Silva, from Brazil, talks about his education in football: "I have learnt so many things *from* football as well. It was one of the reasons why my childhood was full of so much happiness even though the conditions we lived in weren't so good. I don't just mean that I learnt the rules of the game. Look at those in a different way and you see they are rules of life too: when I was young, of course I wanted to win, but I think I understood from early on that to lose sometimes is part of the game too … You must respect the other team you're playing against and respect your own teammates too."[6]

Just like professional footballers, Frank, the little playmaker, loved the feeling of winning. He loved to get laughs in the classroom, he loved to excel, and he loved to be cheered on. But his soccer career also taught him – again like professional footballers – how to lose. He learned how to accept the score, how to pick himself up, how to pull together with his team and aim to win again, how to prevent inevitable losses from feeling like or turning into insurmountable failures.

I'll never forget messing up by giving the other team its winning goal. We lost the championship because of me. It felt terrible but I think it's one of the experiences that taught me how to keep going. There are lots of times in my career when I was reminded of how you can do your best and still get a goal for the other side.

One of Frank's teammates had kicked the ball out of bounds on their side. The referee called a corner for the other team. Frank lined up with the others in front of their goal, all in defence mode. And then, when the ball came at them, Frank headed it – in the wrong direction. The goalkeeper for his team couldn't reach it. Officially listed as "OG," for "own goal," the goal went to the other team, and they won 1–0.

I asked an 18-year-old competitive soccer player to talk about how it feels to do what Frank did. You feel devastated and guilty, he told me. You feel like you've failed everyone. Even if people say it's OK and it's not your fault, everyone's really thinking, "Crap, we lost because of him." But it doesn't bring shame to the team – just disappointment. It definitely didn't count as bringing shame to the family – particularly given the fact that Frank's mother didn't follow her son's soccer career with close attention or understanding. It can happen, it does happen – even in the World Cup – and you learn that it's not the end of the world.

There were other ways in which football-soccer formed part of Frank's education: ways in which it made players like him alert to everything, ways in which it served as a language or culture to bring people together even briefly. Frank didn't become a professional player moving around the country or the world. But the game did take him out of Vancouver and away from home.

When I was working on the Indian Residential School Settlement in 2005, we visited the St. Mary's Residential School in Mission, B.C. We got there, and I suddenly realized I had been there before. I was ten years old and our team went to Mission to play soccer against them. I remembered that they didn't have good equipment, that the kids on their team seemed sad.

Established by the Oblate Order of the Roman Catholic Church, St. Mary's Indian Residential School opened its doors in Mission, British

Columbia, in 1861. One hundred years later, the Catholic school closed down; it was re-opened as a government-run school with the same name and was in operation until 1984. A new gymnasium was built in the late 1950s, ten years after the boys' soccer team played against Frank's visiting team.

The grounds of the original Catholic Mission school have now been turned into the Fraser River Heritage Park, and the buildings of the government school given to the Stó:lō nation. The Mission school students who played soccer at age 10 became some of the survivors for whom the Indian Residential School Settlement was negotiated and whose stories informed the work of the Truth and Reconciliation Commission almost seven decades later.

A snapshot of Frank's childhood comes from his oldest friend, Walter Podovsky: "Frank and I were born in the same month and year in the working-class area of Vancouver ... I believe that playing sports, joining the Vancouver Boys Club, and surrounding ourselves with good friends were the significant factors that helped us develop in our youth.

"One of my favourite memories with my friend Frank takes me back to 1949. Frank and I became business partners; we pooled our financial resources and opened a lemonade stand on Commercial Drive just steps from Frank's house. Unfortunately, the business didn't succeed and only lasted a few hours." (Walter Podovsky)

The short-lived Iacobucci-Podovsky enterprise depended on the pooled energies of two ambitious twelve-year-old boys for whom the sidewalks and streets of the neighbourhood constituted their growing up space. Frank and Walter, classmates from grades 7 through 12, walked or took the streetcar to school every day. Walter remembers that the girls at school appreciated Frank's sense of humour and head of curly black hair, and that Frank was class president in grade 8 and recipient of a Britannia High School medal for academic achievement combined with all-round ability. He also recalls the time the two boys graduated from making lemonade to trying out Gabriel Iacobucci's homemade wine when no one was home: a significant but less than happy experience.

My parents lived in the east end of Vancouver. Some people called this the wrong side of the tracks. But I call it the poor side of the tracks. We had English, Irish, Ukrainian, German, Yugoslav neighbours … in short, we practised multiculturalism before the term was coined. A lot of us had funny-sounding names.

My brother, Danny, played with Bill Esson and Dave Barrett on McSpadden Street, the street where I was born. Bill's family was Scottish; they owned a bakery. Dave's was Jewish; they were fruit-sellers. Bill Esson became chief justice of the British Columbia Supreme Court, and Dave Barrett became premier of British Columbia. Most people didn't become famous. But it goes to show you how far you could go.

My parents moved from there to nearby 5th Avenue, which is where I grew up … near Commercial Drive and not too far from where I went to school: Hastings, Templeton Junior High and then Britannia High School, one of the oldest in Vancouver.

Together, Frank and Walter used to arrive late to class at Britannia on October afternoons after eating lunch at Walter's house and watching the World Series; Walter rooted for the Brooklyn Dodgers, Frank cheered for the New York Yankees. And together, the young Iacobucci and Podovsky were soccer players: members of their high school soccer team the year it won the BC High School Championship, and of the "Daytona 64" team in the Vancouver and District Soccer League. For Frank and Walter – classmates, teammates, and neighbours – involvement in sports combined love for the game, the celebration of individual talent, and respect for the team. You could play no matter what your name was, just like you could live and thrive in East Van in the 40s and 50s wherever you came from and wherever you were headed.

At age 80, Walter was still close to Frank: "I am happy to say that Frank has not changed over the years. I am certain if we were to try hard, and put our minds together, we could make that lemonade stand on Commercial Drive a break-even investment." (Walter Podovsky)

Mistaken Identity

In high school, I got called up to the Pacific Coast Soccer League to play semi-pro soccer. What I remember is the story in the local paper about Frank Yakabuchi — the first Japanese-Canadian kid to make it to that level. Throughout my life, people have heard my last name and thought I was Japanese. It started back when I was playing soccer in Vancouver.

Frank relishes the mix-up in identity with a sense of humour, combined with respect for the Japanese-Canadian community to which he never actually belonged. Finding out that "Yakabuchi" was actually Iacobucci and Italian was an experience for others that Frank watched play out over and over again. He didn't quite set up the play, but he enjoyed surprising the people around him by turning out not to be what others expected or took for granted.

Marvin Storrow, a Vancouver friend and UBC classmate, tells his own version of the mix-up: "Before I met Frank, I had heard a lot about him and became quite anxious to meet the young man who I thought was a Japanese boy. This was just after the Second World War, and the Japanese internees were being released, and I thought that his last name was Japanese. We finally met on the soccer pitch in 1947, and it didn't take more than a minute to realize that the star of the other team was the Frank Iacobucci I had heard about ... and he wasn't Japanese." (Marvin Storrow)

Frank Iacobucci was eight years old as the Second World War came to an end. He remembers going with his mother to check in with the RCMP, as required of members of the Italian-Canadian community, declared "enemy aliens" by the War Measures Act. In 1940s Vancouver, there was an obvious connection between Japanese Canadians and Italian Canadians, both targeted as suspect communities and both subject to efforts to contain and restrict them. And yet Frank acknowledges that the experience of Italians in Canada was nowhere near as horrendous as that of their Japanese counterparts.

Shiyuze Takashima, the Japanese-Canadian artist and author of *A Child in Prison Camp*,[7] writes from the compelling perspective of a young girl interned with her sister, Yuki, and their parents:

> I often wonder about this war. The Japanese are my father's and mother's people. Strange to be fighting them.... I ask father, "Why are we fighting?" "For land and other things," father replies. "This is why we are here." "But I'm not Japanese like you. I was born here. So were you." I look at Yuki. She says, "That's nothing – a Jap is a Jap, whether you're born here or not!" "Even if I change my name?" "Yes, you look oriental, you're a threat." "A threat? Why?"
>
> "God only knows!" Yuki replies. "It's mostly racial prejudice, and jealousy. Remember we had cleared the best land all along the Fraser Valley. Good fisherman. This causes envy, so better to kick us out. The damn war is just an excuse. Dad knows. The West Coast people never liked the orientals. 'Yellow Peril' is what they call us."

Some 22,000 Japanese Canadians were living in British Columbia at the time of the attack on Pearl Harbor; by the spring of 1942, they were all on the move to internment camps in the interior of the province. Not until April 1949 were they officially granted freedom of movement and allowed to move back to the coast.[8] A young Italian-Canadian soccer star with a challenging name was surprising in 1950s Vancouver. For a Japanese-Canadian child to make it to semi-professional competitive soccer in the province by that time would have been truly remarkable.

What's in a name? The mistake made in the context of the Pacific Coast Soccer League was one made decades later by Raji Mangat, one of Frank's law clerks at the Supreme Court of Canada. She reflects on the assumptions she made before knowing how to spell his last name, and on how mistakes can open up opportunities for learning and exchange.

"My first-year notes from law school were peppered with references to cases authored by the Honourable Justice Frank Yakibuchi, a man about whom I created an elaborate personal mythology: I imagined him to be the first visible minority, Japanese-Canadian judge on the Supreme Court of Canada.

"From my first days of law school, Justice Frank Yakibuchi was the most fascinating of the nine members of Canada's highest court to me, with all due respect to the other eight. In my imagination, Frank Yakibuchi was among the first or second generation of his family born in Canada, as either his parents or grandparents had immigrated to Canada from Japan, and they had worked hard and sacrificed so that he and later generations of Yakibuchis would have access to better opportunities. I imagined him to be smart, not arrogant, good-humoured, kind and, of course, scrupulously fair. I imagined that like me, he straddled two worlds – a home life stitching together foreign languages, foods and rituals, and an outside life where identities were shaped by finding common ground on the playground. His life was a Heritage Minute that practically wrote itself.

"I somehow made it through most of year one of law school holding fast to my Frank Yakibuchi origin-story. Why, during all that time, I didn't bother to look at a picture of the justices of the Supreme Court of Canada (and there was one I must have passed hundreds of times in the law library) is a highly relevant question, but one to which I have no answer. When I finally got around to reading the cases discussed in class, I corrected my spelling of Frank Iacobucci's name. At that point, some niggling doubts began to form in my mind about the man I had imagined, but by then I was quite invested in the Japanese-Canadian super-judge myth, so I swept my doubts away.

"Early in my second year of law school, a professor suggested that I apply for judicial clerkships. I had no idea what a judicial clerkship would entail, but it sounded like a respectable way to avoid figuring out what I really wanted to do with my law degree. I finally bothered to look at a picture of the Supreme Court of Canada justices when I started thinking seriously about applying for a clerkship at the Court.

"I don't recall exactly when I realized that Justice Iacobucci is not Japanese-Canadian. It may have been an aha-light-bulb moment, or (more likely) it was a gradual thing, like a compact-florescent bulb that takes a while to reach maximum wattage. After all that, my best course of action was to pretend that I had always known, to never reveal my blunder, and keep my eyes on the prize. At some point late in that first year of law school, I came to learn that he is the son of Italian-Canadian immigrants, not Japanese-Canadian ones, but many of my imaginings still seemed to fit his biography. He is the child of immigrants, and was one of the first generation of his family to be educated in Canada. I came to later learn that Justice Iacobucci does possess all the positive qualities I had ascribed to him (and many more), including a sense of humour that makes dads across the world proud.

"Not surprisingly, clerkship interviews at the Supreme Court were fun, but also stressful. I had brushed up on a few recent SCC judgments in case I was asked substantive questions, committed my résumé to memory, and locked down my list of "best-worst" qualities (too organized, too thorough, too diligent). I arrived for my interview with Justice Iacobucci sweaty palmed, wearing an ill-fitting thrift-store suit, and looking more than a little shell-shocked.

"All the correspondence I had received from Justice Iacobucci's office had been addressed to Mr. Mangat. This did not faze or bother me in the least. Mistaken gender pronouns come with the territory of having an unusual name like mine, and I have made the same mistake with other people's names at least as often as it has happened to me. Justice Iacobucci greeted me at the door of his office, shaking his head, holding his hands up, and apologizing profusely for the mix-up. Apparently, he'd had a male friend in childhood named Raji and had (very reasonably) thought it was exclusively a male name.

"It didn't feel fair to start the interview without revealing my own confusion about his identity, which was so much more embarrassing than his. All my polished, practised introductory small-talk flew out the window, and I blurted out that he shouldn't feel bad for thinking I was a man since I had, until very recently, believed him to be the first Japanese-Canadian

Supreme Court judge. He laughed so hard I think I made him shake. I tittered nervously. We sat down to talk." (Raji Mangat)

When I was a first-year student in law school, one of my professors assigned us the task of writing a short essay on a judge of our choosing. I chose Justice Cardozo – someone I assumed was a famous Italian judge. Of course, I made a mistake based on a name!

Frank reasoned, given the vowel at the end of Cardozo's name, that the American judge and legal scholar must have been a fellow Italian. Not only that, Cardozo must have excelled as an Italian American in order to have his New York Court of Appeals judgments assigned in a Canadian law school classroom. Frank was searching for someone with a name like his, someone with whom he could feel a connection.

As he discovered, Benjamin Cardozo wasn't Italian at all. He came from a Portuguese Sephardic Jewish family, well established in New York. He wasn't the first in his family to go to university or even to become a jurist and judge. Despite the lack of Italian identity, Cardozo was still a good pick. His ethical reputation, famous literary reflections on judging, and memorable writing style as a judge all provided inspiration even if there was no precise match between law student and essay subject. Frank ended up with a long lasting admiration for, and affinity to, "his" Justice Cardozo.

4

Law School

The Wrong Name

Frank Iacobucci enrolled at the University of British Columbia in the fall of 1955. Family resources meant there was no question of leaving town to go to university. Indeed, most of the kids from Britannia High School who went on to college stayed at home. He followed a general arts program in first year, followed by three years leading to a bachelor of commerce degree. It wasn't a very flexible or inspiring curriculum, lacking in the breadth of reading and writing opportunities that Frank would later come to appreciate and recommend to his own children as part of their university education. He checked with UBC early on to see whether he could somehow combine Commerce and Law, but discovered that he had to finish his B. Comm. before heading to law school.

"You don't have the right name."

That was why law school would be a mistake for a student named Iacobucci in the late 1950s in Canada. At least that was the honest and direct assessment offered by his professor of Economic Statistics, a course in which Frank had excelled as an undergraduate student at the University of

British Columbia. Professor Tadek Matuzewski had asked Frank what he planned to do after graduation.

When I replied that I was thinking of law school, my prof said that would be a mistake. Why? Because you just don't have the right name. I didn't expect that. It wasn't what I wanted to hear.

It's unlikely that Professor Matuzewski had any doubts about Frank's abilities; after all, he went on to hire him as a course assistant. Instead, he was concerned about the fit between a promising young student with an Italian name and the prospect of acceptance and success in the universe of law. Odds were not bad that someone with Frank's last name would do well in economics or statistics. In law, they didn't look so good.

Prof Matuzewski suggested that we walk down the hall to ask for a second opinion. We went to see John Deutsch – chair of Political Economy at UBC at the time, and later the Principal of Queen's University. He said Canada was changing, that I should follow my dream and see where that took me.

Before ever setting foot in law school, Frank had been offered a less than rosy picture of what lay ahead and a challenge he was determined to meet. What his university professors didn't know is that the idea of becoming a lawyer had been fixed in Frank's mind from the age of 12.

At my grade 6 graduation ceremony at Hastings School, as I went up to get my diploma, the principal said that I was a great talker, that I should be a lawyer when I grew up, that I could become the next Angelo Branca. I had no idea who Angelo Branca was. My father told me he was a criminal lawyer and a leader in the Italian community in Canada.

Almost a decade later, Frank heard the very different message that he shouldn't go into law with a name like his. But Angelo Branca had a name like his. Branca's very existence proved it was possible. If he went to law school, Frank would be following in the footsteps of someone like him. Frank understood and partially resisted both messages. He would study law; in doing so, he would reject the lack of fit based on his name, and confront any barriers to participation as an Italian Canadian in law. At the same time, he would refuse to limit himself to the precise path of the only Italian-Canadian lawyer he had heard about. Instead he would figure out his own direction.

The Law Class

Whether misspelled or misheard, labelled as wrong or, in his own preferred version, "funny sounding," Frank's name went with him to law school. He didn't move very far from where he had just finished his first degree, but heading to a different building on the UBC campus in September 1959 still felt like a significant change.[9]

In our class, there were two or three Jewish kids, maybe, two or three Asians, one East Indian, one Native Canadian, three women out of, say, 85 or a hundred. Maybe ten "funny-named" students on the class list ... So, you stood out as a member of any minority group.

At the same time Frank selected Justice Cardozo for his first-year essay, he and his colleagues were discovering that it wasn't just Italians who seemed to be missing as members of the Anglo-American-Canadian judiciary. The women would have been hard-pressed to find women authors of any judgments assigned in class, and students from minority groups would have had no luck in finding judges who belonged to their communities. Alfie Scow, Frank's only Aboriginal classmate, went on to become a judge in British Columbia; while he wouldn't have been able to find an Indigenous member of the bench in Canada for his own first year assignment in 1959, he turned himself into a potential subject for later generations of UBC students.

The law students in today's incoming classes constitute a much more diverse population. Sixty years after Frank Iacobucci embarked on a legal education, more than 50 per cent of the individuals studying law in Canada are women, and the mix of backgrounds – racial, cultural, linguistic, socio-economic – in a contemporary law classroom can be striking. The intense and overlapping variety of identities is illustrated by the long list of extracurricular student groups that exist at every law school across the country: groups that bring people together based on everything from faith to sexual orientation, from country of origin to the responsibilities that come with parenthood, from the experience of racial discrimination to political affiliation.

Even without the social diversity of the early twenty-first century, Frank's classmates would have been diverse in terms of the varied reasons for being there – a feature that still characterizes any incoming first year law class. Some, like him, would have held onto the idea of becoming a lawyer since childhood; others, like me, would have applied as a way of continuing to study at university without any concrete idea of a career after graduation. Still others would have had a very clear goal in mind – political office, human rights activism, or corporate leadership – for which legal education seemed like necessary preparation.

Whether perceived as a point on a pre-determined trajectory, or as a kind of default option, law school feels different from university programs in which entering students explicitly indicate some shared and substantive affinity and interest. The fact that there is no prescribed academic path to the door means admitted students come with backgrounds in everything from engineering to anthropology, history to physics, architecture to international development. It doesn't matter what they've studied before, as long as they've immersed themselves in something and have shown intellectual aptitude, curiosity, and achievement while doing so.

First year law students in Frank's class were almost all men, almost all white, almost all Christian, and almost all straight. Their differences primarily lay in their family backgrounds and personal experience: the socio-economic class in which they had been raised, the Church they belonged to, the books they had read, the subjects they had studied, the level of education their parents had attained, the languages their parents spoke at home. Together, they belonged to a generation – born just before the Second World War and already young adults as the 1960s began – collectively marked by a sense of duty to contribute to a country that was growing up with them.

Frank's classmate, Marvin Storrow, proudly notes: "That law class became the graduating law class of 1962 and was arguably one of the stronger, if not the strongest, classes ever to attend UBC's Law School. Many, many members of the class since graduation have been honoured, and four out of the seven Lifetime Achievement Awards given by the University of British Columbia Law School have gone to members of the Class of 1962." (Marvin Storrow)

The Law Classroom

Frank found Law to be a refreshing change from Commerce. He enjoyed being forced into the role of active class participant in what he likes to refer to as the "gymnastics" of his legal education:

The possibility of asking questions as a student ... Law school was the first time I got it in my experience of university education. I think that, pedagogically speaking, the Socratic method is the most difficult technique to adopt if you want to be really good at it. It was the technique that made the greatest impression on me.

Done effectively, the Socratic method in the law classroom invites each individual student into a dialogue with the teacher of exploration and consolidation of knowledge. Famously imagined and implemented at Harvard by the turn of the twentieth century, the Socratic method in teaching and learning law quickly became the preferred technique in case law-based legal education across North America. Often feared and fiercely criticized in the context of a large group of students, the method can go badly wrong. It risks turning into a spectacle and an opportunity for a teacher to expose a student's lack of confidence; it can also convey the sense that the person in front of the classroom is the only one who possesses the right answer.

But, as Frank implies, the pedagogy isn't truly Socratic if it feels like this. Instead, if done well, it can turn the teacher into what Socrates imagined as midwife – someone assisting and supporting students in their learning, understanding, and indeed creation of knowledge.[10] Lecturers who didn't choose Socratic method might deliver carefully structured explorations of challenging issues in different domains of law. But Frank found the technique of asking questions, engaging in dialogue, and demanding critical thinking, truly exhilarating.

Frank had anticipated a certain rough-and-tumble character to the study and practice of law. Warren Mitchell, one of Frank's classmates who accompanied him from undergrad to law at UBC, recalls their shared exposure – definitely entertaining and probably inspiring – to the banter of legal argument:

"On occasions during the summers of 1957 and 1958, we would meet at the home of Frank's great friend, Mike DuMoulin, where his father would sit us down, give us each a large glass of scotch and then perform. Len DuMoulin was a lawyer of the old school and a marvellous raconteur. He would stride up and down the room, using his cigar as a baton to punctuate his tales of legal daring-do, of cases won and lost and characters heroic and villainous. Frank and I were mesmerized."

Warren continues: "Frank's genius was as a crafty, wavy haired soccer player who, just incidentally, happened to be a good student. He had then, and time has not eroded, a marvelous and infectious sense of fun and indeed of mischief." (Warren Mitchell)

On Frank's own admission, he wasn't so serious or hardworking as a law student. He had anticipated being good at the study of law and he was. He could turn up, listen, remember, respond to hypothetical problems, and put up his hand to ask hard questions.

I was a goof-off. I was not the best student. I mean, I was the best in that I finished second in my class, but I was not the best in application. I just crammed and I was smart enough to get by. The class leader always had everything done and all the articles and cases read. You can't get the gold medal by doing nothing.

You probably can't do nothing and get the silver medal either. But Frank wasn't interested in over-investing or impressing others as a serious scholar. The stories told by his classmates and professors make him out to be a brilliant troublemaker, known for his clever comments in class. He knew how to make others laugh, and he figured the law classroom could use some lightening up. So, when Professor Stan Beck turned up at the front of the class wearing a bowtie, Frank said, "Excuse me, sir … I think you have a butterfly on your neck." Told that creditors could use any means to find debtors, Frank raised his hand to ask, "Could a creditor come down the chimney – like Santa Claus?" His reputation extends to the soles of his shoes, on which he purportedly wrote messages aimed at his professors and then sat with his feet propped up on the desk in front of him.

The stories can all be labelled as hearsay – recounted by people at UBC who heard them from others – but Frank wouldn't necessarily deny them. If teachers and colleagues remembered him as a real rascal, with a reputation for creating mischief, all the better. It meant he had succeeded in standing out, not for his stellar grades but for his presence in the classroom, for his contributions to the memories of law school. And anyway it wasn't done with disdain for legal education in general, although Frank didn't have much patience for uninspired teachers and teaching. It was done to test assertions and authority, and to figure out the precise boundaries – of the rules in any area of law, as well as in the classroom. Frank was simply practising what it takes to be an effective jurist.

What makes success in law school seemingly so easy for some students? The answer demands that we unpack "success." At the time Frank was a law student, the final grade in a course would have been based solely on a student's results in a sit-down three-hour exam taken at the very end of the term. Very few professors would have required written assignments during the course; even fewer would have created opportunities in class to be evaluated on engagement with the materials and ability to present or lead a discussion. In this kind of setting, it's true that particular characteristics or talents already developed on the part of a student could go a long way to obtaining excellent grades in law. An outstanding memory for detail, a desire to ask hard questions and to test presented assertions, an ability to articulate convincing justification for an idea or action: all are helpful.

Every year I speak with my first-year law students, one by one, after their first set of mid-term exams. Those who have received outstanding grades are somewhat stunned, not sure how they managed or whether they can do it again. Those with the lowest grades they have ever received in school try to resist despondency; many are eager to figure out what they could be doing better when they synthesize class discussions or structure their responses to questions that require arguments rather than uniform answers. Finally, those who find themselves in the middle of the pack are either relieved to be there or determined to distinguish themselves. It's an intensive process of reassuring everyone that they will indeed figure out how to show that they know the relevant sources by integrating them into their arguments and analysis. It's also a process that happens months before the end of the academic year – such that they are assured opportunities to practise their analysis and writing, through in-class exercises and group assignments, before they receive their final grades.

In contrast to today, law school in the 1950s wasn't known for varied modes of evaluation. Pedagogical innovation came in the form of Socratic-style back-and-forth in the classroom, but it didn't go so far as to recognize diverse modes of student learning and expression.[11] In the context of legal education at the time, Frank shone from first year through to graduation.

One of my friends said that it was in first year law school that I started saying "on the one hand, and on the other hand." I think first year was sort of a turning point in my life, and it was my first year in law that made such an impression on me intellectually and as a person.

There was a fortuitous fit between what Frank was good at, and what was valued highly in persuasive legal analysis: as long as he came to class, held onto the examples and the principles, and could put together a clear and convincing response to hypothetical fact scenarios, then his transcript would be exceptional. He didn't delve into the materials beyond what was required, he didn't always turn up to class with all of his reading done, and indeed, by his own admission, he found writing difficult. But that didn't stop him from impressing his profs when it counted.

"As Far as You Can Go"

On the occasion of Frank Iacobucci's retirement from the Supreme Court of Canada in 2005, Lance Finch – chief justice of British Columbia and member of the UBC Law Class of 1962 – retold one of Frank's stories:

"Frank was 16 years old and anxious to get a driver's licence. He was with his older brother Danny, and one of Danny's friends. Danny had been teaching Frank to drive. The car was parked in a lane near Callister Park, and Danny asked Frank if he would like to drive home. Of course Frank said yes. He got behind the wheel and hit the gas pedal. The wheels spun, gravel flew, and the car took off in a cloud of dust. They rounded the first corner on two wheels and then stopped abruptly when the car plowed into a parked car. The motor was still running, and Frank's foot was still on the gas pedal. Danny's friend leaned over from the back seat, turned off the ignition key and said, 'That's as far as you can go, Frank.' " (Lance Finch)

The end of law school was as far as Frank could go. More precisely, it was the end of the road for him in Vancouver. During his time as a law student, Frank had become a much better driver; the earnings he made from part-time work meant he could buy a second-hand car (which he never crashed). But, in the spring of 1962, he realized it was time to turn off the ignition and leave home. Frank had travelled through Europe in the summer of 1961 with his best friend, Mike DuMoulin, son of the impression-making senior lawyer; during that trip, he had decided he would like to try student life in England.

It was a good thing that I kept my grades up in law school. It meant that my dean, George Curtis, supported my applications for funding. I applied for a Rhodes Scholarship, but it turned out I was too old to be considered: I was turning 25 in the summer of 1962, and that was the cut-off age. Instead, I got a Fellowship in International Law from Cambridge as well as the Mackenzie King Travelling Scholarship for Canadian law students going abroad for graduate school. For my second year, St. John's College offered me a well-paid position as an international law tutor. All of that meant I could afford to leave Canada to do an LLM at Cambridge.

Years after graduation, Frank would describe his three years in the bachelor of laws (LLB) program at UBC as formative, but in a very focused way: legal education felt at the time like it was preparing him specifically to be a practising lawyer, rather than a public servant or a university administrator or a judge. There was little theory (the "why" of law), little practice in problem solving or policy creation (the "how"), little by way of integrating knowledge from a range of disciplines (the "where"). Those were things left to graduate school, although they were also the very things that Frank would later insist, as a law professor at the University of Toronto, were crucial to legal education in general.

As he left his country to pursue a master's degree in law, Frank followed a path still taken by many Canadian law students. It is no longer considered impossible to stay in Canada to pursue graduate legal education of the same calibre as that found at leading universities in other countries. But it is still true that students are often keen to continue their "growing up" as jurists far from where they began their study of law. The tradition continues of young Canadians heading off, usually to the UK or the US or France, to pursue master's and doctoral programs in law – as does the challenge of finding adequate financial backing. At 25, Frank was sure he was ready for a new adventure. He left everything and everyone behind: his car and his city, his university and his neighbourhood, his friends and his family.

5

Legal Education Continued

Surroundings and Substance, People and Partners

Frank discovered at Cambridge a very different world. Not surprisingly, he was struck by the university's extraordinary beauty and its centuries of history, by the mix of people from around the world and the impressive use of the English language. Also not surprisingly, and in the company of generations of fellow students, he noticed the weather:

There was no central heating. My "rooms" or "digs" in first year were freezing cold and my landlady (who affectionately called me Mr. Ybocki) used to put a hot water bottle made of stone in my bed during the winter of 1962–3 when the river froze and the tank of water above the toilet was frozen solid from time to time.

Graduate legal education offered Frank a chance to take courses not offered in his LLB program, to meet and learn from leading scholars in international law, to read more widely and in greater depth than he had done in the past, and to shape and fill out an original thesis project. He was supervised by Professor R.Y. Jennings, later the President of the International Court of Justice in the Hague, and he researched and wrote on "The Proposed International Disarmament Organization: Some Legal Problems."

When Frank talks about his time at Cambridge, he never dwells on the lectures he went to, the books he read, or the time he spent in the Squire Law Library. Neither does he talk about dark winter days, early spring flowers, or even the experience of punting on the River Cam. Instead – and also in the good company of generations of his counterparts – he talks about people. The most significant aspect of life as a graduate student was the opportunity to enter into new friendships that would last for life.

There was Lawrence Collins, to become Lord Collins of Mapesbury and member of the United Kingdom Supreme Court, who introduced Frank to John Cleese, of *Monty Python* fame, and to Jonathan Lynn, director of *My Cousin Vinnie*. Frank discovered much later that David Johnston (with whom he crossed paths in university teaching and administration before David became governor general) and Ian Binnie (with whom he served on the Supreme Court of Canada) studied at Cambridge at the same time he did – which gave them all something to share back in Canada. Martin Friedland, later a colleague at the University of Toronto, became a close friend at Cambridge and was the person responsible for recommending Frank for his first academic appointment.

But most importantly there was Nancy:

The study of international law with the intellectual experience of Cambridge, as good as it was, pales in comparison to the most transformative and significant development in my personal and professional life: meeting Nancy. Far more accomplished and modest than anyone I have ever met, her entering my life made my failure to get a Rhodes Scholarship, which is of course tenable only at Oxford, the best thing that happened to me.

Nancy

Frank's most significant friendship at Cambridge turned out to be the one with Nancy Eastham, a young American woman with a Harvard law degree magna cum laude who had also come to Cambridge to do graduate work in international law. They had arrived in England not only from different countries and universities, but from very different backgrounds. One had working class immigrant Italian Canadian parents, while the other came from a solidly anchored and well-educated New England family. It wasn't surprising that they met far from where each had grown up.

Both Frank and Nancy had wanted to explore the world beyond home and law school – which is why they ended up at Cambridge. And both were willing to shift gears, to make choices that definitely weren't what their parents would have imagined – which is why they ended up together. A brilliant jurist, fiercely proud of her family and roots, and endowed with natural curiosity and easy warmth, Nancy actually had much in common with the person who would become her life partner. Perhaps the outstanding trait they shared was the one that served as a magnet between them: a striking openness to meeting people with diverse backgrounds and experience.

The single most important thing I have done in terms of being educated is meeting her.

After two years at Cambridge, Frank's master's degree in International Law combined with his engagement to Nancy to open the doors to everything that followed. Of course, the reverse is true as well: Nancy's life direction after two years at Cambridge changed due to Frank's presence just as much or more than due to her course of study. They were married on 31 October 1964: both lawyers, both 27 years old, and both with three university degrees in hand.

One of the ways in which Frank describes Nancy is as a "Daughter of the American Revolution." It is shorthand for a context and heritage of which he would have been completely unaware before meeting her. The Eastham family practiced temperance (which meant they were non-drinkers and non-smokers), belonged to the Congregationalist Church, and lived in a community where everyone was Republican. Nancy describes her life growing up in Andover, Massachusetts, as a little cocoon.

Like Frank, she came from a family of three boys and one girl. Both Frank and Nancy were significantly younger than their eldest brothers for whom they felt considerable awe. When Nancy was six years old, her big brother headed off to fight in the Second World War; Frank's big brother was his first teacher, introducing him to the ins and outs of cribbage and the alphabet. Nancy's father was a lawyer with a Harvard law degree, and her mother a well-educated matriarch who had graduated from Mount Holyoke College in 1919. Nancy recalls that family discussions around the dinner table were rarely if ever intellectual in nature, and she took no real interest in politics growing up.

Nancy Eastham majored in Zoology at her mother's alma mater, Mount Holyoke – one of the "Seven Sisters" women's liberal arts colleges understood to be equivalent to the Ivy League. Included in her program were French, German, Sociology, and Psychology courses, making it the kind of well-rounded university experience that Frank would later encourage and regret missing out on. Studying science, in her view, polished the precision in her thinking, something that proved to be a significant advantage at Harvard Law School.

One of a small handful of women in the Harvard Law class of '62, Nancy followed on the heels of Ruth Bader Ginsburg who would later become a justice of the United States Supreme Court. Like Ruth, Nancy excelled as a law student and became a member of the prestigious *Harvard Law Review*. Unlike Ruth, who went through law school already married and with a baby daughter, Nancy graduated ready to continue her university education. With a plan to do post-graduate work in international law at Cambridge, she arrived in England in the fall of 1962, a month shy of her 25th birthday. She had followed a boyfriend, but that relationship quickly ended. Frank remembers meeting her on her birthday and immediately serving as a shoulder to cry on.

She wanted to call her parents and I told her that maybe she should wait, that they would just worry about how things were going for her. She thought that was good advice … that maybe this guy has something to offer. Then people started to say, "You seem to be spending a lot of time with Nancy." It was true. One of my friends from Vancouver came to visit; he thought it was strange that I was denying that something was going on …

When Nancy's parents first learned about Frank Iacobucci, their initial reaction was less than enthusiastic. Nancy recounts that, at first, they didn't think Frank was ambitious enough. The Italian community in nearby Lawrence, Massachusetts, didn't have a good reputation, and there existed general anti-Catholic sentiment in the state – all of which meant that the Nancy-Frank partnership was viewed with considerable concern.

Our courtship was stormy, very stormy. They didn't want her to marry me; they didn't think I was a good choice for her. The mafia was big in those parts of the world, and they thought I was Catholic, which made it even worse. It was tough. The more she tried to keep me in her life and at the same time convince her parents, the more I admired her. What she saw in me, I don't know. Maybe I was like a diamond in the rough.

By the time the wedding was planned, and Frank's parents arrived for the celebration, Nancy had convinced her family that she was serious. In October of 1964, Frank Iacobucci became a member of the Eastham clan, and Nancy became a full-fledged Iacobucci.

Our wedding in Massachusetts was very different than what my family was used to. Not a big, joyous celebration, not like an Italian or Jewish wedding! But Nancy's parents were very kind to my mother, which she always appreciated. In many ways, our families had similar values.

What were the similar values? Belief in education, an aversion to being flashy or frivolous, commitment to hard work and public service: all of these were part of the fabric of the Iacobucci and Eastham clans, something to hold onto even as Frank and Nancy made unexpected choices. Those shared values countered the fact that they came from communities where meeting someone like their eventual spouse was highly unlikely. The mix of similarity and difference meant that each embraced the shaking up, the shift in path, the uncertainty, the sense of adventure, and the feeling of finding a kindred spirit.

The turning point in my life is Nancy ... Every phase of my work has involved her in one way or another. She is the most self-starting, all-rounded, talented person I know.

For someone suspected by the Eastham family of lacking in ambition, Frank ended up proving his ambition over and over, first and far from least by marrying Nancy. She opened up a world of references and experience and confidence and belonging, in which he otherwise would have found full participation tricky if not impossible. It is easy to imagine her encouraging and even pushing him into situations – social and professional – that felt far from familiar or easy. In her advising and editing roles, she became a co-creator even if not an official co-author. Frank had been a playmaker since his days in competitive soccer, but he met his match in Nancy. It is not a stretch to think that she redirected his path from one anticipated to be successful in a general sort of way to one that became truly outstanding.

A Blessing for Those Who Learn

Part of the Evensong service at Corpus Christie College Chapel is a blessing for those who teach and those who learn. Not surprising in the context of Cambridge University where teaching and learning are the stuff of everyday life and centuries of existence, the prayer resonates for a visiting professor imagining the experience of past generations of students in this university town. The Anglican minister continues with a reminder of a shared commitment to ever-enriched knowledge and to the project of creating a new and better world. As I listen, I imagine Frank following Nancy into the Chapel at 6:00 p.m. one early summer evening half a century ago.

The architecture of the Cambridge colleges would have been the same; while there is constant upkeep and occasional construction, the timelessness of the principal buildings is precisely what captures the endless cycle of teaching and learning. The weather would have been the same: continual clouds such that the moments of sunshine breaking through are met with a marked sense of lightness, of gratitude and appreciation for the warmth through the stained glass windows. The order of Evensong would be the same, as would the melody of the hymn chosen to close off the service of thanks and reflection. And the mix of students, fellows, and visitors would be the same – most of whom know the Lord's Prayer by heart and others who know it by reputation.

Nancy could follow along, familiar with the liturgy and with the Church of England mix of faith and connection to the contemporary world marked by the successes and failures of human governance. Frank would show respect for the people and traditions around him, but the ease with which Nancy could insert herself into the tiny congregation would elude him. Familiar and yet foreign, meaningful and yet somewhat mysterious, the Anglican order of things couldn't become second nature for Frank. But the blessing for those who teach and those who learn would be exactly right. After all, Frank was at Cambridge to make the transition from student to teacher, to develop his understanding and knowledge of law in order to integrate practice and theory, to imagine a career dedicated to exactly what this university stands for: learning to teach, and teaching to learn.

Evensong can be imagined as the symbolic prelude to the academic period spent by Nancy and Frank together at Cambridge. But it can also be imagined as the prelude to each academic year: it is the collection of prayers, readings, and hymns meant and able to inspire on the eve of both a new day and, for teachers and students, a renewed cycle of teaching and learning. Every September feels the same, steeped in familiar traditions, structures, words, and call-response behaviours. There is a strong element of communal faith and belonging, of shared devotion and the joy of voices joined in harmony. The tradition and ongoing practice of Evensong at a College Chapel in Cambridge, with its special prayer for those who teach and those who learn, might well have left its imprint on someone like Frank: curious, ready to enter the door to many places and many adventures, blessed, and charged with the task of lifelong learning and leadership.

6

Cutting Stone – Finding a Place in Law

In an address to law students in 1938, Justice Benjamin Cardozo – the judge claimed by Frank Iacobucci as "his" – insisted that a lawyer "be historian and prophet all in one."[12] Lawyers look back to turn to the future; what came before informs arguments as to what comes next. Cardozo may have been talking about the work lawyers do, but the relationship of past to future is crucial to their personal narratives as well. Referring to and reviewing the past – in life as in law - is the foundation for anticipating and appreciating the trajectory that follows.

The welcome to law school is a welcome to a new and particular stage of growing up, of drawing on our past to shape our future and direct our lives. In this sense, legal education is an exercise in cutting stone – becoming familiar with new tools and learning to chisel and polish the basic material we start with. We cut stone in unique ways and patterns, drawing on where we come from and what we have learned before. At the same time, it's by doing the cutting that we figure out what has had the greatest impact on our technique and approach. And, as we become better at our stone cutting, we may start to innovate in unimagined directions.

Just as each person comes "before the law"[13] in a unique way, law students draw on what came "before the law" in their own lives. Knowing what they will be when they grow up – as a 12-year- old Frank Iacobucci thought he did – is less important than figuring out who they are, who they will become, and what they will do. The baggage law students bring with them shapes their knowledge, their experience, their potential, and their understanding of themselves as participants in law. It forms the basis of their necessarily autobiographical voyage.

Frank's stories serve as prelude to, and foundation for, his immersion in the study of law beginning at UBC and continuing through graduate work at Cambridge. They underscore the individual nature of learning and participating in law; they turn into a kind of never-ending personal statement submitted with an application to law school. But it's important not to think of the task of historian as that of discovering and recounting fixed truths. Just as prophecy takes on its substance through the prophet's exercise of voice and choice, the recounting of history is marked by fluidity and interpretation.

"We cannot help but embrace storytelling if we hope to persuade readers of the importance of our subject ... We place human beings at the center of events that they themselves may not fully understand but that they constantly affect with their actions." In "A Place for Stories: Nature, History and Narrative,"[14] historian William Cronon discovers and names a multiplicity of narratives offered to recount history and, accordingly, a multiplicity of different possible endings. "Narrative is (thus) inescapably bound to the very names we give the world. Rather than evade it – which is in any event impossible – we must learn to use it consciously, responsibly, self-critically ... the stories we tell, like the questions we ask, are all finally about value."[15]

We all carve out the particular narratives we share about ourselves, partly by selecting the pieces and people that stand out with hindsight. It's long after Frank's formal legal education that some of his stories evolve to become the truly important ones. The soccer goal story becomes much more significant to Frank's life in law than that of any course taken during his bachelor of commerce program; the first day of first grade matters more than a high school medal or even a master's thesis. They are stories that carry special significance for the storyteller; they are stories that can be gleaned for meaning by the listener and the re-teller.

The stories told by and about Frank Iacobucci convey a range of messages, possible endings, and lessons of value. One of those lessons is that of accountability: survive, learn from, take responsibility for, and even laugh about, loss. Mistakes are inevitable. The lemonade stand ends up as a short-lived endeavour. Despite skills and effort and preparation, the soccer ball can still go in the wrong direction. And the neighbour's rose bushes grow back even after serving as the family goat's snack. There is an emphasis on resilience, on the importance of picking yourself up after a fall.

While Frank's narrative includes bumps along the way – such that it's not all about winning – it never veers into failure or confronts what feels like a dead end. Indeed, a second message, that relationships matter, underscores the way in which adults in Frank's life protected him and ensured that he never actually fell too hard. The stories he tells are a testament to what can go right if early and ongoing "vertical" relationships are positive.

Among the members of my own first year law class was Greg Gilhooly, author of *I Am Nobody: Confronting the Sexually Abusive Coach Who Stole My Life*.[16] Greg was a brilliant student and a gifted hockey player; what he didn't share with any of us as his classmates was that he brought with him the agonizing burden of sexual abuse, sustained through his teenage years, by a respected hockey coach in Winnipeg.

"I would emerge for classes that interested me and for social events I thought would be fun, but I was having a harder and harder time engaging with the world outside my room. Self-doubt, the feeling that you're a fraud, the fear that people know you're a fraud, is debilitating. I wanted to hide ... Withdrawal, living like a hermit, increasingly became my new normal."[17] "I was a larger-than-life character at law school ... But inside, living in my own inner hell, I was no different from before. My achievements were meaningless to me."[18]

Stories like Greg's illustrate the overpowering negative and long-lasting impact that adults can have on young people. Conversely, they serve to underscore the positive potential that individuals can exercise. That is, we are truly fortunate if the grown-ups in our lives hold our hands, literally and figuratively, until we're ready to let go. The opposite – not ever taking a hand, holding on too tightly, crushing a tiny hand in an overpowering grip – fails to honour the trust children need to have in their parents or teachers, counsellors or coaches.

Vertical relationships may tell you where you come from; they clearly influence your understanding of yourself. But they don't determine in a fixed way where you're going. Instead, they co-exist with horizontal relationships that take us in new directions and also inform who we are. These are the relationships with friends, with classmates, with life partners, with the people we meet along our paths: relationships in which we share and give, learn and change.

This brings us to a third message or lesson of value. Identity is crucial but complicated. In other words, be proud of where you came from, but explore beyond the familiar. By choosing law, and by leaving home, Frank Iacobucci refused to surround himself only with people who knew how to spell his name. As a young boy, he carried his mother's messy Italian sandwiches in his backpack to school for lunch. At 25, thanks to Nancy, he was introduced to English orange marmalade for breakfast.

Frank's narrative shows that meaningful human connection – whether with a judge you write about or with a fellow student turned life partner – doesn't require a precise match. The question, "Where are you from?" is one that Frank both welcomes and asks. It offers an opportunity to talk about family background, to express confidence and pride. It can signal curiosity and a desire to make a connection with someone new in your life. Above all, it connects individual history to personal path.

Just after the 40th anniversary of his graduation from law school, the Honourable Frank Iacobucci was invited to follow the dean's speech to incoming law students with his own words of welcome:[19]

The coming days will be full of advice-giving and I am no exception. My advice is to listen to all the advice but heed that which makes sense to you ... Work hard and play hard while you are here. Get to know your classmates for so many reasons ... the greatest assets of this law school are your faculty members and your fellow students.

...

The study of law can teach you to learn how to live. I say this because in your studies of what the law and justice are all about, you will think about what the moral outcome, the right outcome or the decent outcome of a given situation should be. This is of great help not just in practising law but in living your life. In fact, it may well be the most important lesson you learn from the study of law.

Frank's messages are simple: Pay attention to people and connect what you learn to how you live. A speech that welcomes students to law often contains less about the formal period of legal education that lies ahead than it does about the people sitting in the Moot Court. It is an invitation to look around, learn from others, make new connections, and recognize how crucial individuals are to the foundations and development and practice of law. Three years later, the same law students walk out the door and surround themselves with new people. As Frank knew from his own experience, they may do that over and over again, constantly reinventing themselves and finding new ways to connect and contribute.

A framework for connecting individual narratives and interpersonal connections to the process of legal education can come from an understanding of law grounded in the dynamic interplay of distinctive spheres. According to such an understanding, our relationships inform a continuing autobiography of meaning and, more specifically, of legal meaning.[20] That is, we participate actively as creators of law as we engage with others in our lives. Each of us does so at the intersection of the spheres to which we belong and which provide guidance for the decisions we make and the actions we take: so-called normative spheres that can include our family, our neighbourhood, our soccer team, and indeed our law classroom.

Even if he doesn't articulate all of this in words of welcome, Frank Iacobucci himself provides a particularly compelling example of how an individual interacts with different domains or systems of formal and informal law. Like him, and starting on the first day of their legal education, law students engage in an intensive process of narrative imagination *as* jurists. They recreate stories of where they came from at the same time that they construct new stories of how they relate to law. Each law student, like Frank, makes individual choices; their actions and interactions carry value and guidance as elements of law making. Each can serve as source of narrative insight: individual stories, told and retold, sharpen an appreciation of what it means to learn, practise, and live law.

Frank Iacobucci is the reason I went to law school. I had combined arts and science as a University of Toronto student, trying to keep all doors open and unsure of what I wanted to do after I completed a degree in physiology with a minor in English. In the fall of my fourth year, only 20 years old, I went to talk to the registrar of my college about what I might do next. I was told that maybe I should take a break from my studies – I could travel or work and maybe I would meet someone, start a family, and decide I was finished with university. That wasn't what I wanted to hear. I turned instead for advice to the provost and chair of the university committee on which I served as a student member.

Professor Iacobucci thought I might enjoy law. All I knew was that I wanted to keep learning, and I had lost interest in spending time in science labs. So, in the winter of 1986, I walked over to the law school admissions office with my application and academic transcript in hand. That September, I found myself listening to the dean's welcome speech, anticipating the three years I would spend as a law student and hoping I'd received good advice. And ten years later, Frank and Nancy Iacobucci were guests at our wedding, as I married the life partner I had met at age 25 in the year following graduation from law school. Frank likes to joke that he takes credit for my professional path – and is happy to have played a role in supporting my personal choices too.

In *The Truth About Stories: A Native Narrative*[21] Thomas King asserts that "[t]he truth about stories is that that's all we are." Stories are repeated many times, he tells us, and each time they change – sometimes through the voice of the storyteller, sometimes through the response of the listeners, sometimes through the order of the pieces that make up the story. "But in all the tellings of all the tellers," King says, there is a crucial element of the story that stays, something that makes that particular story the stuff of what we are.

Stories fill the baggage of each law student; an incredibly heterogenous group of people comes together to be welcomed to the study of law. But stories also constitute the stuff of legal education itself. Each new class confronts what feel like timeless issues albeit with examples taken from contemporary time and place. We learn and engage in and create law through stories of human conflict, stories of societal transformation, stories told by judges, stories argued by advocates, and stories of the development of ideas and issues. They help us appreciate the rhythm of legal education, and the generation after generation feel of becoming part of the legal community, taking on the identity of jurist, and moving on to do some good in the world.

In an essay on legal education that I wrote as a doctoral student, after my first experience of teaching law students, I started to reflect on the significance of our own stories and the stories that make law resonate for students. "Narrative method in law school can help students learn how law works and how it might be transformed ... In order to do this, we need to look at stories that are effective in turning law students into powerful participants in their own legal education and practice."[22]

As the professor of a first-year law course at McGill, I assign the *Waldick v Malcolm*[23] judgment written by Justice Iacobucci. In the case, the owner of a farmhouse in a rural part of Canada had not salted the icy driveway. A neighbouring farmer came to visit, parked his pickup truck, and slipped as he walked to the front door. Despite arguments referring to customary practice in the region, Justice Iacobucci upheld a finding of unreasonable behaviour leading to liability. The first year I taught the judgment, I was home in Ottawa over the Christmas holidays and drove to the Iacobuccis' home to deliver holiday greetings in person. I parked my car in their driveway. And then, as I got out, I slipped and fell on the ice. No one had salted!

In every year since, the lively class discussion about the case comes to an end with my retelling of the story. Here is my student, Debbie Yeboah, at the end of her first year in law:

"When I think of Justice Frank Iacobucci what comes to mind is ... Professor Van Praagh slipping on his icy driveway. She told us this story just after we read Justice Iacobucci's judgment in *Waldick v Malcolm*. I like the story because it is a reminder that judges are people too.

"During my first year of law at McGill I felt like I had been thrown into a whole new world. I grew up in a house almost completely absent of talk of Canadian law or politics; my parents are Ghanaian immigrants, and before I came to McGill I did not know anything about how the law worked, I did not know any judges or professors, and save one family friend I did not know a single lawyer. It's strange, but there are still moments where I look around and feel as though this is not the place for a person like me. At times I feel like I do not belong. The fact that Justice Iacobucci, a child of immigrants, served on the Supreme Court of Canada resonates with me in a special way because it shows me that this world is not so far away. People like me are part of it. I do belong. His legacy is a concrete reminder that this 'law world' can be the place for the children of immigrants as well – and there is real comfort in that for a nervous first year student."

"Thank you, Justice Iacobucci, for demonstrating that even if your parents grew up in a different place, you do not have to feel out of place here. Thank you for helping me feel like I belong." (Deborah Yeboah)

PART II

$5 a Day – Lawyering in the World

1

Farewell to Law School

"Why study law at university? ... Law is the science of the flourishing of the human community ... It is not just about managing bureaucratic processes or deciding cases. It is to reflect upon ideal futures that contrast with present practices. What would it be for the community of the world to flourish? It is to answer that question that law was instituted as an academic discipline ..." – Martti Koskenniemi[1]

Law students come together again as a class on the day they graduate. They share memories of special moments, class projects, and events in the world that have marked their collective experience in pursuing their degrees. The dean's speech on the occasion of convocation is similar to the one that welcomed them to legal education. But this time it includes a forecast for the future. As students say goodbye to law school, they look ahead to their lives as lawyers. The dean offers counsel regarding the varied ways in which they will share their talents and energy, explore new domains, serve their communities, and "make $5 a day."

There is always a moment at which the graduates are asked to express their appreciation for the people who got them through their study of law. Parents, partners, friends, siblings, children, classmates, and teachers: all are thanked for participating in a network of support. Students are reminded that just as they didn't do legal education all on their own, they won't and can't succeed as lawyers all on their own. As expressed by Professor James Boyd White, scholar of legal education and the culture of law, "none of us acts alone: our minds, our questions, our sense of what needs to be said, of what can be said, are all shaped by interaction with others."[2]

Typically, graduates listen to the advice not only of their dean but also of an invited honorary doctorate recipient, someone who can share words of wisdom drawn from an impressive career. As they say farewell to their study of law, students are meant to feel prepared for what lies ahead. The concepts and competencies they graduate with are meant to connect, even if not in a precise or easy-to-trace way, to the day-to-day work they will take on and the ways in which they will engage in the world. The invited convocation speaker is meant to illustrate, and even embody, the kinds of things holders of law degrees are called upon to do, such that new jurists head off with a heavy sense of obligation and an inspiring dose of anticipation.

"Each day generates fundamental questions whose answers will alter the shape of human experience ... We are at an inflection point in world history – when the ways we learn and teach, do business, handle conflicts, pursue freedom, equality, and security will change. And creative problem-solvers will shape those changes. ... Today and tomorrow, you each will make a difference – in tackling how we all deal with difference and build our world." – Martha Minow[3]

The Honourable Frank Iacobucci received an honorary doctorate from the University of Toronto in 1989, which meant that he delivered the address at that year's Law convocation. It seemed right, and was a nice coincidence, that the person who offered guidance to my graduating class was the same person who had given me personal advice three years earlier. I was proud to share him with my classmates.

Frank was a good choice to talk to us about diverse paths to making $5 a day, although he wouldn't have focused on comparative salary levels. Instead, he would have insisted on finding and enjoying the psychic rewards of a lawyer's work across a wide spectrum of contexts: by 1989, he had practised corporate law, taught as a professor, published as a scholar, helped run the university, devoted himself to public service as the federal deputy minister of Justice, and most recently been appointed chief justice of the Federal Court of Canada.

Years later, as a law professor, I was given the task of introducing Frank Iacobucci to McGill's graduating students at their convocation ceremony. By that time he had added another line to his curriculum vitae – justice of the Supreme Court of Canada. He could talk to students with insider knowledge about yet another way to make a living as a lawyer, another possibility for what you can do with a law degree in hand. This was the job Frank would do for longer than any other – he had the same title, geographical location, and job description for 13 years – but it turned out to be far from his last paid position. His trajectory after retiring from the court includes at least as many stops as he made along the way there.

There's a longstanding joke in the Iacobucci family that Frank has never been able to hold down a job. At least it's the case that, with each position, Frank became a better and better choice as con-vocation speaker, ideally situated to provide insight into what lies beyond formal legal education and how to live and work as a lawyer – whether in ways that receive no monetary payment at all or in others with a market value of many multiples of $5.

Frank Iacobucci as Lawyer

Frank and Nancy lived in Brooklyn and worked in lower Manhattan starting in 1964. Frank practised corporate law for three years at Dewey Ballantine Bushby Palmer & Wood; Nancy was at Debevoise Plimpton until she gave birth to their first child in 1966. It was a challenge for Frank to secure a position in a New York law firm, partly because he hadn't studied law at a top American law school, but also – and, in his mind, more importantly – because of his Italian-Canadian identity. For Nancy as a young woman, even with stellar academic credentials from Mount Holyoke, Harvard, and Cambridge, it was also difficult. After Andrew was born, Frank and Nancy started to think about leaving New York. Frank's good friend, Martin Friedland, already a law professor at the University of Toronto, suggested to both Frank and to his own dean that teaching at U of T might be a good option.

In 1967, Frank was hired, sight unseen, by Dean Caesar Wright to join U of T's law faculty where he would teach primarily in the areas of corporate law and taxation. Frank's later law student and even later colleague, Robert Prichard, characterizes the hire as one of the smartest things that Caesar Wright ever did at the law school. The years as a professor were marked by the birth of Edward and Catherine, Frank and Nancy's second and third children. Frank served as associate dean of Law at U of T from 1973–5, at which point he was appointed vice-president Internal Affairs for the university. After a three-year term as vice-president, Frank returned to the Law School as dean in 1979. His deanship was cut short when he was appointed vice-president and provost of U of T in 1983, to work with President David Strangway and then President George Connell. Years later, upon retiring from the Supreme Court of Canada, Frank Iacobucci moved back to Toronto and to U of T, this time as interim president (2004–5).

In 1985, Provost Frank Iacobucci was thinking about making a change and moving out of university administration. He handed over a curriculum vitae that made its way to the Prime Minister's Office. Frank received a call at U of T from Gordon Osbaldeston, clerk of the Privy Council, letting him know that Prime Minister Brian Mulroney wanted to appoint him deputy minister of Justice and deputy attorney general of Canada. The move to Ottawa was a big one for Frank and Nancy and their family – although it was only their youngest, Catherine, who settled with them in their home on Broadview Avenue and went to high school in Ottawa. As Frank puts it, his job at the Department of Justice meant that he oversaw the largest law firm in Canada with its 1,200 public service lawyers. He served under Ministers of Justice John Crosbie and Ray Hnatyshyn; major government files from 1985–8 included Meech Lake, Aboriginal self-government, free trade, decriminalization of abortion, and official languages.

Frank Iacobucci was appointed chief justice of the Federal Court of Canada by Prime Minister Mulroney in 1988. The appointment brought his time at the Department of Justice to a close, and transferred his administrative leadership skills to a new context while at the same time introducing him to life on the Bench. In December 1990, Frank received yet another call from Mulroney, this time to invite him to join the Supreme Court of Canada. He was officially appointed in 1991, replacing Ontario Justice Bertha Wilson. Frank reports that the first thing he thought at the time of the call was that he wished his mother were still alive so that he could share the news with her.

The Honourable Frank Iacobucci was the first Italian Canadian to be appointed to the Supreme Court. Chief Justice Antonio Lamer spoke Italian, along with English and French, at the swearing in ceremony, video-recorded for Frank's father back in Vancouver. The fact that the prime minister didn't replace an outgoing woman justice with a woman was contentious. Frank remembers his new colleague, Justice Claire L'Heureux-Dubé, saying to him, "I like you Frank, but you should be a woman," to which he responded, "I would do most things to serve my country but a gender change is not one of them." Frank served as a justice of the Supreme Court from 1991–2004. The thirteen years he spent at the SCC – to which he refers as the pinnacle of his professional experience – represents the longest period in his career path without a change in title, location, or responsibility.

Justice Iacobucci's Supreme Court jurisprudence engaged with a broad range of issues and areas of law. His judgments have much to say about administrative expertise and about the appropriate extent of judicial interference in the governance and decision-making that happens within spheres of human activity (e.g., corporate, labour, tax). Individual dignity plays a significant and guiding role, particularly in the task of interpreting the

Canadian Charter of Rights and Freedoms. He issued significant judgments that speak to education, the equilibrium between freedom and responsibility attached to expression, and the significance of religious belief. In general, Supreme Court Justice Iacobucci's jurisprudence indicates a desire to articulate guidelines, and to provide structure and shape for ongoing analysis and development of, for example, equality rights and Aboriginal rights. He has been characterized as a "complex judge,"[4] who incorporated recognition of complex selves (his own and of others) into the task of decision making.

Frank and Nancy moved back to Toronto in 2004, with his first post-retirement office located in Simcoe Hall, a building Frank knew well as the base for University of Toronto's administration. His year as interim president was followed by a move to two simultaneous offices – one at Torys LLP as senior counsel, and the other at Torstar where he held the position of chair of the board from 2005–9.

As a retired Supreme Court judge, Frank combined work as an arbitrator, teaching at U of T and Yale, along with Professor Robert (Bo) Burt and with Justices Dieter Grimm of Germany and Aharon Barak of Israel, participation on boards of directors including that of Tim Hortons, and the role of conduct review adviser to the Canada Pension Plan Investment Board. He advised the Ontario government on post-secondary education, wrote a report for York University on academic freedom, conducted a review of First Nations representation on Ontario juries, directed an inquiry into the treatment of alleged terrorists in Canada, and participated in negotiations regarding the Ring of Fire mining development in Northern Ontario.

Perhaps most notably, Frank Iacobucci served as the Federal Government representative in the process leading to a settlement scheme including compensation for all survivors of the general Indian residential schools experience and of particular abuses suffered during their time as students. The intense five-month process to reach an agreement in principle included over 65 lawyers and the testimonies of survivors and their descendants across Canada. When the agreement in principle was reached in November 2005, the $2-billion in Common Experience Payments represented the largest compensation payment in Canadian history. This was just one component of the overall settlement that included funds for healing, and the establishment of a Truth and Reconciliation Commission that issued its report and Calls to Action in 2015.

As recognition of his contributions and leadership, "Dr." Frank Iacobucci received 18 honorary doctorates between 1989 and 2018: 17 across Canada, and one from the University of Calabria in Italy.

What, How, Why? Elements of a Jurist's Path

A sequential narrative of Frank's contributions over his career provides a snapshot of positions and places, achievements and titles. It could be abbreviated to a more or less chronological list: practitioner, professor, dean, provost, deputy minister, chief justice, Supreme Court justice, university president, negotiator, arbitrator, chair. Classifying the types of roles and responsibilities he has taken on is another possibility: advocate, scholar, teacher, administrator, leader, policy adviser, decision-maker, spouse, parent, and grandparent. Or we could enumerate various ways in which people have addressed Frank over the years: Mr. Iacobucci, Professor Iacobucci, Dean Iacobucci, President Iacobucci, Deputy Minister Iacobucci, Dr. Iacobucci, Counsel, Mr. Justice, Chief, Mr. Chair, My Lord, Dad, and, to his grandchildren, Bucci.

Frank provides a good example of the range of directions in which a person with a legal education can head off or end up taking. His story could be filled out one job or type of contribution at a time. Examined more closely, however, it shows how life as a jurist doesn't proceed in distinct stages. Instead, as with Frank, any individual's post-convocation life is marked by a dynamic and unique overlap of knowledge and skills and responsibilities, of people and places and projects. Even people invited to give convocation speeches because of their experience and impact start again – new diploma in hand – along with all the members of the graduating class. They can motivate and even predict, but they can't specify future job titles for the people they speak to or even for themselves.

It is common for a convocation speaker to offer some advice as you embark on the next chapter of your lives … There has been no more fascinating period to study the law, legal institutions, and the administration of justice than the present … never in our history have we had a generation that is as diverse, talented, enlightened, and energetic as you. Nowadays, we hear so much of the economic or business side of the legal profession with great emphasis on the bottom line rather than on the right line. I realize that economic considerations are an obvious reality but if the practice of law becomes only a business, we will have produced a calling without a spirit, or much worse, without a soul.[5]

Paying attention to Frank's intersecting guises offers insight not only on the diverse options for making a living as a lawyer, but also into the promise and potential of legal education itself. Through the prism of what people do after graduation, we can get a sharper picture of what came before. Whatever they do, jurists will develop their expertise, their skills, and their judgment: there will be a what, a how, and a why to their trajectory. As students, they prepared by gaining substantive knowledge, learning to structure persuasive responses to complex questions, and honing their judgment through critical analysis and commitment to justice: the what, how, and why of formal legal education.

There is a what, how, and why to making $5 a day unique to Frank Iacobucci. Corporate law is the primary "what" on his path as a jurist. Frank has been practitioner, scholar, teacher, judge, and director all within this substantive sphere. Leadership in public service is the "how": whether in the context of university, government, or court, Frank has taken on responsibility for administrative organization and institutional effectiveness. Acting as member of the Supreme Court of Canada underscores the "why." This is where Frank most explicitly took on the responsibility of articulating principles, providing reasons, and setting directions in the pursuit of justice.

Below, in sections 2, 3, and 4 of "Part II – $5 a Day – Lawyering in the World," we will explore all three, incorporating the voices and perspectives of others familiar with Frank's expertise (the what), leadership (the how), and jurisprudence (the why). Imperatives excerpted from an imagined farewell convocation address to graduating law students provide the sections with titles: you will keep learning, you will lead, you will pursue justice.

2

You Will Keep Learning – Frank Iacobucci and the Law of Corporations

Corporate Practice – Frank's First Job

When I went to New York, I found myself in the corporate stream, and I enjoyed that. What really attracted me, what I found fascinating, was the private ordering process. It was not adversarial: lawyers represented clients, of course, and different interests, but there was commonality in wanting to make a transaction. People would gain from trade, gain from agreement. So it was about lawyer as solicitor rather than lawyer as barrister – and that is something that does not get emphasized in legal education, at least not in mine.

That to me was the attraction. It suited my personality. There was also real intellectual challenge: What is directing or facilitating the agreements, what are the underlying motives, where do the incentives and limits come from?

As Frank acknowledges, there was a real fit between his talent at bringing people together and the ordering that characterizes corporate practice. From the vantage point of being Frank's colleague in corporate law first in the early 1970s and then again four decades later, Brian Flood asserts Frank Iacobucci's primary identity: "Before Frank Iacobucci was a law professor, dean of Law, provost, vice-president, and president of University of

Toronto; before he was deputy minister of Justice and deputy attorney general of Canada, chief justice of the Federal Court of Canada and justice of the Supreme Court of Canada, he was a corporate lawyer. That is how he began his career. He was very good. I know; I watched him in action." (Brian Flood)

Frank had studied international law during his master's degree program, but the focus of his graduate work hadn't translated into real passion for the field. He remained open to a range of options and, indeed, his decision to apply for a position at a New York law firm went hand in hand with Nancy's plan for life and work. She had studied law at Harvard, in Cambridge, Massachusetts, surrounded by students for whom becoming lawyers in Manhattan would have been one obvious path. The additional two years in Cambridge, England, simply added credentials to an already stellar Ivy League record. In other words, Nancy was a clear candidate for a position in a leading New York law firm.

Frank wasn't. He had gone to law school in Canada, meaning that his curriculum vitae didn't reflect the usual academic credentials required for entry. The master's degree at Cambridge might trigger attention, but only if the person reviewing the applications knew something about the quality' of graduate education in England. Over fifty years later, the picture hasn't changed so much. It's still the case, as reflected in the popular culture television series *Suits*, that a degree from Harvard Law School carries significant and perhaps disproportionate weight with big law firms in New York City. And it's still the case that a Canadian law graduate, even someone at the top of the class at UBC, can find it challenging to get through the door.

Frank felt that his Italian name combined with his Canadian law degree made it particularly tough to find a job. It turned out that, even with the right law school and New England name and background, Nancy faced different but similarly daunting barriers as a young woman in 1960s New York. She got offers, but often at salaries lower than those received by her male counterparts. Finally, Nancy started at Debevoise Plimpton, a firm with an excellent reputation. And Frank ended up with a position at

Dewey Ballantine, a firm that had hired another UBC graduate a couple of years earlier and where a senior lawyer who had been a Rhodes scholar was familiar with an Oxbridge pedigree. Together, Frank and Nancy settled into a home in Brooklyn Heights and full-time work on Wall Street.

Brian Flood relays Frank's time at Dewey Ballantine, the second largest law firm in New York at the time, and a partnership with huge influence in both business and politics:

"The hours were long, the work challenging, the training fabulous, and the learning curve steep. As with all new lawyers, Frank worked in a number of key areas of corporate and commercial law, in his case mergers and acquisitions, corporate finance, bond financing, and trust indentures to name a few. Frank was clearly excelling at the firm both as a lawyer and as a colleague. In his second year he was appointed to the firm's entertainment committee, a real honour for a young lawyer. The committee was seized with the onerous responsibility of entertaining and embarrassing the lawyers of the firm, of all levels of seniority, at the annual firm dinner. It was a role for which Frank was naturally suited. In his lawyering he worked a great deal with one senior partner on a number of financing and acquisition transactions for a rapidly growing client in the petroleum business. A senior lawyer seldom keeps a young lawyer involved with a client unless the young lawyer is performing very well." (Brian Flood)

Frank fell in love with being in the middle of the action – juggling the many facets of complicated interactions, paying attention to the detail of structures that would facilitate the goals of clients, working closely with other members of the team. In many ways, the practice of corporate law in New York was far removed from the study of international law. And yet there was overlap between the two spheres: key actors, whether corporations or states, create the rules which are in turn reflected and supported, or sometimes shaped and constrained, by law. In the corporate world, corporate law functions best in response to the actors and practices that constitute the everyday reality of corporations.

Frank found a calling in the work of a solicitor that he held onto, even when his later job descriptions seemed to have nothing in common with that of a practitioner of corporate law. He focused on what he referred to as the *psychic reward* of his time in a law firm, emphasizing the flip side of the obvious material reward that is easy to associate with corporate practice. He enjoyed being a small but important player, developing in-depth understanding of corporate organization, coordinating with tax planners, explaining and facilitating the duties of directors, ensuring accountability to shareholders, and feeling that he could help people succeed and prosper. The practice of corporate law prioritizes individual clients and their perspectives and articulated needs. It is grounded in the ways in which people come together to create structures and pursue projects. And it downplays the role of courts and aims to avoid litigation, thus, as Frank points out, eschewing the barrister or courtroom side of lawyering in favour of the solicitor or planning side.

In 1966, baby Andrew was born, and Nancy left the practice of law. In the mid-1960s, women in the profession typically gave up their jobs when they became mothers; there was simply no possibility of a maternity leave at a big law firm. Frank and Nancy started to think about where their family might grow, and to plan their exit from life in New York City. Moving the family to Canada, where Frank's career could continue, seemed like a good option. During their time at Cambridge, they had become friends with Martin and Judy Friedland from Toronto; the Friedlands were now back home where Marty was teaching at U of T. In the winter of 1967, the law faculty was looking for a corporate law teacher and Marty recommended Frank Iacobucci. Neither Frank nor Nancy knew Toronto, but they were open to a move.

Frank was hired over the phone. Caesar Wright, U of T's dean of Law who made the offer, died before ever meeting the junior law professor who joined the Faculty that fall. It wasn't usual practice at the time for people to become law professors without an on-site interview. Today it simply couldn't happen. Future colleagues want to have a sense of the person they might invite to join them. In addition, they – and their university – expect to see a research plan, concrete evidence of publication potential, and teaching experience. Since the 1990s, it has become more and more common to demand that a doctoral degree be completed or at least substantially underway on the part of a plausible candidate for a professorial position. In other words, it's impossible that someone like Frank Iacobucci could be hired now in the way he was, by any contemporary Canadian law school. Indeed, it's highly unlikely that he would be hired at all.

Business Organizations – Professor Iacobucci

I could project that life in a New York City law firm was not a life that I was going to enjoy forever. But the experience gave me confidence to go into the classroom. I wasn't shy about dealing with the issues, with the hard problems. You can't really emulate what you do in a law firm when you're in school. But you can develop skill sets that will help with practice in any setting.

What was it in Frank's background – whether on his curriculum vitae, whether or not noticed or even looked for by Dean Wright – that meant that he walked into the classroom and found teaching a welcome challenge, something he was pretty well prepared for? The two years at Cambridge taking graduate level courses underscored serious intellectual capacity, curiosity, and achievement. His observations and appreciation of the pedagogical aptitude and methods used by effective teachers throughout high school turned them into role models for his own engagement with students. His extensive experience in team sports meant he had practised effective communication, wasn't afraid of hard work, and knew the importance of responsiveness and resilience.

Perhaps most obviously, Frank had been substantially immersed in precisely the kind of law that he was being hired to teach. He points out that you can develop skill sets as a law student that will help with practice in any setting. He could add, *and vice versa*: You can develop skill sets in practice that will help with law school and beyond. For Frank, practice served as preparation for many of the roles and projects that would mark his career, but most immediately it marked his transformation from New York corporate lawyer to Canadian professor of corporate law.

The flagship course in Canadian legal education that deals with duties and relationships in the business or commercial context is typically labelled Business Organizations (shortened to and pronounced "Biz-Org" by students) or Business Associations ("Biz-Azz"). As one of the building blocks in legal education, and a complement to the first-year foundational introduction to agreements, accidents, and notions of property, it is a course that examines the ways in which trust, accountability, and partnership are understood, facilitated, and enforced by legal systems. This is one of the courses in the law school curriculum – along with others including, for example, Taxation, Public International Law, Family Law – that doesn't need to be formally required as part of a university program for most if not all law students to include it. It is perceived as mandatory, whether or not it actually is.

Business Organizations at University of Toronto was Frank's "bread and butter" subject from the late '60s into the early '80s. It's not easy to teach an upper year law course to students who feel they have to be there, students whose attitudes as they arrive in the classroom range from congenial curiosity to bored ambivalence to sharp resentment. Some of Frank's students would go on to specialize in corporate law and finance, securities regulation, or mergers and acquisitions, but many were there because it was just something they felt they had to get through. Success in reaching everyone would have required energy, confidence, patience, and the ability to surprise and convince people into engagement and participation. Professor Iacobucci – or "Yak" for short – seemed to check off all the boxes.

John B. Laskin, Frank's colleague at Torys LLP before being appointed to the Federal Court of Appeal in 2017, remembers Frank as a teacher. "I remember well the first class in the course in Business Organizations that, as a second-year law student, I took with Frank in 1974. Frank's lecture began with a joke about his 'Japanese' last name. That was enough to win the class over. We knew that we had someone special in front of us. There was no doubt that he knew his stuff. But there was also no doubt about his human qualities. They went well beyond self-deprecation; they filtered everything that he taught us. Who knew that Bus Org could be a course in human relations?" (John B. Laskin)

Steve Moate was a U of T law student from 1979–82, and later returned to the university as in-house counsel. "Frank Iacobucci was my professor for the Business Organizations class … What I remember clearly was how he stressed that the entire structure of business law in Canada was based on principles of mutuality, or what would be viewed as commercially reasonable and fair in the circumstances, and that it was designed to facilitate business activity that was aligned with some general societal objectives. He was very much an instructor who asked his students to identify, discuss and then apply the principles underlying the statute law and the case law that he was considering. He wanted us to see the big picture, not just a series of memory-testing rules and precedents. He also stressed a strategic approach to counselling clients regarding business law. These various ways of approaching the interface between law and business have been immensely helpful to me." (Steve Moate)

Professor Iacobucci managed to wear his teaching hat together with his corporate practice hat – bringing what he continued to learn as a lawyer to his students and bringing what he continued to learn as an academic to his clients. He agreed to take the lead on the initial public offering of shares for Consolidated Computer, along with Dave Kilgour, a lawyer who had left a teaching career at U of T to create a small new law partnership, and later to serve as corporate counsel to the firm. Brian Flood describes being assigned as a junior associate to the Bus Org prof-lawyer:

"I joined Kilgour & World as a first-year lawyer in March 1970, just when Consolidated Computer was in need of more money. Dave again called on Frank to help out – more accurately, to lead the transaction. I had never worked on a financing before and served as Frank's junior. Poor Frank! But we got the deal done in what the client and lenders viewed as an impressive performance. I can honestly say that the closing of that transaction was better organized than any transaction in which I have been involved since. Little of that is attributable to my effort; I just did what I was told to do. Frank was most impressive. He had very high standards; was extremely well organized; and was thoughtful and thorough in his analyses and problem solving. And best of all, he was patient with a rookie lawyer.

"As I describe Frank's involvement with Kilgour & World, I must comment on how much fun we had along the way. I still smile when I think of the morning I arrived at the office to find a sign stuck on the bookshelves on which the corporate seals were kept. It read: 'Please don't feed the seals.' There was no doubt who had placed it there." (Brian Flood)

Frank used his sense of humour not only to lighten what could be a very intense atmosphere in legal practice, but also to fit in, to connect with others, and to remind colleagues of his Italian Canadian identity and the importance of diversifying the corporate bar.

Brian Flood celebrates that humour as he continues: "Most memorable of all was the exchange of letters between Sandy World and Frank, after we had asked Frank to become our corporate counsel. With Frank's permission I provide excerpts from the letters:

From the letter to Frank from Sandy.

Dear Professor Iacobucci,
We are in receipt of your application to be included on the letterhead
of our firm. All the partners have given your application mature
consideration and we are disposed to view it favourably subject to certain
reservations concerning the suitability of your name and other matters.
We are of the opinion that our status in the legal community requires a
surname free of any possible dubious ethnic connotations. We are certain
you share our concern.

Accordingly, we take the liberty of suggesting you adopt any of the following surnames which are acceptable to us:

> Abercrombie
> Acton
> Atkins ....

And Frank's reply:

My Dear World,
To say your letter was in poor taste is to promulgate a proposition so patently true as to be unworthy of serious refutation. However, notwithstanding the lack of good taste in the letter, I shall endeavor to meet the two feeble points raised by it.

The first concerns my name. On this point, I am truly amazed by your presumptuous comments. You really don't appreciate my background nor are you sufficiently astute to observe the idiosyncratic nature of those not necessarily iconoclastic but somewhat pragmatic and/or phlegmatic about racial ancestry. You see World, I have already changed my name. It used to be Jacobson and my father and mother decided – some forty-four years ago – to change their name to that of a more hospitable ethnic group........

My answer should now be obvious. My condition of acceptance is that the firm letterhead is:

Iacobucci, Kilgourossi, Worldoro & Floodabella

(Brian Flood)

Critical Analysis – F. Iacobucci, Corporate Law Scholar

The most influential and recognized scholarly contribution that Frank made as a law professor was the creation, in collaboration with others, of course materials in Business Organizations. It's the kind of project that young academics today would be warned away from – not scholarly enough, not peer reviewed, not what gets you promoted or attracts external research grant funding. But, by taking on the task of ensuring that there was a published book with which Bus Org teachers across Canadian common law faculties could plan and deliver their courses, Frank Iacobucci in effect became one of Canada's principal professors of corporate law for students well beyond the walls of the University of Toronto.

Frank's published books and course materials on partnerships and business corporations are all the result of impressive teamwork – whether with colleagues Stan Beck, Leon Getz, David Johnston, and Jacob Ziegel, or with student research assistants Marilyn Pilkington and Rob Prichard. His enthusiasm for approaching the subject area hand in hand with others extended to teaching and pedagogy as well. Frank helped create, and then co-taught, U of T's Business Planning Cluster, a course that integrated different areas of law relevant to the life of a corporation and served as a blueprint for problem-based learning and collegial collaboration. In general, Frank's corner of the curriculum flourished – in substantive and pedagogical terms – at the same time that the legal education curriculum at U of T was becoming more interdisciplinary, more theoretical, and increasingly recognized for expertise and leadership in corporate law and economic analysis.

Later, after becoming dean, Frank had the opportunity to review and share developments at U of T's law school during the 1970s, the decade in which he was intensively involved with law teaching, in an article published in the Dalhousie Law Journal. He described how the Faculty had introduced a signature small-group learning experience for first year students, reached across disciplines to create a range of new upper year courses, and identified law and economics as an important growth area.

This development of broadening the scope of legal education can be seen most clearly in a number of discrete subject areas – law and economics, social welfare law, business law, and clinical legal education and related courses.[6]

Frank spent considerable time in the article outlining the Business Planning Cluster, introduced in the 1974–5 academic year. Meant to lead students through the study of the operation of the legal process as it functions in the business area, the Cluster's goals were as follows:

Placing legal problems in the broader perspective of business problems gener-
ally; ... focusing on legal problems that cut across various areas of business law;
and developing skills such as fact and problem analysis, effective communica-
tion, negotiation and advocacy.... [T]he primary focus of the course ... is on
broadening the perspective of the students by exposing them to accounting,
economic policy and other issues, and in this respect outside professionals...are
brought into the classroom ...

The course concentrates on four stages of the life cycle of a corporation from
incorporation to reorganization.[7]

It was important, according to Frank, that at least one of the co-teachers
be a full-time member of the Faculty of Law, in order to situate the Cluster firmly at the centre of the law school's academic mission. At the same
time, it was clear that the course's raison d'être, content, and shape were
all inspired by the practice that Frank had enjoyed in his brief but intense
time as a New York lawyer.

Les Viner, past student, friend, and colleague in law practice at Torys
LLP in Toronto, describes the experience of participating in the Cluster as
part of a program of legal education:

"I first met Frank about 37 years ago. He was the dean of University of
Toronto Law School, where I was then a student, but I really got to know
him as my professor. He developed and taught the Business Planning Cluster, a small class that focused on corporate law case studies and practical
problem solving. What an honour it was to have been a part of that group,
and to have had the privilege of interacting closely with the dean every
week of that semester. We all knew that this was a special opportunity for
each of us in that class. It was remarkable to have a corporate law professor who had actually practised corporate law! Frank knew the law, but he
also taught us how transactions really worked. His enthusiasm for law was
evident. Yet, it was clear that he also loved the cut and thrust of deals and
he loved interacting with people." (Les Viner)

The 1970s and 1980s were busy decades in terms of substantive developments in Canadian corporate law. Students in Business Organizations were

confronted with a dynamic landscape, and there were plenty of current developments to incorporate into the Business Planning Cluster. As Frank put it, the '70s saw a *"deluge of corporate legislation reform"* in Canada[8] and an accompanying move towards uniformity in corporate law across the country. The new statutes aimed to modernize corporate law and turn the corporation into a more flexible and responsive form of organization in the business context.

At the same time that incorporation was facilitated and made more attractive, accountability was reinforced: shareholder rights, voice, and participation were expanded, as was protection for dissenting or minority shareholders. Significant case law also clarified and introduced greater flexibility into corporate management and the exercise of directors' powers. Perhaps the most important decision, in light of the later upward trend in corporate takeovers, was that related to Afton Mines Ltd., and Frank made substantial contributions to the unfolding critical academic conversation.

Together, legislation and case law illustrated a shift, from the late 1960s and lasting at least twenty years, towards a fair balance between majority and minority shareholders, and an objective assessment of the guiding best interests of the corporation itself. A related issue that began to receive academic attention in the latter part of the 1970s, and that Frank's Bus Org students remember from classroom discussions,[9] was the sale for a premium per-share price of a controlling block of shares in a corporation and the question of whether the profit should be returned to the corporate entity and other shareholders. Accountability for insider trading was tightened and thus underscored. Securities regulation throughout the country was revisited and updated, with the possibility of a pan-Canadian institutional regulator floated for the first time.

Corporate law in the 1980s was characterized by a focus on takeovers and mergers and acquisitions. A federal Restrictive Trade Practices Commission had experienced, in the latter half of the '70s, a strengthening of its mandate to oversee and impose restrictions on mergers that would lessen or squelch competition. A decade later, competition law was even more robust in its targeting of any abuse of dominant position and power. The responsibilities of directors of a corporation on the receiving end of an offer in the context of a takeover bid were difficult to articulate; according to Frank, *"Their dilemma is easy to identify but almost impossible to resolve in a way that will offend no one."*[10] That is, decisions by directors had to abide by securities and corporate law rules; they also had to focus on information sharing with, and protection of, shareholders. Finally, while they could and indeed should offer informed recommendations, they had to guarantee shareholders the opportunity to accept or reject a takeover bid.

Critical conversations with respect to the scope of directors' powers and duties were heating up just as Frank was leaving the university classroom behind. His past students had moved into practice, and some would go on to teach precisely the same issues they had first discussed with Professor Iacobucci. One of the graduate students he supervised, Ralph Simmonds, enjoyed a career as a law professor and a justice of the Supreme Court of Western Australia, incorporating into his own work what he found to be outstanding academic writing and analysis by Frank:

"Frank's article, 'The Exercise of Directors' Powers: The Battle of Afton Mines,'[11] is about what subsequently became one of Canada's best known judicial decisions in corporate law: that of Berger J. in *Teck Corporation Limited v Millar et al.* [1973]. ... The article features a marvellous account of the facts under the heading 'A Mining Promotion Short Story.' It is marvellous because it weaves together the facts that a good first instance judgment would describe, with contextual matter, such as about the mining industry in British Columbia, which gives great flavour to those facts. And it is written most engagingly, even managing to build up an element of suspense, thereby showing that all case law, even in corporate law, contains a story that deserves to be told. ...

"The discussion is a model of its kind. It draws on the factual and contextual matters to address how to locate the judgment in the corporate law of the time, particularly the power of the board of directors to issue shares with effects on control of the corporation. It is heavily footnoted (sometimes to the exclusion of text on that page) with useful ruminations on aspects of the case and reflections on possible future developments of the law in the area of the case and in related areas. The conclusions are clear, comprehensive and concisely stated. One set of those conclusions is worth quoting to illustrate all of this (371–2):

> *In conclusion, the decision of Mr. Justice Berger in the Teck case is correct in validating the agreement between Canex and Afton. The directors of Afton entered into the contract with Canex for a proper purpose – the most advantageous development of Afton's copper property – and in the best interests of the corporation. The proposed issuance of shares under the agreement was quite ancillary to the primary purpose of the agreement, particularly since it was usual in development agreements of this kind; it was therefore not made for an improper purpose, even though the incidental effect of the issuance would have been to affect the control of the company by defeating Teck's majority position. Hence the agreement was rightfully upheld.*

"If there were master classes in academic legal writing about judicial decisions as a means of stimulating interest in the subject matter, 'The Battle of Afton Mines' would feature prominently." (Ralph Simmonds)

Judgments in Corporate Law – Justice Iacobucci

The next time he engaged head-on with the range of corporate law-related issues on which he had developed academic expertise, Frank Iacobucci was a judge, responsible for making decisions that would resolve disputes and provide principled guidance. His contributions to turn-of-the-century corporate and commercial jurisprudence at the Supreme Court of Canada have been subject to in-depth scrutiny and analysis, both formally through scholarship and, more informally, in law school classrooms. The short-hand version of that analysis is as follows: Justice Iacobucci insisted on the institutional limitations of courts, the relevance of context, respect for expertise, and belief in basic values of fairness and decency.

Frank Iacobucci's approach to the powers of directors of a corporation illustrates all of these features. Directors are generally better placed than anyone else to make decisions in the best interests of a corporation, and it would be inappropriate for courts to apply a standard of perfection through hindsight in evaluating their decisions. Put another way, the people responsible for serving a corporation need meaningful latitude to fulfill their mandate. This is far from saying that they have free rein.

Indeed, Frank combines insistence on wide discretion with accountability and the obligation to act in good faith. Context is crucial to assessing decisions and actions, and attention to context by a court should go hand in hand with institutional self-awareness and modesty. Proper judicial understanding of the corporate world does bring with it considerable deference to its participants, and the case of *Blair v Consolidated Enfield Corp.*[12] stands as an instance of unanimous Supreme Court support for Justice Iacobucci's insight and approach.

Jennifer Quaid and Mark Drumbl both clerked for Frank in 1994–5, the year in which the *Blair v Consolidated Enfield* judgment was decided, and many years later Jennifer would teach the case to her corporate law students at the University of Ottawa. They see in the judgment not only a wise decision in the context of business organizations, but a meaningful contribution to understanding the connection between human behaviour and legal rules:

> "'You know the law. I will take my direction from you. What should I do?'
> – Blair (president and chairperson of the shareholders' meeting) to Osler
> (corporate counsel) amid a fiercely contested board election.

"Blair, as it turned out, had made the wrong decision with regard to whether the proxies could be validly voted for Price. In arriving at this decision, Blair had trusted Consolidated Enfield's lawyers who, unfortunately, led him astray on a matter of corporate law that was complex and unsettled at the time. A judge determined the ballots should be counted, a decision upheld on appeal. So Blair was out of his director position.

"It is at this point that the story of the case that went to the Supreme Court formally begins ... Citing Consolidated Enfield's by-laws, Blair filed an application for an order that he be indemnified by the company for the legal costs he incurred in defending his corporate acts. Enfield's by-laws provided for indemnification on essentially the same basis as section 136(1) of the Ontario Business Corporations Act (OBCA), which states that a director may be indemnified by a corporation for all costs 'reasonably incurred' in respect of any proceeding to which he or she is made a party if 'he or she acted honestly and in good faith with a view to the best interests of the corporation. ...

"On its face, *Consolidated Enfield* is a narrow case about interpretation of by-laws. It was a small victory for a director who had otherwise ended up on the losing side of a larger struggle. But big stories often lurk within the smallest and narrowest of cases. This is one of those cases. Whatever the corporate law questions ultimately decided, distilled to its core *Consolidated Enfield* is really a case about justice and fairness. ...

"Blair was a flawed character ... The optics of him serving as chair in the circumstances were terrible and one may wonder why he did not simply head off the entirely foreseeable aftermath by ceding the chair to someone else. But what seems so obvious in hindsight is less so in the moment, especially a moment fraught with tension and conflict.

"Justice Iacobucci's decision is a textbook illustration of the care required in assessing business decisions after the fact. But his decision goes beyond the strict confines of the business judgment rule and the conditions to be met for indemnification. Indeed, he could have stopped his analysis once he concluded that corporate officers seeking indemnification under a regime analogous to s.136 of the OBCA are presumed to have acted in good faith in the interests of the corporation absent proof of *mala fides*. Justice Iacobucci must have felt that something about this case demanded that Blair's conduct be recognized as something more than simply *not bad* for the company (which is sufficient for indemnification) as he devotes the latter part of his reasons to explaining why Blair's conduct be upheld as evidence of *good* behaviour beneficial to the company's interests.

"Why did Justice Iacobucci find Blair deserving of the indemnity? Mostly, because there is a difference between being wrong, and even being self-interested, and being of bad faith. Finding bad faith too easily, and finding bad faith because one was wrong, indeed would be very punitive, in particular when being wrong may only become clear well after the fact, and after all has been said and settled and done. Justice Iacobucci did not find Blair to have improperly used his position as chairperson to further his own agenda. Emphasizing that the detailed organization of a corporation is essentially a private contractual matter, Justice Iacobucci noted that Consolidated Enfield had decided it would be all right for its president to chair these meetings. ...

"Fundamentally, *Consolidated Enfield* is a little case that reveals less about good faith and bad faith than it reveals about Justice Iacobucci's faith in the human condition. Second-guessing is easy; so, too, is triumphalism about being proved 'right.' *Consolidated Enfield* also is a case about time: the passage of time, and the effect of time on the properness of judgement. It is equally a case about the balance between reasonableness in the moment and accuracy in retrospect; duties of care; and what careful reliance on legal counsel means. On this latter note, Justice Iacobucci emphasized that reliance upon legal advice does not guarantee indemnification, but for all practical purposes such reliance, if reasonable and made in good faith, constitutes compelling evidence of honesty and good faith and, thereby, would support indemnification. Here, then, we see a defense of the lawyer, and of legal counsel, or at least the role of legal counsel in the life of a corporation." (Jennifer Quaid and Mark Drumbl)

It is not hard to connect the dots from Frank's time in practice to his teaching and scholarship and then on to his judicial decisions related to corporate organization. In the words of Ralph Simmonds, writing as past student, teacher, and judge, Frank's judicial work in corporate law on the Supreme Court of Canada invites "the flexing of students' legal imaginations" and "in that respect could not be more valuable to another law teacher or indeed to anyone interested in understanding the law."

Expertise gained through practice informed Frank's role as law teacher, and his experience of teaching infused his work as decision-maker and judgment-crafter.

The dots and the lines that join them are not confined to one substantive area. Indeed it is possible to trace them to Frank's judicial approach to issues in administrative law, contract law, and labour law. His appreciation of corporate practice expertise can be linked to a position of considerable deference with respect to expert tribunals and their processes and decisions. His respect for individual actors and their power to organize their affairs can be identified in a desire to line up contract principles with *"modern notions of commercial reality and justice."*[13] And his acknowledgement of the contours and content of business organizations appears to be mirrored in his recognition of the form and vitality of trade unions. It appears that Frank's up-close observation of, and participation in, the corporate sphere encouraged his respect as a judge for other contexts in which people interact with each other and shape the rules that govern those interactions.

Frank's insistence on paying attention to context and practice on the ground is strikingly apparent in the area of tax law. His tax decisions at the Supreme Court of Canada, often for a unanimous Court and usually for the majority, offer a narrow interpretation of the Tax Act provisions at stake, without broad regard as to their intent. This is a judicial approach apparently and explicitly consistent with Frank's solid belief in the importance of context both for understanding the issues at stake and for crafting tailored and effective responses. For Frank, the former practitioner and professor in corporate and tax law, the classic principle that individual actors (persons or corporations) are free to make arrangements to avoid taxation, unless caught by clear and precise rules, provides the relevant contextual background.

David Duff, a U of T law graduate and a tax law professor at UBC, has observed that Frank's Supreme Court of Canada judgments "transformed Canadian tax jurisprudence."[14] In the couple of decades before Frank arrived at the court, the spirit, purpose, and fairness of Tax Act provisions were increasingly emphasized with the result that disputes in interpretation were often decided in favour of the Canada Revenue Agency. In contrast to this seemingly progressive or forward-looking judicial approach, Frank looked back. As Duff notes, he "consistently affirmed the traditional Anglo-Canadian principle that taxpayers can arrange their affairs solely to minimize tax, suggesting that legal responsibility to limit or prevent tax avoidance rested with the legislature, not the courts."[15]

This firm grounding in tradition is examined with a critical eye by Duff, who tentatively explains it by pointing to Frank's personal humility, professional confidence in the institutional abilities of federal government, and, "[a]bove all ... his deep conviction in a conception of the rule of law that emphasized judicial restraint, legal certainty, and individual liberty."[16] While all of this might be right, I would suggest attention primarily be paid to the deep and strong connections between Frank's practice experience and substantive expertise, on one hand, and the task of judicial decision-making at the highest appellate level, on the other. We might say that this is where the $5 a day Frank earned as corporate and tax law practitioner was cleverly invested at a favourable interest rate.

As we will see when we shift to exploring his $5 a day job as judge, Frank understood very well his role and responsibilities as member of the Supreme Court of Canada. As he took on issues related to tax law and corporate law, he could hear the voices of people on the ground in his head. Taxpayers, including corporations, and their lawyers needed to count on clear wording in relevant regulations; they needed to be able to predict and plan with confidence and precision. Frank's pre-court experience of team practice in New York, combined with that of bringing together tax planners and corporate counsel in the design and teaching of the Business Cluster at U of T, informed his judgments. Those judgments in turn, signed by Justice Iacobucci – expert in corporate and tax law – sent out messages received loud and clear by drafters of tax policy, directors of corporations, and individual and institutional actors across the spectrum of commercial reality and justice.

Corporate Governance – Frank's Direction

Post retirement from the court, Frank literally rediscovered the corporate world. He found a place in the boardrooms and governance of Canadian corporations like Tim Hortons and Torstar, and joined the law firm of Torys LLP.

Marc Caira, CEO of Tim Hortons in 2013 and Canada's Business Newsmaker of the Year in 2014, recalls Frank's leadership as the board of the company, famous for its pan-Canadian coffee and donuts, considered the difficult question of whether to sell:

"The unexpected bid for Tim Hortons emerged as a very difficult and emotional issue for our board ... I was recruited, only months earlier, to grow the Tim Hortons brand organically in Canada, the US, and internationally. We never contemplated selling the company or, for that matter, acquiring anyone. Frank diligently reminded us, numerous times, that the board had a fiduciary responsibility to seriously consider the offer ... while we deeply cared for the Tim Hortons brand and the company, it did not belong to us. First and foremost, it was our responsibility and duty to do what was in the best long-term interest of our shareholders, while also taking into consideration the needs of other stakeholders.

"We certainly did not have consensus on our board at first, as you would expect with a very senior and diverse group of individuals. Through dialogue (some heated) and much consultation with our advisers and some soul searching, we reached the unanimous decision to sell Tim Hortons. Frank played a leading role throughout the entire process. Through his quiet, yet meticulous and thorough guidance as the lead director, the Tim Hortons transaction was completed over a 10-month period, resulting in the world's largest restaurant sale ever. The shareholders were definitely pleased, as they received a 47 per cent premium on the previous 30-day average stock price.

"At Frank's insistence, however, this transaction had to be more than just good value for our shareholders. We had to ensure that we protected the

Tim Hortons brand, the franchisees, the Tim Hortons charities, and other stakeholders. As a result, the final language in the sale document included over 40 conditions or, as Frank called them, 'principles,' enforceable by the Government of Canada, requiring those qualities inherent in the Tim Hortons brand to remain well into the future!

...

"Like many things Frank has touched in his life, he left an indelible mark on one of Canada's most iconic brands and businesses. During his tenure on the board of Tim Hortons, the number of restaurants grew from just under 3,000 to almost 5,000. The market cap of the company increased from $6.0 billion to just under $10 billion, and profitability more than doubled. I am certain Frank would accept very little credit for these remarkable results because that is a representation of his humble personality. That's just how he is. He is far more comfortable giving recognition than receiving it, yet there is one statistic that Frank completely owns and cannot pass to anyone else. In the nine years that Frank was on the Tim Hortons board, according to official records, he did not miss one single meeting. Between 15 to 18 meetings per year, including both board and committee meetings, Frank had a perfect 100 per cent attendance every year. That's commitment, determination, and loyalty! That's Frank!" (Marc Caira)

In a piece on legal practice, published when he was chief justice of the Federal Court of Canada, Frank argued that an *over-emphasis on the business side of law* had diminished the professionalism of lawyers. According to Frank, public service – the *constructive involvement in the broad spectrum of activities that enrich the life of our community* – is a key tenet of the practice of law, and efforts need to be made to counter what he worried was an influx of profit-minded individuals and a corresponding decline in the humanity embodied by lawyers. Based on the corporate law practice and academic expertise that had shaped his past, Frank declared that *we must re-discover law as a calling, as rendering high service to our fellow men and women*.[17]

Through re-engagement with corporate governance in the later stages of his career, Frank appeared determined to act in what he perceived as a professional manner and, perhaps, to serve as a model of the kind of public service-minded practitioner of law he had in mind. In particular, he underscored the importance of guiding principles in directing any corporation. In his 2006 report as chair of the board of directors for Torstar (the media and publishing company named for its flagship *Toronto Star* newspaper), Frank underlined the commitment not only to set attainable financial goals but to remain "*mindful of the values that are foundational to the mission of Torstar.*"[18] He referred to the Atkinson Principles – principles that include social justice and community and civic engagement – as a set of guiding beliefs for the corporation. These may not be surprising or particularly original principles for an organization, but they formed part of a regular reminder by Frank to shareholders and board members of the general commitments that should shape corporate decision-making.

Frank's "What"

One of the things a convocation speaker can't do in a speech to graduating law students is dictate what exactly these jurists will become particularly knowledgeable about in terms of substantive areas or issues of law. Each graduate will continue to learn; each listener will indeed develop expertise; each jurist will follow a path partly characterized by a particular answer to the question of "what" that jurist knows and does. For Frank Iacobucci, the "what" that stands out – developed in various ways, with various objectives, within various contexts – is the law of business organizations and associations. It's not the precise "what" that he might have had in mind throughout law school or on the day of his own graduation from UBC or from Cambridge.

The Business Organizations course has served as one of the sites for thrashing out the complexities of what has always been a messy mix of academic and professional governance of legal education.[19] At stake is the place of the course in Canadian law schools: Should it be mandatory or optional, foundational or complementary? Examination for the purposes of entry to the professional Bar or Law Society of every province typically includes testing for knowledge of corporate organization, relationships and powers, and – at an even more basic level – individuals who might end up · as partners in law firms will need to know what partnership means and how it works. But legal academia rightly worries about the ways in which curricular choices can be skewed by perceived expectations in practice, and about the need for appropriate limits on the involvement of regulatory actors in the shaping of the content and form of legal education.

It would be easy and obvious to think that someone like Frank Iacobucci, who taught the course and developed corporate law expertise, would support making Business Organizations mandatory for every law student. Instead, he might describe Bus Org as one on a list of courses – many or most not at all situated in the corporate or commercial context – that focus on human interactions, distribution of power and resources, trust and accountability, ethical practice, and the unpacking and often interdisciplinary resolution of human problems. Exposure to and engagement with ideas related to the intertwining of private law duties and regulation in the public sphere is indeed a crucial part of legal education. But that doesn't or shouldn't translate into a formal requirement on the part of law students to take Business Organizations. That particular course provides only one "what" or substantive field, out of a range of possible candidates, in which to become an expert.

While the lessons don't have to come in the form of a Bus Org course, Frank Iacobucci shows that they can. As Frank's path illustrates, a corporate lawyer can dedicate a career to thinking through the interactions between formal law and organizational norms or rules, the shape of effective restraints on power, the contours of citizenship and service, and the leadership and accountability of Canadian institutions. Frank took his primary area of knowledge as a jurist and sharpened, shared, and developed it through practice, writing, teaching, decision-making, and governance.

Through his understanding of the connections among principles, players, sources, and structures in the domain of corporate law, he figured out those connections in other domains. Through his experience with partnerships in the corporate commercial sphere, he nourished and valued partnerships in other spheres. Frank first learned his 'stuff' in his initial "$5 a day" job. He took it with him through all the jobs to follow.

3

You Will Lead – Frank Iacobucci as Playmaker

Working with Others

In the fall of 1984, Frank Iacobucci was vice-president and provost of the University of Toronto. After delivering a welcome address to the first-year class at University College at U of T, he leaned over to the 19-year-old student president of the College and asked, "Was I OK?" It was remarkable for a university provost to ask an undergraduate student for evaluation and feedback. But checking in with the people around him – making sure he's on the right track with his message or constructive critique or suggestions – seems to characterize how Frank does a job and acts as a leader. It was a striking and memorable way to convey to a student in a position of responsibility that effective leaders don't stop questioning, trying to do their best, and communicating with others.

I was that student. Our conversation that evening led to my being asked to serve as student member on the Academic Affairs Committee that Frank chaired. I gained valuable experience in university governance and I found a mentor who showed me how law and leadership could go hand in hand. For Frank, $5 a day pays not only for what you know but how you contribute to the team. What I didn't realize at the time was that the University of Toronto was full of people who were inspired by Frank, who thought he was doing better than OK, and whose opinion mattered to Frank as he dedicated time and energy to running the place.

In 2004, twenty years later, the Honourable Frank Iacobucci retired from the Supreme Court of Canada. At about the same time, the president of University of Toronto, Robert Birgenau, decided to cut short his term by accepting the position of chancellor of University of California Berkeley. The usual response for the university would have been to appoint the provost as interim president – something it had done 22 years before, when the incoming president had died before taking office. Instead, it turned to Frank Iacobucci, the person selected to serve as provost by that earlier interim president. Frank had left campus life in 1985. This was his chance to return to the world of post-secondary education, and to come home to Toronto.

Janice Gross Stein, professor and founding director of University of Toronto's Munk School of Global Affairs, tells the story:

"The presidency of the university became vacant unexpectedly and the chair of the board of governors did a canvas of the University's academic leaders, asking them whom they wanted for president until a permanent president could be chosen. The consultation was swift and unanimous: the choice was Frank Iacobucci. His judgment, integrity, wisdom, and warmth were obvious to everyone.

"That year was special. Frank brought to the challenges of university leadership not only these obvious but important strengths but a strong moral compass that was unwavering. When the going got tough, out came that moral compass as a guide for everyone. The standard was not only what the rules required – although it was often that; not only what the law required – although it was always that. The standard, whether it was a student, faculty, or staff issue, was what justice required, when justice was rich, complex, nuanced, and fulsome. President Iacobucci held himself and his colleagues to the highest possible standards that represented the very best of what a university in Canada could aspire to be. And he did so always with a twinkle in his eye. How fortunate the University of Toronto was and is to have the devotion and commitment of Frank Iacobucci." (Janice Gross Stein)

By the time he took on the one-year term as university president, Frank had developed his leadership skills in three distinctive contexts: university, government, and judiciary. Each brought its own particular titles, responsibilities, and development of expertise. Each demanded its own set of considerations, each emphasized its own role in Canadian society, each had its own traditions and structures and cast of characters. In all of them, Frank figured out what he could contribute, when he was needed as the playmaker on the team, and how to make sure he did OK.

University Administration

One of the things about administration is that – if you're going to do a good job as an administrator – it takes you away from your teaching, your research, and so on. You can do certain things, but you can't do the full array. You're kidding yourself if you think otherwise.

Frank focused on teaching and research as a professor for a very short time at the University of Toronto. In 1973, six years after joining the Faculty, he received an invitation to serve as associate dean and then proceeded from one leadership position to another: from associate dean of Law to vice-president Internal Affairs of the university, then back to Law as dean, and from there to university vice-president and provost. Each time he answered the call, he became more of an insider – someone who was already appreciated and would be readily accepted and respected. He clearly felt a sense of duty and loyalty, and the fact that he thrived as administrative leader meant fewer regrets at reducing his course load and list of writing projects.

Three University of Toronto colleagues – Martin Friedland, Robert Prichard, and Michael Trebilcock – were special longtime companions at the law school. Marty preceded Frank as dean and Rob followed him, while Michael stayed away from formal administrative leadership positions. Marty takes credit for introducing Frank to U of T, Rob relied on Frank's mentorship throughout his career, and both Michael and Frank adopted Toronto as "their" law school although neither was an alumnus. Reflections by the three friends, each of them a U of T leader in his own way, fill in the narrative of Frank's contributions in university administration.

As a law student, Rob Prichard was Frank's research assistant and co-author; he went on to follow in Frank's footsteps as professor, Law dean, and university administrator. In his words: "It was as an academic leader that Frank's superstar status most fully emerged. He is a natural leader, and at every stage of his career, his colleagues have turned to him to be their leader. People want to be led by Frank: he makes everyone feel valued and respected on their own terms even as he unites them in pursuit of common goals." (J.R.S. Prichard)

Martin Friedland was the dean of Law who selected Frank as his associate dean, and describes the context in which Frank took on the associated responsibilities and then made the transition to university level problem solving and governance:

"The early 1970s were some of the most challenging times in the history of the law school. Many of the student activists from the late 1960s were then in law school and demanded change. Frank was the perfect person to help negotiate the changes. We obtained all of Falconer Hall for special programs, such as the very successful law and economics program, which started in those years. We continued to fine-tune the new first-year small group program, which is still a mainstay of the first-year program. We helped create an active student legal aid program. We introduced a directed research program and what we called 'cluster programs.'

"Frank's skill in solving problems and achieving results became evident to the university Faculty Association and Frank became the chair of the association's grievance committee over a two-year period. At that time there were a number of contested denials of tenure and salary disputes, and Frank negotiated with university officials on such issues as whether the proper procedures had been followed. President John Evans thus became aware of Frank's effective involvement in these matters, and in 1975, when Jill Conway, the vice-president of Internal Affairs, left to become president of Smith College, Frank was asked to take her place as vice-president.

"Not only did Frank take on all the issues relating to student affairs and such other areas as employment equity, he also took on personnel matters and developed written personnel policies throughout the university. He also worked closely with the provost in negotiating with the Faculty Association, which was threatening to seek certification as a union. More than twenty meetings were held during the winter months of 1976–7 between the Faculty Association's negotiating committee and the university's team. This resulted in a memorandum of agreement which contained a list of policies, such as those relating to conflicts of interest and tenure procedures, that became known as 'frozen policies' – policies that could not be changed without the consent of the Faculty Association. Either party after three years of operation could reject the agreement, but that has not happened. The agreement still operates today." (Martin Friedland)

Rob Prichard underscores in a similar way Frank's legacy with respect to labour relations at the university:

"Within six years of arriving at the Law School, Frank was the universally popular associate dean. Two years later, President John Evans called him to the University's central administration as vice-president, Internal Affairs. He enjoyed great success in that role, particularly as he used his skills as a lawyer to devise processes and institutional arrangements uniquely suited to the needs of the academy. He negotiated a creative agreement outside the Labour Relations Act but granting substantial rights to the University's Faculty Association (excluding the right to strike). Forty years later, that agreement still stands, albeit with some amendments, and it has served the University exceptionally well. Recently when the University and the Faculty Association reached an impasse over some potential amendments to the agreement, they turned to Frank as the agreement's original author

to mediate the dispute. This is how well remembered his leadership is."
(J.R.S. Prichard)

Marty Friedland talks about preparing to pass on the reins of leadership of the law faculty: "My period as dean was to expire at the end of June 1978 and Frank, who was then on sabbatical in Cambridge – the only sabbatical he took in his entire career on and off the bench – was the obvious candidate to succeed me. As dean, he continued the momentum he had helped create in the 1970s. He also started the process of planning for a new library building, which Rob Prichard brought to a successful conclusion when he became dean." (Martin Friedland)

It was a new beginning for me and for the law school. The fact that I was a non-alumnus law dean at U of T meant it was important for me to make connections with alumni. And it was important to show professors that I was both their colleague and a leader. It was a time of salary increase for law professors, hand in hand with an emphasis on high quality scholarship and on the development of connections between law and cognate disciplines like economics and philosophy and health. I read every teaching evaluation, and I did my bit of walking around to visit people in their offices. When we hired a new professor, I tried to make sure we asked, "What are we going to do for this young colleague?"

Rob Prichard reflects on the highlights of Frank's deanship and the lessons passed on:

"In 1979, he returned to the Law School to serve as dean where he again demonstrated superb leadership. He greatly strengthened the Law School's relationship with its graduates and the broader community, and set an example followed ever since by not just his successors in law, but by professional faculties across the University...

"Frank was a terrific university administrator because he was first and foremost a teacher and scholar, but he was also a fine lawyer. As he told me once, the dean of Law should be the University's attorney general, giving wise and independent counsel to the university's leadership and carrying influence far greater than the law school's size alone would dictate.

Frank did this brilliantly and became the university's most trusted adviser."
(J.R.S. Prichard)

It might sound pretty corny, but I think it's right to say that the dean has to be the voice of the law school in the deliberations of central administration, and the voice of the university in deliberations of the school.

From Michael Trebilcock comes a different kind of memory of, and lesson from, the Iacobucci deanship, recalled in a speech directed to Frank upon his return to the University in 2004:

"In your four years as dean, I recall that we both were early morning persons and that we came to an agreement that you and I would share coffee making duties on the third floor of Falconer, just outside my office and immediately above the Decanal suite. Despite our agreement, I swear that over this four-year period I made coffee at least 80 per cent of the time. You would listen for my footsteps on the floor above performing the disagreeable task of cleaning out the coffee machine and then refilling it, at which point you would come racing up the stairs explaining (to pick one of your more credible excuses) that you had been diverted on your way up the stairs by a distraught student who needed urgent counselling.

"Over early morning coffee each morning during this four year period, you and I would start with the outer perimeters of the world – the intensification of conflict in the Middle East, the imminent collapse of communism in Eastern Europe, the latest military coup in Latin America – and work inwards to the current concerns in the Faculty, such as what should be done with the latest of a seemingly endless stream of proposals to revise our grading scheme for students' courses.

"From this experience with you, I learned the importance of strategic behaviour in most walks of life and have applied these concepts rigorously in a wide range of academic and personal pursuits." (Michael Trebilcock)

Frank didn't finish his term as dean; four years in, he was called upon once again to head to Simcoe Hall, the home of U of T's central administration. He became the university's chief academic officer, taking on the new title of vice-president and provost. Marty Friedland points out the connections between the work Frank had done previously and the particular challenges that confronted him in the mid-1980s:

"Partway through his deanship, Frank was invited by President David Strangway to become the provost of the university and continued in that position under President George Connell. Once again, the most difficult issue he had to deal with was collective bargaining with the Faculty Association and whether an arbitrator's award was binding on the university. It was resolved when Frank presented a compromise formula: an arbitrator's award could be rejected by the Governing Council of the university, but the following year an award would be binding. As far as I am aware, that compromise arrangement, like the memorandum of agreement, is still in existence over thirty years later." (Martin Friedland)

When Frank reflects on his role in developing a sustainable hybrid model for the Faculty Association, he admits he was *probably the key player*. His engagement with academic colleagues in reaching an agreement everyone could live with was a recurring aspect of his work as a vice-president. It was part of the reason that U of T came back to him in 2004 to convince him to return as interim president – an offer to which Frank reports Nancy as saying, "I think you have to do it." When asked why someone would want the job of university president, Frank answers, *It's an important position in society … You have to be passionate about what universities do; you have to have a desire to lead. And it takes courage.*

In his book *Leadership under Fire: The Challenging Role of the Canadian University President*, Ross H. Paul describes a successful university president's role in setting the direction for an academic institution and in underscoring the virtues of achievement, teamwork, and celebration:

The president has primary responsibility for ensuring an organizational climate that encourages and builds these virtues, and most successful leaders have demonstrated by example how best to fulfill them. The president's role is not nearly as much about formal strategic planning as it is about identifying, through an open and thorough process, the strategic priorities that best represent the institution's mission and mandate and working tirelessly to communicate these priorities, to assign appropriate resources to them, to insist on the highest standards of performance, and to celebrate success.[20]

Frank earlier had declined consideration for the presidency through the usual process. He had worked closely with individuals who served as successful university leaders, including David Johnston and Robert Prichard, two of the Canadian university presidents selected for attention in Paul's book. But he had decided not to follow what might have seemed an obvious path to the president's door from the provost's office down the hall. Instead, he came to the position in interim mode: perhaps an ideal way to lead a university he loved without quite having to invest energy in the full range of responsibilities that fall on a president's shoulders. He had a short time period in which to leave the place in a better position than it had been when he arrived, and he managed to do precisely that. In Rob Prichard's words, Frank reminded U of T it could be a place of "joy and optimism."

Steve Moate, U of T's in-house counsel, describes the context as Frank arrived from the Supreme Court: "It was not an easy time. There were many issues that could have erupted into disharmony. This being a university, a lot of strident voices enjoyed making themselves heard (sometimes, it seemed, primarily to have the pleasurable – for them – experience of hearing their own voice). Frank repeatedly said, and I believe this is a quote, 'I am just here to keep a steady hand on the tiller.'

"He was a brilliant interim president … He is a leader. And he leads by example. He would not raise his voice, but by his calm, reasonable, compassionate, and insightful approach to every single issue he would gently (or sometimes very firmly) nudge things in the direction they had to go. He listened and could be persuaded of a different course of action than that which had been initially put forward. Even with very contentious issues, his wisdom and humility, and the fact that he was at the university to serve rather than to advance his own interests, made a huge difference. On rare occasions we got to see his skill in conveying displeasure, usually about

behaviour, in a way that did not produce confrontation and almost immediately got the offending person or people to back down. He was able to
assist the many voices in the university's large Governing Council to move
in a common direction at a time of transition." (Steve Moate)

In the quote shared earlier to introduce Frank's work as university leader,
Frank reflects on what has to be given up if you're going to take the path
of administrator in the academic context: *If you're going to do a good job
as an administrator it takes you away from your teaching, your research, and
so on.* His time dedicated to the classroom and scholarship, without any
administrative title and set of responsibilities, was limited. He moved from
professor to associate dean to university vice-president to dean to provost,
each role taking him further away from full-time teaching and research.
He particularly missed the classroom dynamic in which he engaged with
students and received constant feedback on the effectiveness of what he
was doing as a teacher. On the other hand, administration offered positive
feedback as well. Much less lonely than research and writing could be, it
kept Frank in a position he excelled at: that of inspiring, directing, and
bringing together people in shared projects.

Indeed, Frank proved to be so good at university administration that it
would have been difficult, if not impossible, to return to the life of a professor. By 1985, perhaps without explicit recognition on his part, Frank
was ready for a change and a new challenge. By handing over his curriculum vitae, albeit with the insistence that he was happy where he was, he
opened the door to exiting the context and community in which he had
become a known and highly valued entity.

Canada's Lawyer

*When Mulroney got elected, he said it was time to shake up the civil service and
bring in some new blood ... I was asked to meet with a couple of his supporters
in Toronto over breakfast and they asked me whether I was interested in going*

to Ottawa. I said "No" ... I was provost at that time. "I'm very happy in the
university, I'm not looking for anything."
"What do you think about down the road?"
I said, "I don't know." I was in my 40s.
"Well, could we get your cv?"
I said, "OK, but please, on the understanding that I'm not applying for any-
thing." There was nothing to apply for anyway!
And then one day, out of the blue, I got a call from Gordon Osbaldeston, who
was the clerk for the Privy Council, and he said, "Frank, we'd like you to come
to Ottawa to be deputy minister of Justice."
I said, "Wow! Are you sure you've got the right guy?"

When Frank Iacobucci, appointed by Prime Minister Brian Mulroney, walked into the Department of Justice in 1985, the lawyers in the civil service probably asked themselves the same question. Was this the "right guy" for the job? What did he know about working for government? How would he adapt to them and vice versa? And, for the francophones in the department, what would it mean for them to have a boss who didn't speak French? He might be a law professor (specializing in private and commercial law – not an obvious fit with the Department of Justice, but of value under the new, business-oriented management style of the Mulroney government), and a big shot at a university (which at least indicated political neutrality), but what could he bring to the post of Senior Legal Officer of the Crown?

This was a big change for Frank. He had left the comfort of Simcoe Hall – the home of the leadership of U of T – for the Department of Justice on Wellington Street in downtown Ottawa, where it wasn't going to be easy to receive support and admiration. He was, he admits, completely under-prepared in some ways. He had no French – his high school teacher unfortunately had advised him to take Latin rather than French when she learned that he wanted to become a lawyer – and he had no idea what the job of deputy in the public service entailed. But Frank was excited to be going back to the practice of law, albeit public law, something he hadn't focused on since his days as a graduate student. He arrived at Justice as someone without any party affiliation or loyalty, which meant that civil servant lawyers didn't perceive him as a political insider brought in to supervise. With those advantages in hand, he set about getting to know everybody.

I spent hours with everyone, asking them what their plans were ... basically saying "Look, I'm the new guy, I want to learn, I don't have the answers, but I want them." I was told that the success rate wasn't great for bringing in people from the outside. So, I just immersed myself. I used to say to the Justice lawyers: you can't have a better client than the people of Canada. It's a big message. The overall ethos of the organization was so important ... I gained great respect for the public service.

I started taking French lessons and gave strong signals of support to the francophone membership of the department ... even though I was linguistically challenged. I'll never forget what Anne-Marie Trahan (lawyer at Justice and later member of the Quebec Superior Court) said at the end of my three years: "Although we have a deputy minister who is not as bilingual as we might like, we could not have had a stronger supporter." I was in tears when she said it; it meant so much to me.

Douglas Rutherford served as Frank's associate deputy minister of Justice and recalls the arrival of Canada's newest top lawyer:

"One might have thought that breaking into the culture and society of Ottawa's senior mandarinate by an outsider might have required time and adaptation. But Frank's energy, intellect, and engaging personality made such a challenge look more like an amicable take-over. He made friends very quickly throughout the deputy minister cadre, from line departments, through central agencies and to the heart of the Privy Council Office. Always ready to match strokes with anyone who could keep up, Frank deepened a number of collegial relationships through his very competitive tennis game, outdoors in good weather and indoors in winter. In no time at all he made friendships and forged bonds of confidence and trust throughout the Capital such that his effectiveness not only as the deputy senior law officer of the Crown, but as deputy-head of the Justice Department was immediately palpable." (Douglas Rutherford)

Mary Dawson was associate chief legislative counsel at the time, responsible for the English versions of Canada's federal statutes. She learned of Frank's appointment while at a Canadian Bar Association conference in Halifax. Like many of the lawyers around her, she had never heard the name "Iacobucci"; like others, she didn't recognize its Italian origin before seeing it in print and speculated that the new deputy minister might be Japanese Canadian. In her words: "It was quite unusual to have a deputy minister appointed who had not already served in the federal Public Service. But then, Frank turned out to be quite unusual. I don't think I ever met anyone who was quite so adept at fitting in so quickly. After a short time, it was as if he had been in Ottawa for a long time. … Frank was only at the Department of Justice for a few short years, but they were important ones both for me and for the country. It was Frank who convinced me to move from the Legislation Section when, in 1986, he appointed me as the assistant deputy minister of Public Law." (Mary Dawson)

Frank's mode of leading the department and making decisions regarding appointments is described by Doug Rutherford, the person he named as the deputy minister's associate:

"In managing the Justice Department, the new deputy minister took his time assessing the resources he had to work with. He accepted what he considered to be good advice, namely, to wait at least six months before making significant changes in his senior personnel or departmental structure, because early on he would likely be met with a number of bright and ambitious suggestions for advancement and change from within, only to appreciate later that some may not have been as bright as they were ambitious.

"In due course, however, Frank made significant choices about the way he wanted the department to operate and put in place a senior staff team of his own choosing. In doing so, he instilled in all his senior colleagues a sense of a special relationship of trust and confidence and an expectation on his part of a high level of achievement." (Douglas Rutherford)

The deputy minister of Justice is the senior bureaucrat in the Department of Justice or, in other words, the top-ranking unelected official in that Cabinet portfolio. The simultaneous hat of deputy attorney general of Canada makes that person the lead general counsel to the government of the day. Frank had ample opportunity to guide a whole range of important projects, some to a satisfactory conclusion and others frustrated in the process. Under Ministers of Justice John Crosbie and Raymond Hnatyshyn, Frank worked on the constitutional aspects of the North American Free Trade Agreement, the elimination of capital punishment, the decriminalization of abortion, war criminals legislation, and Indigenous self-government. The self-government file was unsuccessful. So was that of the Meech Lake Accord, meant to bring Quebec into the Canadian Constitution and the highest profile dossier during the time Frank was at the Department. It was Meech Lake that situated Frank at the very centre of Canada's self-defining projects and priorities.

More than thirty years after Meech Lake, students of Canadian Constitutional law are unlikely to spend much if any time on the details of constitutional promise and failure in the 1980s. In general, accounts and understandings of the constitution (small "c") and the Constitution (big "C") of Canada no doubt display considerable diversity across first year law classrooms as well as across the country's geographical, linguistic, and socio-cultural communities. The story of Frank's role as would-be playmaker against a backdrop of the characters and conversations that made up Meech Lake provides a picture of the substance and process at stake at the time, and insight into the context that continues to shape Canada's identity.

What were the principal hurdles embodied in the Meech Lake project and process? There were two: the exercise and scope of the federal spending power, and the recognition of Quebec as a distinct society.[21] With respect to the first, Quebec wanted a constitutionally entrenched limit on the federal spending power – a power that can be used to circumvent constitutional barriers to federal involvement in areas formally under the jurisdiction of the provinces. For example, while the federal government cannot legislate in healthcare (which falls within provincial competence), it can make funding grants conditional on the faithful participation by provinces in the administration of a national public health system. With respect to the second, Quebec wanted the distinct society wording to provide an interpretive clause that applied to the entire Constitution, reflecting a narrative of Confederation as a marriage of French and English nations. Critics responded with an alternative narrative according to which Quebec was one among equal provinces. Further, they worried that the rights of minority linguistic communities in Quebec might be limited; in this, they were joined by other supporters of Pierre Elliot Trudeau's vision of a uniform countrywide guarantee of fundamental human rights.

Douglas Rutherford recalls the immediate aftermath in late April 1987 of the drawing up of an agreement at Willson House situated on the shore of Meech Lake: "Anyone speaking with Frank Iacobucci that night or in the ensuing days could tell that his participation in the affair and contribution to its success had been a career highlight for him." Frank was there as member of the federal delegation, headed by then Prime Minister Brian Mulroney. Also included were Rutherford, associate deputy minister, and Mary Dawson, head of Public Law and drafter of the proposed constitutional amendments.

It wouldn't have been hard to tell how happy Frank was on that spring evening. Frank's smiles typically show remarkable warmth, and the accomplishment at Meech Lake must have made him beam. He had accompanied Mulroney, along with the first ministers of every Canadian province, in devising a solution to the constitutional impasse created by the absence of Quebec's signature from the 1982 Constitution. As Doug Rutherford recounts, a usually modest Frank Iacobucci admitted, "When the prime minister of Canada puts his arm around your shoulder in the presence of the whole company and announces, 'Frankie, you're my lawyer,' you can't help feeling a bit good about yourself." (Douglas Rutherford)

Without Quebec's agreement, the Constitution, indeed the country, had felt somehow incomplete. After five years of hesitation, the officials of the day had decided to make the leap. As Frank would later suggest, and historians of Meech Lake mostly agree, the most significant factor in the emergence of a new constitutional solution was the coincidence of Brian Mulroney and Robert Bourassa in office. Both the prime minister of Canada and the premier of Quebec eagerly wanted a solution, and they worked together to prime the electorate for change. Mulroney made public overtures to Quebec, while Bourassa responded with a set of strict conditions under which his province would sign.

That was the show. Behind the scenes, the two leaders already agreed on almost everything. An intergovernmental consensus emerged with uncommon speed in the months leading up to the Willson House meeting, such that on April 30 at Meech Lake, the first ministers needed only nine hours to finalize an agreement in principle. Mary Dawson remembers, "We were in a state of euphoria"; Doug Rutherford recalls, "Ottawa was in celebration that night."

According to the Meech Lake Accord, Canada's Constitution would be modified through the following five crucial elements:

- Quebec would be recognized as a "distinct society" in s. 2 of the *Constitution Act, 1867*. This would operate as an interpretative clause for the entire constitution;
- Prospective constitutional amendments would now be subject to s. 41 of the *Constitution Act, 1982*, which meant they required the approval of every province and the Federal government;
- Provincial powers with respect to immigration were to be increased;
- Provinces were to be granted the right to reasonable financial compensation if that province chose to opt out of any future federal programs in areas of exclusive provincial jurisdiction;

- The appointment of senators and Supreme Court judges, traditionally a prerogative of the prime minister, would be drawn from a selection of names provided by the provinces.

A little over a month later, the elation had dissipated. There was a deal formally in place, and a signing ceremony was held at the Ottawa Convention Centre on 3 June 1987, to mark the agreement. But, as revealed in one striking photograph at the time, the happy smiles were gone. Brian Mulroney looks down without joy, pen to paper, as his chief of staff, Norman Spector, watches over his left shoulder. Next to him, federal Minister of Justice Ray Hnatyshyn looks into the distance. Frank, seated in the background, makes a stiff attempt at a smile, nothing like the April version would have been.

The tense atmosphere anticipates the Accord's eventual failure. No one had slept the night before. What was supposed to have been a routine confirmation of the terms had turned into a bitter slog, with details settled in the hours leading up to the moment of signing. Ian MacDonald, an adviser to the prime minister at the time, remembers Frank Iacobucci and Ian Scott, attorney general for Ontario, in the middle of the night "in an unseemly shouting match in which they very nearly came to blows."[22] Even if exaggerated, the moment was obviously intense and difficult for everyone. It posed what would become a central question for all Canadians and an ongoing personal and professional struggle for Frank as lawyer, citizen, and consensus-builder: Can we have unity while preserving difference?

Patrick Monahan, at the time a young policy adviser on the legal team that accompanied Ontario Premier David Peterson to Ottawa, recalls the details of that night:

"We had originally expected the June 2 meeting to be relatively straightforward, since our task was simply to translate the political commitments in the Accord into a legal text. But in the weeks leading up to the meeting concerns had been raised about various aspects of the Accord, culminating in a 27 May newspaper article by former Prime Minister Pierre Trudeau which condemned the Accord as a 'total bungle.' Trudeau was particularly concerned over the potential impact of the Accord's 'distinct society' clause on *Charter* rights in Quebec.

"As the discussions continued through the day and into the evening of June 2, we had settled the legal text for most of the Accord, with the only outstanding item being the wording of the distinct society clause. Ontario's lawyers, led by Attorney General Scott, were continuing to press for clarity that the distinct society clause would not diminish the rights of the English-speaking minority in Quebec. At the same time, Quebec Premier Robert Bourassa had made it clear that such an amendment was both unnecessary and unacceptable.

"By 3:00 a.m., with no agreement in sight, what was emerging was the possibility of a split between Premiers Peterson and Bourassa on the distinct society issue. This was a nightmare scenario, since it would turn a process originally intended to enhance national unity into one that would open fresh divisions between Quebec and the rest of the country.

"In an attempt to break this impasse, Premier Peterson suggested that the Ontario legal team be invited into the conference room where the prime minister and the premiers were gathered and be provided the opportunity to make their case directly to the first ministers. Attorney General Scott and Professor Peter Hogg, who was one of Ontario's legal advisers, argued that wording needed to be added to the Accord to make it clear that *Charter* rights would not be negatively affected.

"Fortunately, Prime Minister Brian Mulroney had had the good sense and foresight to ensure that Frank Iacobucci was in the room for this critical discussion. After Ian and Peter had concluded their arguments, the prime minister invited Frank to provide his comments. Frank reviewed the terms of the draft text, agreeing with Scott and Hogg that the distinct society clause would confirm the role of the Quebec government to promote the French language in the province. But this was nothing new, Frank argued, since the courts had already recognized that such efforts were entirely legitimate. Frank also noted that the draft text included reference to the English-speaking community as a fundamental characteristic of Canada, thereby indirectly referencing their *Charter* rights. Thus, Frank concluded, the distinct society clause, with or without the amendment Ontario was proposing, would merely confirm the direction that the courts had already adopted in their interpretation of the *Charter*. In his view, Ontario's amendment was not needed and the text before the first ministers should be approved.

"There were other interventions, including by noted jurist Roger Tassé, following which the legal advisers were dismissed and the first ministers resumed their private deliberations. They emerged around 5:00 a.m. with a unanimous agreement, one that did not include the proposed Ontario amendment to the distinct society clause. In the end, David Peterson had been persuaded by Frank Iacobucci that the wording his own advisers were advocating was not needed." (Patrick Monahan)

In 2009, Frank was invited to the European University Institute in Florence, Italy, to speak at a conference on courts and democracy. His presentation was entitled "The Quebec Secession Reference: Law, Politics and Nationhood";[23] in it are the connections he saw between constitutional law and politics in the construction and sustenance of his country. By the time he prepared and delivered the talk, he had participated in the Supreme Court of Canada's response to the federal government's questions regarding the procedural parameters of potential Quebec secession.[24] Among the members of the court, he was the only one with extensive experience on the side of the questioner – that is, as chief lawyer for the federal government, albeit at a different stage of this perpetual piece of Canada's constitutional puzzle. Parts of Frank's presentation are excerpted here:

"Historically the challenge of forming Canada as a country was particularly difficult in recognizing the needs and attributes of Quebec as part of a country that was to be Canada. The rather unique features of Quebec that included its language, its civil law tradition, its institutional differences and its

impressively rich culture are matters that required accommodation in creating the constitution of the country ...

"However, the aspirations of Quebec and many Québecois did not disappear upon the creation of the Canadian Constitution in 1867 ... There were a series of issues and events that manifested Quebec's longing for either increased recognition under the Canadian Constitution or, for many Quebeckers, having a separate nation to better reflect the Québecois political, linguistic, cultural, and social reality.

"This political goal of increased Québecois recognition if not secession was heightened when former Prime Minister Trudeau led the efforts to repatriate the Canadian Constitution from the United Kingdom and to introduce a Charter of Rights and Freedoms for Canada. The political leadership of Quebec at the time was opposed to Trudeau's efforts, and Quebec never did sign the constitutional amendments that were ultimately passed into Canadian law in 1981–1982. This represented something of a wound in the Quebec body politic, and efforts to bring Quebec into the constitutional family subsequently failed on several occasions. These failed constitutional efforts to give greater recognition to Quebec while preserving the major features of the federalist model also added to the controversy. I should point out that Quebec's adherence to the Constitution was not necessary from a legal viewpoint, but from a legitimacy perspective it remained something of an open sore that led to increased efforts on the part of separatist leaders to push for either a separate nation or some form of sovereignty association with Canada. ....

"Obviously, the court was faced with a very large task, namely, how to respond to questions revolving around secession when the Constitution of Canada had no specific provision dealing with secession ... The methodology that was chosen by the court was to look at the underlying constitutional principles that were in play ...

"In the view of the court, the Constitution of Canada is more than a written text. It consists of the global system of rules and principles which govern the exercise of constitutional authority in the whole and in every part of Canada. In the court's view, four fundamental and organizing principles which are

relevant to the issue of unilateral secession are federalism, democracy, constitu-
tionalism and the rule of law, and respect for minorities. Those principles must
inform an overall appreciation of constitutional rights and obligations ...

"The role of the court is to identify the relevant aspects of the Constitution in
their broadest sense. The court has clarified the legal framework within which
political decisions are to be taken under the Constitution, but the court will
not usurp prerogatives of political forces in that framework. The court has no
supervisory role over the political aspects of the constitutional negotiations.

*   ...*

"The Reference engaged the full participation of all members of the court,
and there was a collective sense that this case ideally should be written by the
court, and therefore an effort would be made to try to achieve that consensus if
that proved to be practicable ... In my time on the court, I know of no other
decision that collectively engaged all the members of the court as much as the
Quebec Secession Reference because the stakes were so high: arguably the unity
of the country."[25]

Patrick Monahan reflects on what he learned from the experience of
participating in the Meech Lake negotiations: "As I think back on those
events, my first thought is how fortunate Canadians were that Frank Iacobucci was there at that pivotal moment in our history. It was his wise
counsel and advice, at a critical point in the final stages of the process, that
enabled us to avoid a split between Canada's two largest provinces on a key
national unity issue.

"But what I now also understand, with the benefit of hindsight and some
experience, is that Frank's persuasiveness and value as legal adviser reflected
the fact that his analysis was informed by a larger vision of Canada. That
vision was an expansive and inclusive one, intended to make space for the
diversity and the competing perspectives that permit human flourishing
on the northern half of this continent." (Patrick Monahan)

I never thought really seriously about going into politics, even though I did
think about it sometimes. First, I thought that Nancy would never enjoy that,
and I didn't want to do something she wouldn't be content with. Second, I

think you've got to develop a really thick skin. I thought I would be good at it in a way … I would have been accessible, approachable, committed, honest. But I may have had too much sensitivity, been too sensitive to people's reactions. You have to seek an equilibrium in life: you don't want to have so thick a skin that you're insensitive to others or to issues you have to deal with, but you can't be so sensitive that you're paralyzed. And third, I had seen how politicians sometimes depreciate their professional skills, and I really didn't want that to happen.

Frank never ran for office. He might have won, but he knew he wasn't a politician. As a leader, he wasn't by nature an entrepreneur or surprising innovator or taker of high risks. He wasn't someone inclined to try out true failure. On the other hand, each successive leadership position gave him further practice at the experience of losing and then coming back to win, facing difficulty and finding a way to overcome it, turning challenging people into allies and directing demanding projects toward success.

If Frank's aversion to going into politics suggested a preference to stay away from high-risk initiatives, Meech Lake showed that he could work with extreme risk, at a level where the stakes for the country were incredibly high. In this context, his sensitivity was exactly what was needed; rather than scaring him off a strikingly risky venture, it meant he could act as go-between, translator, persuader, and patient behind-the-scenes builder. There was no highly visible chance of individual failure or messing up; instead, it was the entire team at the Department of Justice, headed up by Frank as key play maker, that felt the country's constitutional failure as an institutional blow.

Even in the aftermath of Meech Lake, Frank's particular gift for leadership rather than politics made him a highly appreciated civil servant. When it came time for him to move on, he left behind – in the words of his Associate Deputy Minister Douglas Rutherford – "a Department of Justice full of pride for its former leader and for itself, an institution on which much of his lustre remained and in whose people much of his character had been infused."

The "Chief"

Frank talks about *getting my law back* as deputy minister of Justice. For three years, he was the top lawyer for the country, the person overseeing the research, analysis, and drafting work of a team of people committed to public service. He enjoyed being a generalist, becoming an expert across the board in law. In particular, it was a position that allowed him to combine development of his leadership skills with intensive learning of Canadian constitutional law and engagement with Canadian constitutional lawyers.

He had become a true insider by the time he got a call in the fall of 1988 about a new job. Prime Minister Mulroney, obviously appreciative of Frank's work, picked up the phone on a Wednesday to offer him the position of chief justice of the Federal Court of Canada. That evening, Frank spoke with Nancy; he accepted the position on Thursday, and the announcement was made on Friday.

As he moved to his new office, Frank walked once again into a context in which he was a total outsider. In an interview for the Osgoode Law Society,[26] Frank described the shift to the court as a *double whammy* of apprehension. First, he worried about becoming a judge and, second, he worried about becoming chief justice.

While this new job meant he was continuing explicitly in law, the judiciary was a new universe. *There was no period of training; there was obviously a period that I had to get my feet wet and find out the nature of the job and get to know the people. But, no, there was no training as such. I don't think you really know anything about being a judge until you are a judge ... you don't really know the job until you are in it.*

He would have been even more worried if he had been asked to serve as a trial judge. At least at the appellate level, Frank felt that the experience he had accumulated counted for something. Indeed, he had some legal expertise relevant to Federal Court jurisdiction, specifically in tax and in federal legislation and regulations. *I did teach tax, so I did follow the decisions of the Federal Court in terms of that subject. It was an intriguing jurisdiction to me because I saw this linkage of tax and trademarks and intellectual property and maritime law.*

The warm welcome he received from other members of the Federal Court meant he never felt unwanted as he found himself on the bench. In addition, as he recalls, there was a little booklet prepared by past Chief Justices Wilbur Jackett and Arthur Thurlow that provided a nuts-and-bolts orientation to new judges, and Frank was a quick learner.

Perhaps the hardest thing for Frank as an outsider to the judiciary was adjusting to the change in pace and interaction with others. The phone didn't ring all the time; he wasn't moving from crisis to crisis; he wasn't reporting to someone or receiving reports from the people he supervised. That change in day-to-day work would have been even more dramatic if he hadn't taken on the position of chief justice.

In his new leadership role at the helm of a national institution, Frank's work was far from limited to preparation for hearings and the writing of judgments. Instead, as the administrative head of the Federal Court of Canada, he assigned his colleagues to panels for the hearings, oversaw and responded to needs on the support staff front, and ensured the effective functioning of a committee on the library and another on the hiring and supervision of law clerks. He introduced a process of reporting on the work of the court and identified a press liaison; he worked with architects to ensure progress on a Federal Court building in Ottawa; and he interacted with Brian Dickson and Antonio Lamer, who each served as chief justice of the Supreme Court of Canada while Frank was next door.

In practice, the chief justice is the administrative head of the court – in other words, the chief manager. I felt it important to sort of manage the court, if I can use that term, from the point of view of a partnership, that we were all partners. There is accountability for financial administration, dealing with support staff and office needs of the judges, responsibility for the court's overall growth and development, addressing what we could do to do our work better.[27]

The institutional responsibilities and governance that came with the position of chief justice of the Federal Court were right up Frank's alley. He had proven his capacity to adapt to new contexts, and to put his people skills into practice in order to ensure institutional effectiveness. Distinct from his university and Department of Justice positions of authority, this job required learning how to be a member of a group of peers while at the same time taking on the burden of overseeing that group.

I like to think that the chief justice is first among equals. He or she is there because the appointment power and the statute provides for a role, but I don't think that means I am less of a judge because I am chief justice or more of a judge because I am chief justice. I really feel that quite profoundly, and the same principle applies in being dean of a law school. I was not a stronger professor because I was dean. When I was dean, I think I learned about what was involved in being a chief justice.[28]

The prime minister brought Frank to the Federal Court as someone with a proven record as a lawyer and a leader. The position he held for two and a half years was an intensive introduction to the particular identity and weight of being a judge. It handed him a unique opportunity to apply his legal knowledge to a very different setting and to explore a new set of substantive topics and issues. This was new terrain for merging meticulous focus on legal principles, on one hand, with broader attention to the people affected by, and engaged in, law, on the other.

Chosen primarily for his capacity to take on the task of assessing and reinvigorating the institution, he had arrived with no judicial baggage. By the time he moved to the Supreme Court, he had become an insider in the Canadian judiciary and was ready to take a break from administrative leadership.

Frank's "How"

The narratives of people who worked with Frank, whether in Toronto or Ottawa, are remarkably similar. He is described as a highly successful leader: someone who invested and believed in people, adapted to context, made confident decisions, was able to bring others along in a desired direction, and welcomed accountability. Frank describes himself as a team builder, as someone who gets to know everyone, and as a believer in honest professional public service.

Camille Nelson, one of Frank's Supreme Court law clerks, went on to become a dean of Law in the United States and describes Frank's influence on her own understanding of leadership:

"My notions of leadership and professionalism in action are attributable to the patient teaching, modelling, inclusiveness, and humility so profoundly demonstrated by Justice Iacobucci in everything he does. To me, he is a most authentic leader. Importantly, I do not intend to understate the obvious and deep brilliance of this man. Often when people speak of one's approach to life, personality, demeanour, and other so-called soft skills, it is assumed that such aptitude is a parallel, natural and, therefore, easy form of intellect.

"Mastery of the law can be learned with sufficient time, commitment, and tutoring, if need be. However, few people master accessible and inclusive demeanour that is simultaneously disarming and reaffirming. In my opinion, this is the icing on the cake. When combined with the utter brilliance of his formidable intellect, the equally rare superlative EQ (emotional quotient) is what makes Justice Iacobucci a legal leader unlike any other." (Camille Nelson)

Frank tells the story of how one thing led to another as a series of unexpected opportunities, requests, and appointments. Respected as a remarkable administrator in every context in which he served, from the university to the federal government to the Federal Court of Canada, Frank never actually applied for most of the jobs at which he excelled. Instead, it was all about "who he knew": not in the sense of a network into which he had been born or through which he had grown up, but rather via relationships he had built and nourished.

Of the leadership positions he held – as vice-president Internal Affairs, dean of Law, university provost and vice-president, deputy minister of

Justice, and chief justice of the Federal Court of Canada – the deanship is the only one Frank acknowledges actively seeking out. To be chosen to lead his colleagues and peers at the Faculty of Law, a little over a decade after joining it as a junior professor, was something he wanted and explicitly prepared for. He was keen to take a turn at guiding U of T Law, at facilitating productive relationships within and beyond the law school, and supporting the teachers and researchers, students and staff who made up the small community. He wanted the chance to welcome students to the study of law, and to send them off to discover their own paths to earning $5 a day.

Camille Nelson continues: "I mean to elevate some of the 'icing' which intersects every aspect of the intellectual heft of Justice Iacobucci. And that is the way he moves through this world. It is not just that he is an extraordinary jurist, it is the *way* he dons that task. As I say to my students, it matters not only what you do with your law degree; the *way* in which you do your work matters as much as *what* you do. Specifically, the '*how*' matters as much as the '*what*.'" (Camille Nelson).

As we have seen, Frank thought of the position of chief justice of the Federal Court as akin to the deanship – one with little authority and lots of responsibility. In between those two leadership roles, he showed he could combine considerable authority with significant responsibility. The fact that he didn't search explicitly for positions from which to exert top-down control goes hand-in-hand with the recurring observation that Frank sought to serve the common good, to use his skills and experience in law to work with others on projects ranging from university-professoriate relations to constitutional reform to court administration.

Perhaps it explains the remarkable desire on the part of Steve Moate at the University of Toronto to offer a tailored 80th birthday blessing for Frank as a way to express appreciation:

"There were some very special moments, and one stands out. It was at the time when his interim presidency was drawing to a close. There were events to honour him and for him to convey his best wishes. How many university presidents, at a farewell speech attended by many (and which for others might have been full of rhetorical flourishes and the like, as per usual for university speeches) would have the confidence and perceptiveness to talk about 'the human need to love and to be loved' as the thing he wanted his colleagues to focus on? He cut right to the heart of the matter.

"I have not had the opportunity to speak with Frank about spirituality and religion, but I know he remains very interested in these subjects. So, this is not just a happy birthday wish, it is a 'birthday benediction':

"Thank you for your service to others and for being such a positive influence in the lives of many, for showing compassion, and for demonstrating leadership throughout your career in each of the roles you have undertaken. Thank you for the light you bring into the world. May God bless you and your family always, keeping you in good health and always surrounding you with the love that you so richly deserve." (Steve Moate)

Frank's close friend and colleague Michael Trebilcock insists that it would be a big mistake to think that Frank was somehow angelic or passive: "The second vignette from this period is the frequent table tennis games that you, I, Dick Risk, and David Beatty participated in in the basement of Falconer on many Friday afternoons. Despite your cherubic appearance, you were a ferocious competitor, with a fierce forehand smash that made Boris Becker look like a wimp. From these games I learned the value of the competitive instinct in all walks of human endeavour, and, again, have attempted to apply this insight to all my academic and public policy making endeavours, even in some contexts where, arguably, to my chagrin, competitive forces work imperfectly at best." (Michael Trebilcock)

As a young soccer player, Frank had been the playmaker and team leader. He wasn't one of the forwards explicitly recognized for their goal scoring prowess. Neither was he the goalkeeper, prepared to take all the shots in plain view. He sometimes made mistakes, most painfully with an "own goal," but mostly he saw the field, watched for opportunities, and facilitated the best game possible on the part of his teammates. To borrow Michael Trebilcock's words, he was a "ferocious competitor," someone keen to succeed and to bring his team along with him.

4

You Will Pursue Justice – Frank Iacobucci at the Supreme Court

Nothing Magical

Frank had held down the job as chief justice of the Federal Court of Appeal for a couple of years when he received yet another call from Prime Minister Mulroney. This time, the offer was to jump into judging at the highest level, as the newest member of the Supreme Court of Canada. Unlike the jobs he had done for a decade, this one didn't come with any formal administrative title or responsibility. From "chief" at the Federal Court, he became one of the eight "puisne" justices on the Supreme Court. As he was sworn in by the Right Honourable Antonio Lamer, chief justice of Canada, in English, French, and Italian, Frank joined a new team. His new colleagues constituted a group of jurists all carrying a significant burden on their shoulders, each expected to develop a distinctive and profoundly individual "signature" on Canadian justice.

The term "puisne" is used to refer to the judges associated with the chief of the Supreme Court. But it looks, and – if slightly mispronounced – sounds like "puny." Frank, and everyone around him, appreciated the disconnect between the adjective and the prestige of the position. His description of himself as an athlete provides introductory insight into his contributions over the 13 years he would serve as puisne justice:

Soccer is a game where physical strength and being big aren't crucial. I've never been that strong in terms of brute strength; instead, I'm blessed with good hand-eye coordination. As a playmaker, you make the passes, you distribute the ball, you use the space well. That's what I was good at.

Frank didn't mind the shift from a formal leadership role, whether "big" and explicit or "small" and somewhat in the background. After all, he had had only limited experience as a judge, and this new position offered an intensive opportunity to learn, listen, and make decisions situated at what most people would consider the pinnacle of a jurist's career. He had been working hard all along for his $5 a day, but this kind of work seemed special: it was something seen as having maximal importance and impact on Canadian law and society.

The January day that Frank got appointed to the Supreme Court of Canada stands out in my own memory. I was in Ottawa, home for a break from Columbia Law School in New York where I was doing graduate work in law, and had been in touch with Frank to see if he had time to catch up. He took me to lunch at The Mill, just down the road from the Supreme Court and Federal Court complex on Wellington Street. As we were finishing, he invited me to drop by the Iacobucci home at the end of the day to see Nancy and the kids who all happened to be around. In between lunch and my visit, the new addition to the Supreme Court was announced to the country. I turned up at the house with warm congratulations – Frank had of course said nothing about this at lunch – and was still there when the CBC television team arrived. That night, on national news, astute viewers caught a glimpse of someone who might have been an unknown fourth Iacobucci child in the background!

That story helps me keep the Supreme Court stage of Frank's career in perspective. The move to the Supreme Court was something to celebrate: it was truly exciting for Frank to be selected as the new justice from Ontario, and as the first Italo-Canadian to join the highest court in Canada. At the same time, captured by the warmth and ease with which the Iacobuccis treated the moment and me as a visitor, this could be seen as just another transition – a new job that simply indicated justified appreciation of what Frank could do, and of what he was ready to contribute at the age of 54. The Supreme Court appointment was important enough to make the national news, but not so important as to eradicate the normal routine.

For any observer or commentator focused on a Supreme Court or on the body of jurisprudence generated by any one of its members, there is a risk of glorification or even something close to idolatry. This might be a phenomenon more obviously associated with the judiciary in the United States – recognized and warned against for a long time before the movies about Ruth Bader Ginsburg publicly proved the point. Judicial biography, simply through sustained attention to one person on the bench, can too easily place a halo over that person's head.[29] The warning isn't only about approving or championing an individual justice. It is just as relevant when the observer disagrees with that judge's work. The trap is that of exaggerating significance and power, of treating what a Supreme Court justice does as necessarily worth more than $5 a day.

The trap exists not only for followers of biographical trajectories; it is a constant presence for all jurists and perhaps especially for law professors.[30] A second year law student once put up his hand in one of my classes – a course which immersed participants in the form and methods of English common law – and suggested that his teachers were all "seduced" by judges. We were engaged in preliminary brainstorming on the key characteristics of a good common law judge, recognized as the central player in the common law tradition. As my student reminded everyone that day, there is a real risk of over-fascination.[31] Judgments matter; indeed, they can serve as the bread and butter of much of the learning and shaping of law. But it is crucial to step back and remember that the words and contributions of even a judge of a top court aren't inevitably more important and influential than those of other speakers, actors, and institutions.

"The work of a judge is in one sense enduring and in another sense ephemeral. What is good in it endures. What is erroneous is pretty sure to perish. The good remains the foundation on which new structures will be built ... I sometimes think that we worry ourselves overmuch about the enduring consequences of our errors. They may work a little confusion for a time. In the end, they will be modified or corrected, or their teachings ignored. The future takes care of such things." – Benjamin Cardozo[32]

In the fall of 2000, Frank invited me to speak at a conference at the Supreme Court of Canada marking the 125th anniversary of the court. As a relatively junior scholar who had just achieved tenure as a law professor, I was asked to address the court's relationship to, and impact on, social diversity and multiculturalism in Canada. I suggested that the court is only one partner in the determination of our interactions and identities, albeit with a unique and heavy responsibility in working with concepts that have an impact on the meaning and promise of diversity:

"As a participant, the court is never solely determinative of our relations and interactions, but its presence is significant in our collective existence and our shared experience of living our pluralist lives ... the court's role is one of partner and participant in a shared framework."[33]

The challenge of articulating the significant yet necessarily constrained role of the Supreme Court in shaping Canadian society is similar to that of underscoring the important yet necessarily limited work and impact of any member of that court. Years later, as Frank and I talked about his time at the court, I was trying to figure out how to highlight his contributions as a Supreme Court justice without allowing them to take over either his own story or the stories of Canadian law and society. I got help from Frank himself:

I don't really see anything omnipotent or magical about courts.

Pithy and precise, Frank's comment is, I think, exactly right.

Doing the Right Thing

If Frank's work of practitioner and teacher/scholar was grounded in the "what," and his work of administrator the "how," the work of judging shifts him explicitly to the "why." In exercising judgment, Frank engaged in the "why" question and offered answers to issues that, by definition, people needed help in sorting out. "Justice" as job title is also the content of the job: to be a justice is to do justice. We have seen that earning $5 a day as a jurist is about learning and the development of expertise, and about leading and governance. It is also about listening, responding, and decision-making.

In this capacity, Frank speaks through written judgments, sometimes co-authored and usually joined by colleagues on the bench. Unlike with his stories or his answers to interview questions, no intermediary is necessary to hear what he has to say. On the other hand, judgments cannot be treated as personal narratives or reflections; reading a judgment is not quite the same as listening to the voice of its author. As students of law quickly find out, the exercise of reading judgments is not always straightforward. It benefits from guidance and careful attention to context and purpose and, as Benjamin Cardozo reminds us, can be enriched by recognizing the connections between the work of judging and the experience that precedes and surrounds it:

"There is in each of us a stream of tendency ... which gives coherence and direction to thought and action. Judges cannot escape that current any more than other mortals. All their lives, forces which they do not recognize and cannot name, have been tugging at them – inherited instincts, traditional beliefs, acquired convictions; and the resultant is an outlook on life, a conception of social needs ... which, when reasons are nicely balanced, must determine where choice shall fall."[34]

The case of *Waldick v Malcolm* is an example of an everyday story that travelled all the way to the Supreme Court of Canada. I have already mentioned it as a case that belongs in a first-year tort law course. This is a small case. It is not one of the principal or most important contributions by Justice Iacobucci to Canadian Supreme Court jurisprudence at the turn of the twenty-first century. But it serves as an interesting if modest introduction to Frank's work as a Supreme Court judge.

A man fractured his skull when he fell on the icy path that led to his sister's door. The home was a farmhouse in southern Ontario and, as recounted by its occupants, farmers in the area generally don't put salt or sand on their driveways in the winter. The snow gets cleared, pick-up trucks can get around, and everyone wears boots designed for icy conditions. Despite wearing the right boots, and being as careful as usual as he walked across what he knew was snow-covered ice, Norman Waldick fell. When he claimed insurance to cover his losses, his insurance company brought a claim against Roberta and Marvin Malcolm as the occupants of the farmhouse. That claim alleged that the failure to salt the path was inappropriate, and thus that the Malcolms (and their own insurance company) were responsible for the costs associated with the injuries sustained by Norman.

Justice Iacobucci, writing for the entire bench of seven Supreme Court judges in 1991, agreed. Even if it were the case that no one in rural Ontario sanded the paths leading up to their front doors, that was no excuse for Roberta and Marvin to fail to do the right thing.

Waldick v Malcolm reinforces the special character of law as a system of norms or rules for behaviour. It underscores the vocation of the judge as decision-maker within that system. It reminds us that there are always human stories involved in the unfolding of legal principles. It exemplifies the rich potential for engaged learning grounded in legal text. Finally, it invites us to recognize the difficulty in labelling judgments as right or wrong.

At the core of the case is the difference between "custom" and "habit." If someone can point to an established custom, should that change our assessment of that person's behaviour? After all, in some circumstances, custom can constitute the law governing the way in which we treat each other. If, however, the behaviour simply reflects collective habit – falling into a pattern of conduct rather than acting according to expectation – can or should a judge play an important role in redirecting or remodelling that behaviour?

Waldick v Malcolm provides rich terrain for exploring the definition of "reasonable behaviour." As first-year law students learn, the tort of negligence – or more broadly, the private law of civil wrongs – concerns itself with allocating responsibility for the outcome of action that fails to meet an expected standard. That standard is classically captured by the notion of the "reasonable man," replaced in contemporary language by the "reasonable person": a fictional character who always takes risk into account and acts precisely in the way that avoids excessive injury. The students quickly come to realize that what appears to be fairly straightforward as a concept is anything but.

Reasonable isn't the same as rational: carefully calculating the risk involved doesn't necessarily let you off the hook. Intelligent doesn't guarantee reasonable: very smart people can still – sometimes fatally – fail to do the right thing or take the necessary precautions. The meaning of "reasonable" shifts over time; the example of how to put a baby to sleep, whether on tummy, side or back, is a good illustration. What's reasonable for an experienced surgeon or plumber might not be the same as what's reasonable for a first-year medical intern or apprentice. Perhaps most relevant to a critical understanding of *Waldick v Malcolm*, reasonable isn't the same as average. In other words, saying "But everyone else does it" is not persuasive; everyone else, it turns out, might be doing the wrong thing.

At first glance, *Waldick* seems to send the quick and fairly obvious message that a bad habit is not the same as acceptable behaviour. In underscoring that point, the judgment turns for help to Allan Linden – a tort law professor turned judge, and a past colleague of Frank's on the Federal Court of Appeal:

"[C]ustomary practices can provide a fairly precise standard of care to facilitate the courts' task of deciding what is reasonable in the circumstances. Like penal statutes, customs can crystallize the ordinarily vague standard of reasonable care."[35]

Frank dismisses the arguments made by the Malcolms to the effect that the practice of not salting or sanding was customary. He says that no such custom was established in the testimony, regardless of the fact that the Malcolms indicated that they knew of no one who salted, including Norman Waldick himself. But then he goes on to consider the situation were it indeed the case that such a custom existed.

In short, no amount of general community compliance will render negligent conduct "reasonable … in all the circumstances"… If, as the lower courts found, it is unreasonable to do absolutely nothing to one's driveway in the face of clearly treacherous conditions, it matters little that one's neighbours also act unreasonably … In my view, it is far from self-evident that the "practice" of not sanding or salting the driveways in the area should earn the acceptance of the courts.

Here, Frank underscores the responsibility, and indeed power, of the court and the common law to define "reasonable behaviour." That is, rather than rely on a definition internal to a community, such as that of farmers in rural Ontario, Frank insists that the court can and should determine what path-clearing practices are necessary during the long winter months.

The judgment isn't filled out or nuanced on this point. Frank's confidence is palpable, bolstered by the approval of his Supreme Court colleagues and by similar conclusions of the judges at the trial and appellate levels. The message is delivered almost like a ready-made lesson, a reminder that the court has an important role to play in deciding what standard of behaviour is required, regardless of the context. Students who read the judgment typically take away the basic message that customary doesn't equal reasonable. Without further probing, they like the idea: courts and law – which, after all, are what they're focused on – get the final say on how we should act vis-à-vis each other.

But, if given a more careful look, the content of the judgment might not warrant the satisfied tone in which it's delivered. There is considerable slippage between the terms "practice" and "custom"; no sustained attention is given to what the difference might be. That is, as Allen Linden suggests in the excerpts from his scholarship cited in the judgment, we might accept that true custom receive respect as a reference point for establishing reasonableness. If particular human behaviour is persuasively customary, that means it has been adopted as correct or desirable, and thus reasonable. On the other hand, practice is simply the way things are done; it might constitute "bad" practice given its inappropriate or careless character, and thus should never define "reasonable" comportment.

Thus, for example, it might be the case that the teenagers at a summer camp never bother with sunscreen. But that doesn't make it reasonable behaviour. Indeed, it's helpful to distinguish practice from custom in this way. Practice, or "how things are," isn't sufficient or convincing if we're figuring out what's reasonable. But custom might be defined as "how things should be," and then it's very helpful for assessing reasonable actions. The same summer camp might include an opening day custom of writing names on sunscreen bottles and making campers cover themselves head to toe. In an important sense, that custom sets the requisite standard; it becomes the rule or even the law for everyone at camp. When Frank rejects arguments that simply point to the typical – and minimal – snow clearing efforts in the vicinity, he rightly refuses to equate practice with reasonable behaviour. By failing to delve further into the distinctiveness of custom, however, he misses a chance to consider when and whether true custom can and does overlap with reasonableness.

The case of *Waldick v Malcolm* invites the examination of the dichotomy between descriptive and normative, between is and ought. It's an invitation that the court doesn't fully take up, probably because the arguments weren't fully presented, but which they pass on to readers of the judgment. If there were to be a snow-clearing custom with normative implications, where would it come from? How would it develop? Who would the participants be in its creation and development? What consequences would flow from its violation? It might be that, in the end, there really is no custom that could lend support to the Malcolms' insistence that they behaved in the right and reasonable way. But there's a missed moment for rich reflection on these fundamental issues – issues that form part of every law student's first year of legal education, and that continue to arise whether noticed or not.

Another, related, aspect of the judgment also mirrors the foundations of legal education. That is, we might focus on the apparent gap between residents of rural Ontario and the Supreme Court justices ensconced in their urban setting. It is far from clear that Frank Iacobucci and his colleagues have much to say to farmers and the choices they make about how to run their farms. It's even less clear whether snow-clearing behaviour would have changed one bit after the court condemned it as unreasonable. In an earlier related judgment, referred to in *Waldick v Malcolm*, the court acknowledged a practice among professional notaries in Quebec as an accepted, expected, and reinforced rule.[36] It then went on to deliver a collective rap to notarial knuckles: from the perspective of the law – which the judges had the ultimate responsibility to interpret and apply – the notaries' apparently customary behaviour was simply unreasonable. In that case, the court appears to pull out its obvious expertise in law to dispute that held by the notarial profession. In *Waldick*, there's no equivalent judicial expertise in rural snow-clearing at play.

The case thus raises obvious, universal, and never-fully-resolved questions about the power of judges, the relevance of appellate judgments, and the distance between a judge's experience and that of the people whose stories and conflicts form the basis of case law. Maybe this is precisely the issue that Frank speaks to with such confidence. Perhaps, as he dismisses the "custom" argument and the notion that farmers themselves can tell the Supreme Court of Canada what's reasonable in the circumstances, he ends up telling us something larger and more significant. Law in its evaluative mode, Frank says for the court, belongs everywhere. The very responsibility of private law in particular, and of the judges who interpret and apply it, is to articulate the standard of behaviour expected in human relations. Regardless of whether others have addressed that very question – through practice or custom, through norms that are formal and written, or informal and assumed – Frank and his peers must ask it again. It is their responsibility to provide the answer. The path leading up to one's front door simply has to be ice-free.

It was in 1995 that I first taught the foundational Tort Law course at McGill. I included the case of *Waldick v Malcolm*. The students and I talked about the interaction among collective practices, community norms, and the central, if necessarily nebulous, notion of human reasonableness. Those familiar with life on a farm found it simply unrealistic to expect people to follow the Supreme Court directive as to reasonable ice management. Others suggested the possible existence of a stronger justification for avoiding salt and sand, based on environmental concerns or the health of farmers' crops. We contrasted the usual deference of courts to norms of practice within the medical profession to the reluctance to adopt a similar approach to the behavior of the Malcolms: the exercise of recognized expertise generally falls within required reasonableness.

Earlier, in talking about the experience of first year legal education, I recounted the story of how I visited the Iacobuccis' home in Ottawa over the 1995 Christmas holiday break. It had snowed the night before and the temperature had dropped that morning. There was a thin layer of ice on the ground. As their first guest on that wintry day, I fell on the slippery path. The story continues, however, past the moment I found myself on the ground.

I picked myself up, reached the front door, and rang the doorbell. Nancy Iacobucci answered. "How can Frank write what he did in *Waldick v Malcolm*, and then leave ice on the front path?" I asked, laughing, after greeting her with a "Merry Christmas!". "Well," said Nancy, "He was wrong on that one ... and I've told him so!" Every year since, I have included this story, including Nancy's critique, in my teaching.

Who else, besides Nancy Iacobucci, might pay close attention to Supreme Court of Canada judgments? Who reads them with a critical eye, who cares what they say and how they say it? Who agrees or disagrees, who finds them right or wrong or partial or problematic?

The parties who bring the case all the way to the highest level appear to be the obvious readers. They might be individuals like Norman Waldick and Roberta and Marvin Malcolm; indeed, given the all-in-the-family nature of their case, we might imagine them discussing the outcome over coffee at the kitchen table. But that picture is somewhat skewed: in fact, their respective insurance companies carried the litigation, and the lawyers for those companies would be the people charged with reading the judgment with care. In other cases, the parties aren't individuals at all, but rather corporations or government actors and agencies. In criminal law appeals, one party is figuratively the Queen – representing Canada in the case against the accused. All have to pay close attention to what the Supreme Court has to say.

Nancy Iacobucci points us in the direction of another kind of reader. Albeit the spouse of the judgment's author, she reads as a jurist, interested in the Supreme Court's interpretation of, and impact on, the law beyond the case at hand. Jurists look to judgments for guidance, for direction, for the resolution of complicated issues. As practising lawyers, they may refer to relevant Supreme Court judgments to provide counsel, or articulate arguments, or refine expertise. As law professors, jurists subject those judgments to careful scrutiny, and incorporate them into their teaching and writing about foundational problems or of contemporary developments. As policymakers, jurists follow the Court's jurisprudence as they shape and reshape rules and regulations, constitutions and codes. As judges of lower courts, they follow the lead of the Supreme Court; as judges of appellate courts in other countries, they may pay careful attention to how the Canadian judiciary responds to shared or similar challenges.

For the parties involved, a Supreme Court of Canada judgment represents a final decision with specific consequences. For everyone else, it informs governance, or teaching and learning, or the meaning and scope of rules relevant to our everyday lives. Seen in this way, a judgment should be accessible not only to jurists but to any reader interested in the issues at stake. The neighbours in rural Ontario are invited to read what Frank has to say, even if – like Nancy – they might not agree with the bottom line.

I tell the story of Nancy's disagreement as a reminder to law students that the right thing to do is not always clear, whether in dealing with ice or in writing a judgment. As jurist and spouse rolled into one, Nancy was Frank's closest critic; she was a particular expert on Frank in all of his guises, including that of appellate judge. Her critique illustrates the fact that even, or perhaps especially, those closest to a judgment (and judge) can disagree. It shows that even Supreme Court judgments can open ongoing conversations rather than close off discussion.

This might seem obvious, but it is a hard thing for students to figure out. On one hand, they need to appreciate that Frank and his Supreme Court colleagues – and judges in general – aim to do the right thing with their judgments, and to ensure that others do the right thing in their respective spheres of activity. On the other hand, they are asked to read closely and carefully, to articulate their own reactions to judgments and other legal texts, to go much further than simply agreeing or not with the outcome.[37] That is, figuring out whether a Supreme Court judgment is right or wrong is complicated. Given the equally complicated impact of judgments on never-ending conversations in the law, that particular assessment might not be the principal task at all.

Dialogue and Dignity – A Framework

"The work of deciding cases goes on every day in hundreds of courts throughout the land. Any judge, one might suppose, would find it easy to describe the process which he had followed a thousand times and more. Nothing could be further from the truth." –Benjamin Cardozo[38]

Despite Frank's assertion of the non-magical nature of courts, judging demands and entails what can seem like a magical mix of integrity, experience, reliance on past sources, compassion, and prophecy. It is not easy for judges – including Supreme Court judges – to describe what they do, although Benjamin Cardozo, Frank's non-Italian judicial touchstone, famously tried to do so in a series of lectures at Yale University, published in 1921 as *The Nature of the Judicial Process*. Neither is it easy for non-judges to describe and offer analysis as to what it is that judges do as they exercise judgment.

As underscored by Robert J. Sharpe – one of Frank's colleagues at the University of Toronto, a justice of the Ontario Court of Appeal, and author of a 2018 book entitled *Good Judgment. Making Judicial Decisions*[39] – the ways in which judges exercise crucial power to make law, even as that power is shaped and limited by the law's existing framework, are often left unarticulated. "The subtle play of forces that empower judges to make law and that constrain judges in the choices they make is not well understood by the lay public, by politicians, or by scholars of other disciplines. Judges are at least in part responsible for that lack of understanding."[40]

An exploration of the contributions of Frank Iacobucci as a Supreme Court justice could take many forms. We could proceed from one substantive area of law to the next (for example, tort law to criminal law to administrative law to tax law to international law). Alternatively, we could cluster by theme (for example, fairness, collective organization, identity) or by sphere (for example, education, family, corporation) or by fundamental rights (for example, liberty, equality, expression). In sketching a portrait of Frank at the Supreme Court, I have not aimed for broad, comprehensive coverage; neither have I delved into particular areas with the objective of providing substantive expert critique. Instead, I have relied on two words that Frank himself uses: dialogue and dignity. Found both in his judgments and in his narratives about them, these two words offer a prism through which to view the anthology of work signed by Iacobucci J. of the Supreme Court of Canada.

In shaping what follows around dialogue and dignity, I have taken my lead from a post-SCC seminar taught by Frank together with Robert Burt, his friend and colleague at Yale Law School.[41] In the 2013 version of the course, entitled Judicial Supremacy in Constitutional Interpretation: Comparing the US and Canada, students began by exploring the imagined place and role of the Supreme Court in the constitution (and formal Constitution) of a country. In particular, they played with the notion of dialogue as a way to think through the interaction between legislators and judges, between, on one hand, the projects put forth by the government of the day and, on the other, the constitutional framework and restraints within which successive governments must operate. The interaction between policymakers and judges serves to shed light on the contours of the court as institution. We can think of the court as partner in many different dialogues: the dialogue with federal and provincial governments regarding potential secession of Quebec (a topic included on the Burt and Iacobucci course syllabus), the dialogue with corporate organizations over the outer limits of self-regulation, and even the dialogue with residents of rural Ontario over practices of ice management.

Participants in the Yale seminar then moved on to examine the particular responsibility of a Supreme Court to interpret and apply constitutional guarantees of fundamental rights. This is where we find Frank's insistence on the guiding notion of human dignity. For him, dignity grounds any discussion of equality and liberty, whether in a judgment or in a classroom. There is no explicit text on dignity included in the course syllabus. Yet the notion's primordial significance would have informed class conversations on race discrimination (focused on the history of racial segregation in the United States, and of subordination of Canada's Indigenous peoples), gender equality (focused on LGBTQ rights and same-sex marriage in both countries), and individual privacy (focused on abortion and assisted dying). For Frank as judge, the commitment to human dignity grounded the exercise of responsibility as interpreter of human rights and freedoms. In this, he drew on conversations with Aharon Barak, past chief justice of Israel, author of *Human Dignity. The Constitutional Value and the Constitutional Right,*[42] and another one of Frank's colleagues and co-teachers: conversations that began during the time both were on their respective Supreme Courts and continued long after both had retired.

The course Frank Iacobucci taught with Robert Burt combined dialogue and dignity: students started with constitutional and institutional contours, and then focused on the impact of judicial decisions on individuals, groups, and societies. Likewise, as we will see, Frank's Supreme Court jurisprudence is marked by that combination. Dialogue captures Frank's understanding of the Supreme Court as an institution in interaction with other institutional organizations and structures; dignity captures his approach to claims for respect, in the form of equality or fairness or liberty, by individuals and groups.

We will see examples of cases that convey Frank's sense of the court's scope and limits of jurisdiction, expertise, responsibility, and power. And we will see examples of cases that convey the centrality of the individual in his approach to rights claims in the contexts of free expression, faith-based identity, sexual orientation, and Aboriginal justice. The themes are inextricably connected. That is, it seems that Frank's approach to dignity, as he articulates a test for equality or suggests sentencing guidelines for Indigenous offenders, is shaped by his approach to dialogue, and his sense of the court as one (albeit special) institution among many. Conversely, his understanding of institutional interaction is shaped by his sensitivity to human identity, integrity, and flourishing.

For Frank, the complexity of human beings mirrors the complexity of institutional relations, and vice versa. Jurists and judges are called on to grapple with that complexity; as we see from even a small selection of Frank's judgments, they may internalize and exemplify it. As Canadian law professors Brenda Cossman and David Schneiderman suggest: "[I]n the course of his constitutional decision making, Frank Iacobucci called upon his complex self (the internal dimension of complexity) in order to resolve difficult rights claims (the external dimension) ... [He] allowed for the differing and complicated aspects of our selves to remain in play, to the extent that he feasibly could, while maintaining fidelity to the strictures of the Constitution."[43]

Cardozo reminds us that the judicial process – in general, and for any specific judge – is hard to describe. I will not try to define dialogue and dignity, but rather incorporate them, as words Frank himself highlights, into an appreciation of Frank's judicial footprint. Perhaps the best we can do as we consider a judge's work is shed some light on the complexities at play, realize that there are many ways of reading what is always a mix of the ephemeral and enduring, and try to glimpse the impressions of a judge's outlook on life upon the approach that judge takes to law.

The judgments from Frank's Supreme Court repertoire that I have chosen to explore below have two things in common. First, and obviously, they share a signature. They are the work product of a complex individual shaped by experience and of a complex judge self-consciously inspired by dialogue as form and dignity as substantive commitment. Sometimes they are the product of a sole author, sometimes they were written in collaboration with colleagues on the bench. Second, also obviously even if not usually acknowledged, they are never the last word. The court itself may revisit, reinterpret, modify or even overturn the approaches embodied in particular judgments. More generally, as we will see, there is a post-judgment story for every judgment, a story out of the hands of the judicial author, a story that shifts to actors, policymakers, institutions, and individuals beyond the court.

This second characteristic underscores the hard to trace line between a judge's responsibility to offer guidance and the need to retain humility as to the scope and impact of any given judgment. It is one of the toughest things for law students to understand and work with. While they need to pay careful attention to Supreme Court judgments, they also have to realize that the Court never has the final word. Instead, the Court offers one point – sometimes a truly significant reference point – along an ongoing path. It participates in a particular and influential way in shared and multi-faceted projects. Individual Supreme Court justices can shape the nature of that participation, but they cannot complete the projects on their own.

These two features – the signature by a complex individual and the place of a judgment in an evolving context – invite us to read Frank's jurisprudence with the curiosity common to students of law. We read not for finite clarity or certainty, but for the interactions between the words of a judgment and the actions, practices, and evolution of the members of a society. In this vein, law students specifically asked to comment on Justice Iacobucci's judgments notice his "gradual, thoughtful manner" of advancing the court's jurisprudence and the ways in which some of his decisions serve as "building blocks for further progress in legal thinking."[44] Like them, we can focus on the questions asked, the lessons learned, the reflections and actions that come in the wake of a judgment – rather than fixating on whether it was right or wrong, short-lived or long lasting. And we can explore the intersections between other ways in which Frank made $5 a day as a jurist, and the contributions he made on the court.

The structure of "conversation" may prove helpful as we turn to cases. As I have written with a co-author – at the time a doctoral student in law – viewing the "law as a conversation gives us a metaphor with which to explore and define its unique characteristics, constraints, and contours." "The idea of conversation helps to contextualize the partial nature of any particular moment ... to see how each speaker is responding to someone else, and that their words are always liable to adaptation and re-use." "Understanding judges as conversants highlights their obligation to attend to what has come before to position themselves within a continuing tradition, and to remain open to what may lie ahead ... Courts and judges are by definition caught in a constant process of reading, learning, reflecting, testing, and shifting direction. Nothing that is said or done ... is lost and nothing is final; everything is part of an ongoing conversation that both precedes and outlives what we have to say."[45]

James Boyd White, law professor and scholar of law and literature, similarly insists on the dynamism of law when he suggests that we see it "as a community of speakers of a certain kind; as a culture of argument, perpetually remade by its participants."[46] In this light, we turn to the shaping of Frank's Supreme Court jurisprudence within this special community of speakers: a community of law students and jurists connecting the dots between an individual's words, institutional contours, and societal fabric, while at the same time joining the ongoing conversations as participants in their own name.

Institutional Interaction – Dialogue

To engage in meaningful dialogue as the highest appellate court in the country requires considerable listening capacity and restraint. It entails respect for knowledge, expertise, and decision-making power in the hands of people other than members of the judiciary. Frank's role as chief justice of the Federal Court of Appeal would have prepared him for precisely that kind of dialogue. As judicial assessors of administrative actions, Federal Court judges spend much of their time revisiting the processes and decisions made by others (in the realms, for example, of immigration, competition, and taxation). Experience in that context would have an obvious impact on attitudes and instincts vis-à-vis the contours and scope of institutional power.

The basic issue at stake is that of attitude in the exercise of responsibility. When confronted by a controversial decision made by someone whose role, understanding of context, expertise, and consideration of relevant factors all make her an appropriate decision-maker, in what circumstances might it be appropriate to overturn that decision? How and why would we allocate power to someone to do so? With what degree of respect should the original decision be treated? Should the approach be one of deference? Of humility? When might it be the case that too much humility or deference amounts to abdication of responsibility? Is it possible to articulate a test or standard to be applied whenever a court is asked to review the actions of a tribunal or decision-making body operating within a particular and often specialized framework?

These are both simple and extremely difficult questions, Never-ending in nature, they receive constant attention by administrative law scholars as well as by the administrative institutions and courts implicated in their answers. Referred to as the cornerstones of Frank Iacobucci's strong legacy in administrative law,[47] his judgments of *Southam* and *Ryan* indicate, both times for a unanimous court, that "it's complicated." Rather than avoiding the complicated nature of the landscape of judicial review, Frank seemed to welcome it. Can we – indeed must we – live with complexity? Frank's answer was a resounding yes. To get it right, we need a range of possible answers characterized by flexibility, sensitivity, transparency, and cooperation. To appreciate the challenge, we can turn to situations close to home.

"Mommmmm!!!!! Dad turned off the television and says I have to practice piano … I wasn't even finished my game, and anyway I didn't have my whole hour yet … It's not fair!" The young speaker – imagined or real, and replicated with variations every day within the framework of well-rehearsed child-adult repertory – isn't happy. The unwilling subject of a decision perceived as inappropriate and even unjust, she appeals to another person with authoritative power in her life. She wants her mother to overturn the original decision: to hear her appeal and to change the outcome. Perhaps she even wants her father to learn a lesson in the process, to realize that his actions vis-à-vis his daughter might be properly subject to review.

This scenario will be familiar to readers who know children, are responsible for children, or remember having been children. They know that the Mom in the picture will probably decline the invitation … at least if she and Dad are keen to maintain a structure for family relations where each has an equal authoritative voice. If Mom offers an alternative judgment, one that questions the weight of Dad's decision or assesses it as inappropriate in some way, the chance of real conflict between the two adults has just gone way up. The power balance would be knocked askew, the structural integrity of the family would be under threat. That is, the decision made by one parent isn't something subject to easy review by the other. There might arise a situation in which it is indeed appropriate to imagine resort to a parent with specialized knowledge or expertise for the final call, but usually the assumption is that each adult can pronounce a decision that then demands respect and support.

Law students asked to reflect on such a situation as part of an introduction to the contours of administrative process and judicial review might be quick to point out that some decisions should be subject to a second look. Indeed, there are concrete examples in the day-to-day aspects of legal education that provide guidance. In contrast to the structure of shared parenting within a family, the structure of evaluation of student work, for example, assigns one kind of power to the evaluating professor and another to a professor asked to review a grade assigned by a colleague. This isn't meant as a way to undermine the hard work of reading and assessing exams and assignments, and the exercise of discretionary power associated with that work. Instead it is recognition that a mistake might happen, and that a fresh second look can ensure consistency in the allocation of grades and fairness to the student asking for a review.

The typical parameters provided for the task of review ensure that appropriate respect is paid to the first evaluation. Instead of asking, "What would I give as a grade for this work?" the reviewer asks, "Was it reasonable to assign this grade?" To make this example even more concrete, students might be given actual language found in the grade review policy adopted by a Faculty of Law:

> The original grades awarded are treated with significant deference by the co-examiner or reviewer and are only changed when the reviewer finds that the original grade assigned is an unreasonable assessment of the merits of the student's work. This recognizes the possibility that another grade could have been awarded, but maintains the original grade unless it falls outside the range of acceptable outcomes, giving consideration to the justification and intelligibility of the original decision …

The task of co-examiners or reviewers is not to determine what grade they would have assigned the work in question, but to determine whether the grade assigned by the Instructor was reasonable. In reviewing the grade, the co-examiner or reviewer shall consult, the case permitting, at least three other examinations or other evaluation exercises from the same class. Where this procedure cannot be followed, any procedure deemed appropriate by the co-examiner or reviewer may be adopted, including consulting with the member of Faculty or Instructor originally responsible for the student's evaluation.[48]

Law students who receive a grade that appears inappropriate or mistaken may indeed call out for justice, albeit in a more sophisticated way than our mythical child whose voice initiated this discussion. A professor will take seriously the task of reviewing the evaluation carried out by the instructor with whose grade the student takes issue. But that task comes with clear contours. Only in a situation of unreasonableness in the allocation of a grade to the work in question can that grade be adjusted. While "reasonableness" receives no further definition or explanation, the suggested process offers guidelines. That is, by comparing the grade and reasons offered for one student with those offered to her peers, the reviewer can figure out whether something has gone wrong or whether the evaluation under scrutiny is in line with the overall grading scheme in the course.

Whether through reference to personal or professional context, anyone can grasp the principal and recurring themes that characterize the study of judicial review of administrative decision-making. The particular examples provided above might resonate with particular force in the lives of law students. They also remind us that Frank Iacobucci himself would have drawn from knowledge and experience in parallel contexts, whether that of family or university, corporations or constitutions, as he crafted his contributions to the notion of deference in Canadian administrative law.

The judgments in *Southam* and *Ryan* arise in contexts that indeed anyone can understand but that also require specialized knowledge and capacity for effective governance. The first centres on the challenges and risks of monopoly in the Canadian newspaper industry; the second on the ethical and professional responsibilities of members of the legal profession.

In the 1997 case of *Canada (Director of Investigation and Research, Competition Act) v Southam*,[49] the Federal Court of Appeal had ordered the Competition Tribunal to reconsider its decision in response to a request to limit Southam's control of local community newspapers in the Lower Mainland of British Columbia. The owner of both Vancouver daily newspapers at the time, Southam embarked on a project of taking over existing community papers, action that was alleged to cross the lines set by rules governing fair competition. The expert tribunal found insufficient evidence to show unacceptable market competition. On appeal, the Federal Court of Appeal found that the tribunal's decision-making on the issue deserved no particular deference and indeed that the tribunal had made a mistake by failing to consider all relevant factors.

For a unanimous nine-member court, Frank articulated the need for a distinctive standard of review that invites courts to ask whether a decision can be labelled "reasonable": "*That this standard is appropriate and sensible becomes clear when one considers the complexity of economic life in our country and the need for effective regulatory instruments administered by those most knowledgeable and informed about what is being regulated.*"[50] When subjected to that standard, the original decision of the Tribunal was upheld.

The standard articulated in *Southam* was confirmed and applied six years later in *Law Society of New Brunswick v Ryan*.[51] A lawyer who acted in an egregiously unethical way vis-à-vis his clients was disbarred by the provincial discipline committee for the legal profession. Frank, again for a unanimous court, confirmed that three possible standards of review exist: deciding which one applies then tells us what level of deference is appropriate. The reviewing court can interfere only if the original decision was incorrect (correctness standard), unreasonable (reasonableness simpliciter standard), or patently unreasonable (patent reasonableness standard). In *Ryan*, the standard applied to a decision of the discipline committee of the Law Society of New Brunswick was one of reasonableness simpliciter; as a result of the "somewhat probing" examination demanded by that standard, the decision to disbar was upheld by the Supreme Court of Canada.

Taken together, *Southam* and *Ryan* provided an opportunity for Frank to emphasize the importance of preserving and respecting the expertise of the membership of tribunals. Whether in the sphere of competition related to the print advertising market, or in that of discipline of members of the legal profession, the bodies charged with decision-making are owed significant deference by a reviewing judge. As the Supreme Court had affirmed and reaffirmed, a court in its administrative law mode – the Federal Court of Appeal in *Southam*, the New Brunswick Court of Appeal in *Ryan* – could not search for the right answer by overturning what it deemed a wrong one. Rather, it should engage with the reasoning offered by a tribunal in reaching a particular result. If justifiable as reasonable – even if not compelling or correct – that reasoning and result should stand.

Excerpts from Frank Iacobucci's judgments that articulate the approach labelled a "reasonableness simpliciter" review include the following:

"An unreasonable decision is one that, in the main, is not supported by any reasons that can stand up to a somewhat probing examination."[52] *"In the final result, the standard of reasonableness simply instructs reviewing courts to accord considerable weight to the views of tribunals about matters with respect to which they have significant expertise."*[53] *"Even if there could be, notionally, a single best answer, it is not the court's role to seek this out when deciding if the decision was unreasonable."*[54]

In the two decisions, Frank insists on the existence of this "reasonableness simpliciter" standard, falling between "correctness" on one hand and "patent unreasonableness" on the other: a standard that provides a vantage point between the insufficient deference associated with the former and the sometimes inappropriately high level of respect associated with the latter. He recognizes that different standards may belong to different kinds of situations. Thus, the first task of the court is to determine the appropriate standard by looking carefully at the relevant regulatory language, the kind of expertise required, the objectives of the statutory framework, and the character of the issue at hand.

To explain the difference between a search for "unreasonable" as opposed to "patently unreasonable" decisions, Frank points to the *immediacy of obviousness of the defect … [I]f it takes some significant searching or testing to find the defect, then the decision is unreasonable but not patently unreasonable.*"[55] Once the standard is chosen, the second is to apply it with care. Guided by the degree of deference communicated by the applicable standard, the court balances appreciation of the reasons provided with the requirement that their reasonableness be ascertainable.

Where did Frank's comfort with at least two standards that incorporate what he calls "*deferential self-discipline*"[56] come from? When we take a close look at the way in which he highlights the economic and commercial expertise of the members of the Competition Tribunal in *Southam*, we see an insistence on judicial self-awareness and indeed humility. Perhaps that approach should come as no surprise from someone who came to the court with extensive experience with institutional integrity. Frank knew very well the importance of supporting the people and processes responsible for the workings of all kinds of regulation of human behaviour.

"*As I have already said, the Tribunal's expertise lies in economics and in commerce. The Tribunal comprises not more than four judicial members, all of whom are judges of the Federal Court – Trial Division, and not more than eight lay members, who are appointed on the advice of a council of persons learned in "economics, industry, commerce or public affairs" … The preponderance of lay members reflects the judgment of Parliament that, for purposes of administering the Competition Act, economic or commercial expertise is more desirable and important than legal acumen.*"[57]

Whether participating in the running of a university, studying the intricacies of corporate governance, analyzing the coordination of a multitude of factors relevant to federal justice legislation, contributing to the administrative law jurisprudence of the Federal Court of Appeal, or articulating and enforcing rules of home life for his own children, Frank had cultivated a wealth of knowledge of, and appreciation for, a striking spectrum of kinds of institutional decision-making.

Given that background, Frank seemed to see the well-travelled landscape of administrative law as something that required a freshly drawn map – one that incorporated past versions but cleaned up bits that had faded or didn't reflect the changing neighbourhood. It wasn't surprising that he rejected a simplistic "bright line" rule or standard. It wasn't that he didn't like clarity, but he did know that such a rule, even if superficially clear, would be not only unworkable but unjust in its failure to incorporate enduring and necessary complexity. Instead, he accepted a range of standards, a range that could mirror his own combination of humility and responsibility, whether in making decisions in some circumstances or providing appellate-level review in others.

All of this might lead us to question Frank's hesitancy to embrace a more fluid spectrum of review. In *Ryan*, he insists that the "reasonableness simpliciter" standard does not *float along a spectrum of deference*;[58] instead there are fixed points in the form of distinctive standards to be applied. In response to this, commentators who have otherwise celebrated his wisdom in taking the Supreme Court in the direction of what they see as an appropriately complex approach, have suggested that a spectrum would have been both desirable and manageable.[59] Indeed, they suggest that a move towards such a spectrum would be the best way to nourish and build on Frank Iacobucci's legacy in this area of law.

Instead, the court seems to have headed in the opposite direction: to the adoption in 2008 (*Dunsmuir v New Brunswick*)[60] of one labelled standard, albeit influenced by prior case law on deference, including that penned by Frank.[61] Intent on offering some resolution to the recurring questions at the heart of administrative law, the court in *Dunsmuir* defined "reasonableness" as a clear or bright line standard: a standard the content and contours of which can be adjusted to each context without ever being subject to a name change.

The one and perhaps only sure thing in the ongoing jurisprudence is that the complexity won't go away. The search for clarity in law doesn't necessarily get us there. As suggested by Frank's contributions, it might not be the right quest. Even with the adoption of one standard of deference on review, the never-ending discussions go on – whether in classrooms devoted to the study of administrative process and judicial review, over the regulatory language used to create tribunals and express the scope of their authority, or by courts constantly confronted by new challenges in the form of distinctive institutional contexts. To sustain true institutional integrity, all the participants are doomed to a day-to-day existence that often feels confusing.

The adoption of a "legal pluralist" sensibility helps deal with that complexity. A lens for thinking about the functioning of co-existing institutions of regulation and justice, legal pluralism focuses on multiple sites of lawmaking. Instead of directing a search for a precise definition of the scope of either a tribunal's discretion or a court's power of review, a legal pluralist viewpoint searches for the ways in which institutions coordinate their specific responsibilities and interact with each other in the governance of any particular sphere of human behaviour.[62] Rather than trying to describe a hierarchy between variously named decision-making bodies that do the regulatory work in most domains of everyday life, and those we call courts that do the highly specialized job of providing a check on that work, legal pluralism emphasizes their distinctive character.

The interactions among different actors all engaged in the setting and applying of norms become the focal point of a pluralist analysis. Respect for the worlds of business, labour, human rights, or professional organizations remains fundamental. But the permeability of those intersecting worlds requires constant attention. That is, the interactions are crucial: institutional integrity depends on them, and peaceful co-existence depends on getting them right.

Without ever resorting to the theory of legal pluralism – at least in any explicit way in his judgments – Frank displayed a pluralist sensibility on the question of deference and review. Administrative law called out for his careful attention, but so had the law of the university, of the corporation, of Canadian federalism. Perhaps it was through keeping those systems in mind that Frank showed an acute sensitivity to the efforts and processes associated with making hard decisions. The ease with which a court should overturn a conclusion reached by people prepared to deal with the issues and to exercise their responsibility, will always depend on the context. It's nothing but complicated.

Human Interaction – Dignity

I suggested earlier that, for Frank, the complexity of human beings mirrors the complexity of institutional relations. If institutional interaction is complicated, human interaction is even more so. Students of law only figure out how a legal tradition sees and shapes the individual by analyzing the law's recognition of human actions and their consequences: bodies, minds, emotions, words, behaviours, and movements may be encouraged, limited, prohibited, rewarded or punished by law. The law's voice articulates the difference between a free person and his imprisoned counterpart, between a person unable to consent and her caregiver or substitute decision-maker. Liberty and security, equality and autonomy: all are terms in law's vocabulary and all provide a portrait of the human beings for whom they are crucial defining notions. Frank might give that portrait the title *Human Dignity*.

I have also suggested that a pluralist sensibility appears to characterize Frank's understanding of the law's engagement with co-existing worlds of business, labour, human rights, and professional organizations. A dissenting judgment focused on the fundamental freedom of association, co-authored by Frank with fellow Supreme Court Justice Peter Cory, illustrates the central significance of the individual as actor in all those worlds. Collective spheres of activity depend on the ability and desire of individuals to come together in all kinds of contexts and communities; so does human dignity.

"The human animal is inherently sociable. People bind together in a myriad of ways, whether it be in a family, a nation, a religious organization, a hockey team, a service club, a political party, a ratepayers association, a tenants organization, a partnership, a corporation,' or a trade union. By combining together, people seek to improve every aspect of their lives. Through membership in a religious group, for example, they seek to fulfill their spiritual aspirations; through a community organization they seek to provide better facilities for their neighbourhood; through membership in a union they seek to improve their working conditions. The ability to choose their organizations is of critical importance to all people. It is the organizations which an individual chooses to join that to some extent define that individual."[63]

With these sentences, Justices Cory and Iacobucci introduce their analysis in *Delisle v Canada*, a case that they see as all about *"the basic freedom of employees to associate informally together in pursuit of their mutual interests."*[64] The same sentences trigger a reflective inquiry into Frank's approach to collective projects and meaningful communities, and the ways in which self-worth and self-reliance appear inextricably tied to working together with others.

Frank's appreciation of the importance of association went beyond the pages of a judgment to his working relations with his fellow judges. He often wrote together with Peter Cory; their words in *Delisle* underscore their camaraderie and sharing of perspective. Another one of Frank's colleagues, Justice Michel Bastarache, recounts how Frank welcomed him to the working community of the Supreme Court of Canada:

"When I was appointed to the court in September of 1997, there had not been a change in the composition of the court for a number of years. At the time, there was no judge's manual and little information on court policies and practices ... During those first days at the court, Frank invited me to have lunch with him and Justice Cory on most days. This was a great occasion to learn about court practices and policies, but it was also an occasion to share views and discuss not only cases, but anything of interest.

"Frank was the first colleague to establish a personal contact, to offer assistance, to be open to lively discussions ... I was a little insecure, participating in decision-making at that level with eight judges who had experience and had been working together for years. Like lower court judges and practitioners, I did not really know how the Supreme Court functioned and was under the impression its members were some of the best jurists in the country, a club to which it was still hard to imagine I could belong. Frank made me feel comfortable; he inferentially told me I was just like the others when it came to decide a case.

"In practice there was good collegiality at the court, but not of the kind I had experienced before. It was friendly, but not very warm; it is hard to explain. This is why Frank's openness was so well received. Frank was sincere, committed; he worked hard and wanted justice to be done. He was convinced we could do a lot to improve the administration of justice. He was still a bit of a romantic, like most of our clerks, in the good sense of the word, at least as a francophone like me understands it. He was not at all pompous. It was easy to be his friend, and to admire him for his commitment to his duty as a judge." (Michel Bastarache)

A closer look at the 1999 Supreme Court of Canada judgment in which the paragraph about *the human animal* is found provides the context for this picture of the relationship between individuals and the organizations to which they belong. Gaétan Delisle, a member of the Royal Canadian Mounted Police, had been involved in the creation of an informal association of RCMP members in Quebec, and challenged the way in which the Public Service Staff Relations Act limited the scope of such organizing by these particular employees. Although the claim was not specifically one based on the right to form a union, with its attendant certification and collective bargaining features, it did assert that the government's desire to prevent possible unionization had led to an unjustifiable infringement of the freedom of association of individual RCMP employees.

The majority of the court, in a judgment written by Justice Bastarache, found no violation of Gaétan Delisle's *Charter* right to associate; that is, the government has no obligation to facilitate or even contemplate the creation of RCMP employee organizations. But Justices Iacobucci and Cory disagreed. For them it was clear, upon a review of the legislative history and social context, that the federal government's purpose in excluding the RCMP from the framework in place for public service staff was to deny the possibility for members to come together in meaningful employee associations.

The tone of the judgment is definite in its convictions; it offers strongly worded support for a *Charter*-guaranteed individual freedom that fundamentally favours groups. The very meaning of membership – particularly in an employment setting – is addressed with real empathy. Individuals develop their sense of self through the connections they have with others; respecting those connections is part of what it means to recognize individual integrity and identity. Further, the judges insist that individuals can, and must be able to, exercise choice in their associations.

Before turning to the message that the dissenting judgment holds for Canadian labour relations law, trade unions, and freedom of association jurisprudence, it is worth noticing the way in which it offers a nuanced picture of human beings. Handed down roughly a decade after the high-point of an intense and prolonged liberal-communitarian debate in legal and political theory,[65] the *Delisle* dissent appears to reject or at least circumvent the conflict. The individual cannot exist as an atomistic, isolated self; she must situate herself within a web of commitments, affiliations, and relationships that provide her with a unique and multi-faceted identity. At the same time, however, the judgment's authors never imagine individuals submerged within the group, wholly subject to collective structures and communities. Instead, they are understood to choose to belong, to shape the significance of their membership, to take responsibility for participating in the flourishing of the organizations to which they commit. Extremely clever and yet simply and passionately expressed, the judgment both centres the individual and provides a lens of dynamic interaction and human connection through which to bring that individual into focus. As they suggest, the organizations which individuals choose to join define them to some (and an important) extent.

This combination of autonomy and association is precisely what Frank acknowledges as the basis of collective mobilizing in the workplace. For someone who would not have labelled himself a labour law expert or practitioner, Frank's contribution to the field has invited high praise from leading scholars. As noted by Brian Langille and Patrick Macklem, Frank "had a robust understanding both of unions as collective bargaining entities and of bargaining itself ... [flowing] from his basic understanding of the importance of work and the vulnerable position of workers in the labour market."[66] In other words, if the starting picture of the individual in the *Delisle* dissent is someone for whom belonging to an organized group of fellow workers may be essential to self-understanding and self-worth, then the freedom of association clearly encompasses the right to create and participate in the strongest form of workplace organization.

Indeed, as Justices Cory and Iacobucci indicate, free expression and association are intertwined in their significance for individual well-being.

"Simply to join a trade union is an important exercise of an individual's freedom of expression. It is a group which so often brings to the individual a sense of self-worth and dignity. An employee association provides a means of openly and frankly discussing work-related problems without fear of interference or intimidation by the employer."[67]

The focus on, and empathy for, individual workers and their choices might in some contexts be expected to detract from recognition of the distinct collective character of a union itself. That is, arguments aimed at weakening collective bargaining and the power of trade unions sometimes point to the diminution of individual contracting autonomy in the employment context. In a second labour law judgment at the Supreme Court, Frank made clear that his support for workplace organizations, although built on respect for the individual, would not waver in the face of arguments better suited to private law. Rather than subscribe to a historical view of unions as unincorporated associations sustained by webs of bilateral contracts between their members, Frank recognized a trade union as a distinct entity engaged in relationships with every individual worker.

This second judgment, *Berry v Pulley*,[68] handed down in 2002, is one in which Frank wrote for a unanimous Supreme Court. His dissenting voice from *Delisle* is transformed into a strong, clear, and convincing message about the character and functions of unions in contemporary Canada. In *Berry v Pulley*, one group of union members – Air Canada pilots – left the Canadian Air Line Pilots Association to create their own union, and then were personally named by their ex-co-union members in a private law claim for interference with contractual relations. Faced with arguments based in confusing and messy historical assumptions and legal fictions, Frank opted for clarity and accountability: clarity in defining the nature of a trade union in law, and accountability to the Canadian public perception of what unions are and do.

"The time has come to recognize formally that when a member joins a union, a relationship in the nature of a contract arises between the member and the trade union as a legal entity."[69] "[...] In today's labour relations context, the public has come to view unions as associations with the responsibility to discharge their obligations to members; it would be inconsistent with this view to deny unions the right to enter into legally enforceable contracts with these members."[70]

The judgment pares down the issues to the fundamental question of how to see unions and their relationships with their members. As a real entity in law, the union has a distinctive personality and power. It also has obligations to the people who work together, organize together, and pursue their individual and collective goals. Those individual workers are far from lost in the judgment's acknowledgment that a union is more than a bunch of contracts embodying connections among members. Instead, they are crucial to the very creation and nourishment of their own organizations. Together, they take on hard work: not only the work assigned in the workplace but that needed to build and sustain their organization with which they each have an individual relationship.

The story continues. In 2015, a majority of the Supreme Court of Canada followed what had been the dissenting direction in *Delisle*, and struck down the long-standing prohibition on collective organizing by the RCMP. In 2019, members of the RCMP overwhelmingly voted to certify the National Police Federation as their bargaining agent.

The judgments in *Delisle* and *Berry* combine clarity and fairness in the domain of labour relations, link respect for workers' organizations to fundamental recognition of individual liberty, and underscore the replacement of paternalism with respect for employee-directed and governed collective entities. This is not an extensive legacy for Frank Iacobucci in Supreme Court of Canada labour relations jurisprudence. But the pair of judgments – one dissenting and co-authored, the other written for a unanimous court – is enough to send strong and striking messages. Both resonate with real confidence and compassion whether speaking of human nature, the need to respond to contemporary realities, or the importance of ensuring free association in the workplace.

That confidence and compassion come as no surprise if we read the judgments while connecting the dots between Frank as the son of a steelworker, Frank as university administrator with substantial engagement in labour relations, and Frank as Supreme Court justice. As his University of Toronto colleague Martin Friedland reminds us, Frank Iacobucci served as chair of the grievance committee for the university's faculty association. In that capacity, he developed experience in the context of disputes over salary, tenure, and promotion, and sensitivity to the ways in which these are the principal markers of academic success. Further, as provost of the university, Frank was responsible for overseeing internal affairs including human resources. In that capacity, he negotiated with members of the Faculty Association with respect to potential unionization, and participated in designing and implementing governance structures and policies. Beyond firsthand involvement in labour relations, a provost works closely with deans and department directors in approving appointments, overseeing promotion processes, and assessing and supporting distinct academic units or sub-communities of the university.

Frank's concrete experience within the university context meant that he was acutely conscious of the meaning and functions of membership and collective organization at different levels. Different employee associations serve the needs of different categories of workers crucial to the functioning of a large university, and he would have been familiar with all of them. At the University of Toronto in particular, academic communities are shaped along different trajectories and overlap in various ways. The undergraduate colleges all have professors who, while members of the college, also belong to their particular departments within Arts and Science. The professional faculties are separate, as is graduate studies administration and programming. For such a large university, small communities are crucial. Within them, members can enjoy true collegiality, show loyalty to each other and the collective, and develop self-reliance and distinctive paths.

A Faculty of Law – precisely where Frank first served as leader – is an intense and particular example of a small community within the university. Professors work to ensure the smooth governance of all aspects of the faculty's collective life. From admissions to fundraising, designing curriculum to ensuring consistency in grading, alumni relations to faculty recruitment, law professors contribute to the sustenance of the community; in doing so, they not only get to know each other extremely well but rely on each other in important ways. As dean, Frank Iacobucci had to figure out the best routes and decisions for the Law Faculty as an institution, and then lead it along those routes and through the decision-making process.

Frank's colleague David Beatty, also a labour law scholar, suggests that the role attributed to Frank as team player and consensus builder at the Supreme Court reflects precisely the kind of professor he was: "He was a leader by example long before he was elected dean. He was the team player *par excellence*…Loyalty to the larger institutions and communities to which a person belongs is one of [his] ten commandments."[71]

The fact that this colleague remembers the way Dean Iacobucci gave credit to others and maintained a self-deprecating approach to leadership, underlines Frank's sense that institutions flourish if their members are supported and vice versa. People appreciate and thrive in a collegial atmosphere when they have some part to play in creating and contributing to the community. Indeed, recognizing human sensitivities and individual dreams and constraints is key to ensuring sustained commitment to a shared enterprise, to a community incorporated into the very sense of self for its members. That was precisely Frank's message as a Law dean and, years later, as a judge grappling with the promise and scope of freedom of association.

The quoted paragraph from *Delisle* that opens this discussion of human interaction offers an array of examples that show how we are social animals in the choices we make to work, live, and flourish together, to form a family, join a union, belong to a nation. The fact that Frank co-authored the judgment with Justice Peter Cory is telling on this point. The very act of working with a friend and close colleague to create a shared product mirrors the kind of chosen association that the two judges say is core to the case. Beyond addressing the importance to human dignity of organization in the workplace, the judgment illustrates true collegiality in the development of an ongoing conversation about freedom of association in Canada. If David Beatty says that we can't understand Frank's professional persona without an awareness of his human qualities, Frank might reply that no one, including himself, can understand that persona without taking into account the ways in which he joined with others in every one of his workplaces.

Never-Ending Conversations: Dialogue, Dignity, and Doing the Right Thing

The judgment in *Delisle* came out in 1999. In that same year, as the court approached the turn of the century, Frank Iacobucci handed down three other judgments, all of which constituted significant markers of his time and contribution as justice of the Supreme Court of Canada. In two of them, *Gladue* and *M v H*, Frank wrote together with Peter Cory on behalf of the entire court; in the third, the *Law* case, he wrote on his own, again for a unanimous court. In different ways, all three incorporate aspects of Frank's commitment to dialogue, human dignity, and the importance of doing the right thing.

On their substance, the decisions belong under the headings of Indigenous justice, sexual orientation discrimination, and gender equality. Specifically, they address sentencing for Aboriginal individuals within Canadian criminal justice (*Gladue*), the extension of spousal benefits to individuals in same-sex relationships (*M v H*), and the need for guidance in applying the guarantee of equality found in the *Canadian Charter of Rights and Freedoms* (*Law*).

More broadly, the three judgments present three kinds of challenges or responsibilities for the Supreme Court: first, informed engagement with Canada's Indigenous Peoples; second, innovative responsiveness to contemporary claims for inclusiveness and visibility; and third, careful articulation of structures or tests for constitutional analysis.

The most obvious way to explore the three challenges, as embodied by these three contiguous judgments, might be to start with Frank's theoretical approach to equality as set out in *Law*, and then to turn to the application of that approach vis-à-vis, first, LGBTQ individuals, and then, members of Indigenous communities. Instead, I suggest that Frank's approach to Aboriginal offenders sets the stage for delving into his recognition of sexual orientation as a prohibited ground of discrimination and, more broadly, for appreciating his attempt to integrate human dignity into the promise of equality. That commitment to dignity and equality then circles back as the driving force behind Frank's engagement with Indigenous justice at the court and beyond.

Flexibility and Engagement with Canada's Indigenous Peoples

Two decades after the 1999 judgment in *R. v Gladue*,[72] co-authored by Justices Iacobucci and Cory for a unanimous Supreme Court, the name

"Gladue" had become the equivalent of a household term in the principles and practices of criminal justice in Canada. *Gladue* is a core element of Canadian sentencing law. The submission of "Gladue reports" and the existence of "Gladue courts" are elements of criminal procedure found, albeit not uniformly, across the country. All students of Canadian criminal law learn about the Gladue principles; all learn that, in words taken from the judgment, *"the circumstances of aboriginal offenders differ from those of the majority because many aboriginal people are victims of systemic and direct discrimination, many suffer the legacy of dislocation, and many are substantially affected by poor social and economic conditions."*[73]

The *Gladue* judgment set out the proper interpretation of s. 718(2)(e) of the Criminal Code of Canada: a sentencing provision, found in a new part of the Code introduced in 1996, that directed courts to take into account the particular circumstances of Aboriginal offenders. The Supreme Court unanimously found that Aboriginal offenders must be treated differently in the search for a truly appropriate sentence: *"... the logical meaning to be derived from the special reference to the circumstances of aboriginal offenders, juxtaposed as it is against a general direction to consider 'the circumstances' for all offenders, is that sentencing judges should pay particular attention to the circumstances of aboriginal offenders because those circumstances are unique, and different from those of non-aboriginal offenders."*[74]

Identified in the recently enacted part of the Criminal Code was a principle of restraint in sentencing and a move away from rampant incarceration; indeed, Justices Iacobucci and Cory saw this as a response to the overrepresentation of Aboriginal people in prisons resulting in their *"estrangement [...] from the Canadian criminal justice system [...]."*[75] The judgment emphasizes the importance of restorative justice as a different approach to sentencing, one more consonant with community values than the approach of deterrence, denunciation, and separation traditionally found in Canadian criminal justice.[76]

In deciding on a sentence, trial judges must include two inquiries in an assessment of the particular circumstances of Aboriginal offenders:

"(A) The unique systemic or background factors which may have played a part in bringing the particular aboriginal offender before the courts; and (B) The types of sentencing procedures and sanctions which may be appropriate in the circumstances for the offender because of his or her particular aboriginal heritage or connection."[77]

The judgment goes on to acknowledge the fact that the result of such inquiry might well disrupt consistency in sentencing for similar offences: *"the appropriateness of a sentence will depend on the particular circumstances of the offence, the offender, and the community in which the offence took place. Disparity of sentences for similar crimes is a natural consequence of this individualized focus."*[78]

As Jamie Tanis Gladue's story moved through the criminal justice system on its way to the Supreme Court, it was reduced to that of a young, intoxicated woman who stabbed to death her fiancé and father of her children, on the basis of her belief that he was having an affair with her sister. Charged with second degree murder, she pled guilty to manslaughter. In deciding on a sentence of three years imprisonment (with conditional parole after six months), the trial judge considered the fact that she had been beaten on previous occasions, and that she had now undertaken drug and alcohol counselling and gone back to school. Significantly, despite the directives found in s. 718(2)(e) of the Criminal Code, the judge declined to include consideration of Ms. Gladue's Cree heritage, partly because she was living off-reserve. On appeal, the Supreme Court focused on the scope and mandate of the Criminal Code provision, making it clear that the judge should have considered Ms. Gladue an "Aboriginal offender," but left the sentence intact.

In writing with Peter Cory, Frank spoke to the role of the judge in remedying injustices in Canadian society, and integrated into the judgment an awareness of social realities and an acknowledgement of a shift in approaches to sentencing:

"It is clear that sentencing innovation by itself cannot remove the causes of aboriginal offending and the greater problem of aboriginal alienation from the

criminal justice system. The unbalanced ratio of imprisonment for aboriginal offenders flows from a number of sources, including poverty, substance abuse, lack of education, and the lack of employment opportunities for aboriginal people. It arises also from bias against aboriginal people and from an unfortunate institutional approach that is more inclined to refuse bail and to impose more and longer prison terms for aboriginal offenders. There are many aspects of this sad situation which cannot be addressed in these reasons. What can and must be addressed, though, is the limited role that sentencing judges will play in remedying injustice against aboriginal peoples in Canada. Sentencing judges are among those decision-makers who have the power to influence the treatment of aboriginal offenders in the justice system. They determine most directly whether an aboriginal offender will go to jail, or whether other sentencing options may be employed which will play perhaps a stronger role in restoring a sense of balance to the offender, victim, and community, and in preventing future crime."[79]

The judgment proceeds to examine the notion of restorative justice, indicating a willingness to go beyond what was strictly necessary to decide whether to uphold the sentence handed down by the trial judge in this particular case. The dialogue opened up in *Gladue* is on several levels: between sentencing judge and the accused in individual and collective context; between appellate court and trial judges trying to do the right thing in the cases before them; and, at the most general level, between the Supreme Court of Canada and alternative versions of criminal justice.

"In general terms, restorative justice may be described as an approach to remedying crime in which it is understood that all things are interrelated and that crime disrupts the harmony which existed prior to its occurrence, or at least which it is felt should exist. The appropriateness of a particular sanction is largely determined by the needs of the victims, and the community, as well as the offender. The focus is on the human beings closely affected by the crime."[80]

In underscoring the relevance and potential of restorative justice, *Gladue* didn't bring with it an end to Aboriginal over-representation in Canadian prisons; neither did it eradicate and replace all principles and practices of sentencing across the country. Fundamentally, however, it reminded all actors in the criminal justice system that small decisions about individual offenders are part of a bigger picture of paying attention to and moving towards reconciliation on the collective experience and confrontation of Indigenous persons and peoples with Canadian criminal law. In other words, and as an important piece of Frank's Supreme Court jurisprudence, it insisted that respect for the dignity of individuals demands dialogue with the communities to which they belong.

The judgment in *Gladue* is part of an ongoing conversation in which Frank continued to participate long after leaving the court. In the introduction to his 2013 independent review of First Nations representation on Ontario juries,[81] commissioned by Order in Council of the Ontario government, Frank described juries as the "*cornerstone of our justice system, as well as a fundamental institution in the administration of justice.*" He then acknowledged, "*it is clear that the jury system as it has developed and operated in Ontario, like Ontario's justice system in general, has not often been a friend to Aboriginal people.*"[82]

Based on visits and meetings with leaders and members of 32 First Nations and four First Nation organizations, Frank and his review team explored striking cultural barriers, indicators of systemic discrimination, gaps in knowledge and awareness, and inadequate control over community justice matters. As the resulting report made clear, all these things stood in the way not only of meaningful representation on juries but of effective realization of broader justice.

"In my experience dealing with Aboriginal issues as a lawyer (in both public and private practice) and judge, too often I have seen evidence or examples of mistrust and disrespect between Aboriginal and non-Aboriginal Canadians, whether the latter are government or private institutions or individuals. Although the evils of racism and discrimination have diminished over time, much more is needed to foster a relationship of harmony and enlightened co-existence ... Without building a foundation of mutual respect and mutual trust for each other, the recommendations below will achieve nothing. And

that respect and trust has to be earned not proclaimed. Concrete proposals and mutual effort are required.[83]

Responsiveness to Claims for Inclusiveness and Visibility

Frank's collaboration with Peter Cory continued in the case of *M v H*,[84] issued in 1999 along with *Gladue* and *Delisle*. Here, the Iacobucci-Cory partnership produced a judgment, supported by a majority of the court, focused on the definition of "spouse" as a term found in provincial family law legislation. In extending spousal support to same-sex partners, the judgment grapples with the promise of equality for individuals and, at the same time, the significance of context for understanding support within marriage.

M and H (initials, or even numbers in some jurisdictions, often stand in for names in family law litigation, so as to preserve some degree of privacy) were two women living together in a long-term relationship. They shared household responsibilities and expenses, as well as a business. When the relationship broke down after a decade, M made a claim for spousal support under Ontario's Family Law Act. In order to do so, she challenged the validity of the legislation's definition of spouse.

Justices Iacobucci and Cory had recently decided the case of *Vriend v Alberta*,[85] in which they had divided up the task of addressing equality on the basis of sexual orientation on one hand (Cory), and the strength of offered justification for discrimination, on the other (Iacobucci). In that case, Mr. Vriend had lost his job after coming out as gay; his complaint, filed with the Alberta Human Rights Commission, was dismissed given that the province's human rights legislation included no explicit protection against discrimination on the basis of sexual orientation. The Supreme Court decided to read in that protection as an implicit and previously invisible guarantee. In doing so, it exercised what Frank refers to in his part of the *Vriend* judgment as its responsibility as trustee of constitutional rights and freedoms:

"*To my mind, a great value of judicial review and this dialogue among the branches [of government] is that each of the branches is made somewhat accountable to the other. The work of the legislature is reviewed by the courts and the work of the court in its decisions can be reacted to by the legislature in the passing of new legislation (or even overarching laws under s. 33 of the Charter). This dialogue between and accountability of each of the branches have the effect of enhancing the democratic process, not denying it.*"[86]

Again in *M v H*, the two justices split up the judgment writing. The first part, by Justice Cory, found that the restrictive definition of spouse found in the *Family Law Act* infringed the guarantee of equality, thus constituting a breach of s. 15(1) of the *Charter*. In the second part, Frank turned to section 1 of the *Charter* to scrutinize the legislative objectives against the backdrop of a free and democratic society. "*Providing for the equitable resolution of economic disputes when intimate relationships between financially interdependent individuals break down, and alleviating the burden on the public purse to provide for dependent spouses*": these were the Act's spousal support goals.[87] Frank read them as objectives serving to *promote both social justice and the dignity of individuals*, and found no persuasive justification for refusing to extend the protection of spousal support to same-sex partners.

The result of the judgment was the striking down of the spousal definition section of the provincial family law legislation, and the resulting extension of spousal support coverage to individuals in same-sex relationships. At the same time that consideration of individual dignity led to that conclusion, the judgment also acknowledged the traditional and strikingly gendered socio-economic backdrop of marriage, and the meaning and importance of support in that context. But while Frank referred to "*the economic vulnerability of heterosexual women, their tendency to take on primary responsibility for parenting, the greater earning capacity of men, and systemic sexual inequality,*"[88] he refused to confine the policy of the Family Law Act regarding spousal support to situations of economic dependency of wives on their husbands. "*In my view, this general social reality does not detract from the principle that dependencies can and do develop irrespective of gender in intimate conjugal relationships.*[89]

Skewed economic dependency within a personal partnership – what Frank refers to as the true mischief that the support provisions are meant to address — is not restricted to heterosexual relationships. As illustrated by the story of M and H, real need and dependence can arise, in either direction, in any long-term relationship. If promotion of dignity was part of the mission of spousal support directives, as the majority judgment suggested, then individuals previously excluded from coverage could and should be eligible.

For law students keen to see the promise of equality extended to gay, lesbian, and bisexual individuals, the Cory-Iacobucci collaboration in *Vriend* and again in *M v H* was both refreshing and exciting. It wasn't the case that there weren't co-existing developments in the same direction to be found in other areas of law and practice, or that the *Charter* on its own was crucial or responsible for recognition of same-sex marriage and LGBTQ identity.[90] But the decisions in those cases, reached through explicit and collegial dialogue between two judges, intersected with and helped open up broader conversations about sexual identity and justice across Canada.

In 1998, the opening class of my Foundations of Canadian Law course took inspiration from the *Vriend* decision as I invited first year students in their first week of law school into a preliminary discussion of the dynamic back-and-forth between society and law, between legislating and judging, between policy and *Charter* analysis. In 1999, a student in my Social Diversity and Law seminar wrote a short personal reflection piece on how Frank Iacobucci seemed to speak directly to people whose rights were not yet fully recognized, and on how non-straight sexual identity felt like it was moving out of the margins, thanks in part to the Supreme Court of Canada.

Ten years earlier, in the hallway outside one of the large classrooms at University of Toronto's Faculty of Law, there was a bulletin board maintained by and for members of the group Gays and Lesbians at U of T.

Documents relevant to equality on the basis of sexual orientation were routinely posted and updated. I noticed that no one was ever seen putting up or taking down the articles. All of that action was invisible; it appeared to happen "off hours." It was awkward, and noticed, to stop in front of the board to read the posted documents. In 1988, as a second-year law student, I spoke to a professor about what our Women and Law group had learned from a student at Queen's University who had spoken out at a student conference about how it felt to be lesbian in law school – and how we might address similar problems in our own classrooms and corridors. The response was that we didn't need to worry: there weren't any lesbian law students at University of Toronto. I knew that couldn't be right. For law students emerging from that invisibility within their legal education, Justice Iacobucci seemed to know exactly the same thing.

Identifying and addressing discrimination on the basis of sexual orientation, in all the places it has existed and continues to exist in this country, is necessarily a task that requires more than what the Supreme Court can offer. Norms of behaviour, governing assumptions and rules only shift as a result of intersecting energies and initiatives on the part of many people and institutions. This is a telling example of how the *Canadian Charter of Rights and Freedoms*, interpreted and applied by the court, could make a real difference – but also of how the court's contribution to change was necessarily partial and incomplete.

Frank himself, as a Supreme Court justice, went further than the context of equality in the workplace or marriage in recognizing the spectrum of human sexual orientation. In what became known as the *Little Sisters Bookstore* case,[91] decided a year after *M v H*, his dissenting reasons showed that he understood the importance of protecting gay and lesbian erotic materials from ignorant and discriminatory censorship. In the following excerpt, his past law clerk, Matthew Milne-Smith, comments on the power of a judgment written by someone whose background, Matthew speculates, was unlikely to have "exposed him to the world of gay and lesbian erotica."

"Little Sisters was a lesbian and gay bookstore. It was not an Adult or XXX bookstore; most of its inventory was entirely innocuous. However, among travel guides, AIDS/HIV educational materials, and general interest periodicals, it carried gay and lesbian erotica. For 15 years, Little Sisters had been engaged in an ongoing battle with Canada Customs over its importation of this erotica from the United States, where the vast majority of such content was produced.

"By the time the case had wound its way to the Supreme Court of Canada, the government had conceded that a great deal of non-obscene materials had been wrongly detained at the border. Books that were imported by general interest bookstores, or even the Vancouver Public Library, were detained or excluded entirely when destined for Little Sisters. Prominent literature featuring far more graphic depictions of (heterosexual) sexual violence, such as Bret Easton Ellis's *American Psycho*, were granted special pre-clearance to mainstream bookstores, while far more innocuous homosexual literature intended for Little Sisters was seized at the border.

"This importation struggle caused significant hardship to Little Sisters. Shipments had to be paid for within 30 days, but were not delivered for months, if at all. Putting aside the commercial harm to the bookstore, there were also significant intangible harms to the Vancouver gay and lesbian community from being denied access to literature that depicted people with their desires and interests.

"The majority acknowledged that the customs legislation had been implemented in an unconstitutional manner, and held unconstitutional a reverse onus provision requiring the importer to prove that material was not obscene. With that small exception, however, the majority held that the general system of prior restraint at the border was constitutional and required no further remedy. Customs simply needed to stop discriminating.

"Justice Iacobucci, joined by Justices Arbour and Lebel, dissented. Regardless of whether the customs legislation was non-discriminatory *in theory*, the reality was that *in practice* it had inevitably and consistently been applied in a discriminatory manner. It was not enough to simply say that Customs needed to stop applying the law in a discriminatory manner. The law structurally lent itself to abuse, not necessarily because of ill will on anyone's part, but because homosexual erotica was so foreign to typical Customs officers that they could not be expected to determine what was or was not obscene. Customs officers receive extensive training on things like the proper tariff to apply to different fruits and vegetables. They had little or no background or training to prepare them to distinguish permissible erotica from prohibited obscenity.

"The result was that an obviously marginalized community was further stigmatized and isolated by being denied access to a significant form of self-expression: '*In a society which marginalized sexual difference, literature has the potential to show individuals that they are not alone and that others share their experience.*' I can't imagine that much in Justice Iacobucci's background or upbringing exposed him to the world of gay and lesbian erotica. Nonetheless, he was able to vicariously 'share their experience' and understand why the law had violated their constitutional rights." (Matthew Milne-Smith)

Equality and the Evolution of Analytical Tests

Frank's 1999 judgment in the *Law* case invites a different kind of analysis and commentary, this time centred primarily on methodology. Here, Frank wrote on his own as he set out a test on behalf of the entire Supreme Court: a test explicitly meant to be used in interpreting and applying section 15 – the equality section – of the *Canadian Charter of Rights and Freedoms*. As *Law* illustrates, both potential and peril attach to the creation of a test in law: while always intended to clarify and guide legal analysis, a multi-faceted test can lead instead to confusion. As *Law* also indicates, while respect for human dignity might seem an obviously good thing, the form and consequences of insisting on that respect pose significant challenges.

One decade before Frank's judgment in *Law v Canada (Minister of Employment and Immigration)*,[92] the Supreme Court of Canada had handed down *Andrews*,[93] its first and landmark judgment on the promise of equality in the *Charter*. Following that case, *Charter* analysis at the first stage of a claim of equality rights violation focused on whether the complainant could show a disadvantage impermissibly based on one of the grounds listed in s. 15(1). Successful claims of discrimination, on the basis of citizenship or sexual orientation, had established that the list could be enlarged by analogy. Once the infringement of equality was established, the burden shifted to the implicated government actor to show that there was persuasive justification for the differential treatment.

The judge's task within this framework of analysis was roughly as follows:

1. To assess the policy or decision in question for the way in which implicit or explicit distinctions are made based on race, sex, age, etc.
2. To work through the analogical reasoning required to treat an unenumerated ground for differentiation as if it were included in s. 15 protection
3. To examine the purpose, rationale, and methods employed in order to determine the existence of persuasive justification for the discriminatory treatment

In accepting to hear the appeal in *Law*, the court indicated that it was time to revisit and elaborate on the constitutional guarantee of equality, and to provide fresh guidelines for analysis of an individual's claim of unjustified infringement. Frank's judgment for a unanimous court turned to the centrality and significance of human dignity in giving meaning to equality.

"It may be said that the purpose of s.15(1) is to prevent the violation of essential human dignity and freedom through the imposition of disadvantage, stereotyping, or political or social prejudice, and to promote a society in which all persons enjoy equal recognition at law as human beings or as members of

Canadian society, equally capable and equally deserving of concern, respect and consideration."[94]

In explicitly linking failures in equal recognition and respect for members of Canadian society to violations of human dignity, Frank added a dimension to the decision-making process. Beyond acknowledging the impugned legislation's differential treatment on the basis of an enumerated or analogous ground, a decision maker would look further in order to establish whether the legislative effect is to perpetuate or promote the view that an individual is less capable or less worthy of recognition or value as a human being or as a member of Canadian society. Without any such effect, it would be unlikely that differential treatment would constitute discrimination within the purpose of s. 15 (1) of the *Charter*.

Aware that precise definition of human dignity – and of harm to dignity – is difficult if not impossible, Frank offered some guidance:

"What is human dignity? There can be different conceptions ... Human dignity means that an individual or group feels self-respect and self-worth. It is concerned with physical and psychological integrity and empowerment. Human dignity is harmed by unfair treatment premised upon personal traits or circumstances which do not relate to individual needs, capacities, or merits. It is enhanced by laws which are sensitive to the needs, capacities, and merits of different individuals, taking into account the context underlying their differences. Human dignity is harmed when individuals and groups are marginalized, ignored, or devalued, and is enhanced when laws recognize the full place of all individuals and groups within Canadian society. Human dignity within the meaning of the equality guarantee does not relate to the status or position of an individual in society per se, but rather concerns the manner in which a person legitimately feels when confronted with a particular law. Does the law treat him or her unfairly, taking into account all of the circumstances regarding the individuals affected and excluded by the law?"[95]

It is difficult to disagree with the idea that our dignity as human beings is nourished by, and partly dependent on, our sense of being treated fairly and with equal consideration. But the way in which the *Law* judgment introduced human dignity into the analysis of whether government action constitutes discrimination under s. 15 of the *Charter* became the subject of ongoing concern and critique. Commentators focused on the adequacy of the connection between the listed factors for consideration and the impact on a somewhat nebulous concept and perhaps even more nebulous subjective experience of a blow to human dignity. In addition, regardless of the intent of a judgment's author, a list of factors has a tendency to evolve into a rigid test that loses the desired flexibility and responsiveness of a constitutional guarantee of equality. Finally, critical analysis of the judgment pointed to the potentially heavy addition to the burden on the claimant to persuade a court of impairment of human dignity.[96]

As author of the Supreme Court's unanimous judgment, Frank might find the critique a somewhat bewildering response to what he (and the court) no doubt felt was an in-depth examination of a part of the *Charter* that had continued to attract disagreement and active discussion. Indeed, the exploration of how human dignity is affected when someone's equality is undermined seems like a way to pay close attention to the individual involved. Frank might add that he anticipated the possibility of a rigid test and explicitly warned against it. And he might say the proper place for a full assessment of the claim to discrimination must be within s. 15 itself and thus the responsibility or burden of the claimant. If establishing a blow to human dignity is central to the analysis, as it is according to *Law*, it is a fair hurdle to clear for any equality claimant.

This brief sketch offers ample room for debating the substantive strengths and weaknesses of the judgment's approach to equality. Instead of directly taking up that offer, however, I turn to *Law* as judgment to examine particular and recurring features of law in general. The *Law* case certainly has a place along the trajectory of equality rights in Canadian law and society, a trajectory that moves from provincial human rights codes and the federal Bill of Rights to the drafting of s. 15 of the *Charter* and its development and application in the hands of advocates and courts in the late twentieth century and into the twenty-first. At the same time, and in a way I focus on below, it draws our attention to always present challenges for legal reasoning, decision-making, and responsiveness.

First, the *Law* judgment sheds light on the attraction and power of legal tests, and on how tests can feel and work in the hands of those charged with applying them. Second, it allows us to question the desirability, or at least to appreciate the perils, of unanimous Supreme Court decisions. Third, *Law* can be imagined as a site for the coming together of judge, commentator, and protagonist in the story that led to the judgment; it invites us to notice imagined and real interactions among the law makers who shape future paths. Together, these are key themes in thinking through the shaping, influence, and limits of law. In addition to contributing to discussions focused on the substance of equality rights law in Canada, Frank's judgment in *Law* provokes a revisiting of the restraints and risks that characterize the role and responsibilities of the judge.

First then, we consider the contours and consequences of the presentation of a test. In proposing a question to be asked within the framework of constitutional analysis, followed by a non-exhaustive list of factors to be considered in arriving at an answer, Frank's judgment in *Law* was far from breaking new ground. Utilized at other key points of Canadian *Charter* jurisprudence – whether in framing the analysis of state justification for rights infringement (*Oakes*)[97] or the meaning and scope of recognition of Aboriginal rights (*Sparrow*)[98] – the test approach is meant to organize arguments and reasoning in a consistent and clear way. It casts the judge as both shaper and interpreter of principle, responsible for providing content and guidance to legislative language. This understanding of the responsibility of the decision-maker is not unique to the realm of constitutional interpretation. Multifactorial tests can be found in other areas of law as well, including in the domain of private law governing the interactions of individuals.

Yet a fixed test can lead to a loss of the flexibility needed to respond to the complicated and unforeseen contexts that inevitably arise. Specifically, the test offered in *Law* seems to invite the task of interpreting the principle of protection of human dignity to dislodge that of comparing the impugned action and its impact to those previously found to constitute a violation of equality. That shift could be a problem. In assessing claims of inequality, analogical reasoning – asking, for example, whether discrimination on the basis of sexual orientation is "like" discrimination on the basis of another prohibited ground – can go a long way in developing the content and promise of s. 15 of the *Charter*.[99] Insisting, at a preliminary stage, on giving meaning to dignity by reference to factors that risk turning into a formal checklist arguably shifts the focus away from inequality itself.

Second, the clarity and apparent finality of a unanimous judgment can turn out to be anything but. While *Law*'s appeal to a grounding commitment to human dignity reflects a desire to smooth over and better define a somewhat bumpy path for equality jurisprudence in Canada, it risks the creation of a major pothole. In a 1994 House of Lords judgment, albeit in the far-removed context of the relationship of tort to contract, Lord Goff warned against what he strikingly referred to as the "temptation of elegance."[100] The aim of clearing up confusion, by producing a sophisticated and streamlined set of guidelines for the future development of the law, can backfire.

Human dignity as a notion might provide a kind of all-encompassing framework for understanding the protection of human rights including equality. Turning it into the touchstone of anti-discrimination under s. 15, however, introduces a real and structural difficulty: how could it ever be justifiable for the state to trample on someone's human dignity? Section 1 of the *Charter*, by which the burden shifts to the state to justify actions that appear to infringe a guaranteed right, is potentially gutted of its function.[101] Either human dignity has been breached, in which case there is discrimination that would be almost impossible to justify. Or, as was found in the *Law* case itself, what seems to be discrimination doesn't qualify for its apparent lack of a human dignity destroying aspect, and thus no justification is required.

The attempted elegance in the judgment is found in the way it purports to enrich and clarify our understanding of equality. The fact that the court speaks in one voice appears to cement its role in providing guidance for all equality cases to come. Interestingly, the absence of a dissenting voice in the judgment may be a big factor in this problem of "elegance." While Frank might have been proud to get unanimous support for his judgment, there is something lost in the absence of multiple voices. Further reflection and precision in a majority judgment are often the result of interaction with the disagreement provided by dissent; the lack of that disagreement in *Law* may be responsible for the somewhat fuzzy guidance provided by an appeal to dignity.

To be fair, the need to make the assessment more concrete had been recognized by Frank through the suggestion of four contextual factors that might assist assessment of the impact on human dignity of allegedly discriminatory treatment. Those four factors were (1) pre-existing disadvantage, stereotyping, prejudice, or vulnerability experienced by the individual or group at issue; (2) correspondence, or lack thereof, between the ground or grounds on which the claim is based and the actual need, capacity, or circumstances of the claimant or others; (3) the ameliorative purpose or effects of the impugned law upon a more disadvantaged person or group in society – relevant when the claim is brought by someone more advantaged; and (4) the nature and scope of the interest affected by the impugned law.[102]

Even with those factors in hand, a later judgment of the court – *R. v Kapp* in 2008[103] – revisited *Law*, and referred back to *Andrews*, in an attempt to provide the precision perceived to be necessary but lacking:

"There can be no doubt that human dignity is an essential value underlying the s. 15 equality guarantee ... But as critics have pointed out, human dignity is an abstract and subjective notion that, even with the guidance of the four contextual factors, cannot only become confusing and difficult to apply; it has also proven to be an additional burden on equality claimants, rather than the philosophical enhancement it was intended to be.

"The analysis in a particular case, as *Law* itself recognizes, more usefully focusses on the factors that identify impact amounting to discrimination. The four factors cited in *Law* are based on and relate to the identification in *Andrews* of perpetuation of disadvantage and stereotyping as the primary indicators of discrimination. Pre-existing disadvantage and the nature of the interest affected (factors one and four in *Law*) go to perpetuation of disadvantage and prejudice, while the second factor deals with stereotyping. The ameliorative purpose or effect of a law or program (the third factor in *Law*) goes to whether the purpose is remedial within the meaning of s. 15(2). (We would suggest, without deciding here, that the third *Law* factor might also be relevant to the question under s. 15(1) as to whether the effect of the law or program is to perpetuate disadvantage.)

"Viewed in this way, *Law* does not impose a new and distinctive test for discrimination ... The factors cited in *Law* should not be read literally as if they were legislative dispositions, but as a way of focussing on the central concern of s. 15 identified in *Andrews* – combatting discrimination, defined in terms of perpetuating disadvantage and stereotyping."[104]

With these words, the Supreme Court's approach to equality sidelined the consideration of dignity in favour of a concrete analysis of discrimination. The disagreement over the form and substance of s.15 of the *Charter* – remarkably missing when the *Law* judgment was handed down – had emerged almost a decade later. The offered test was no longer to be understood or applied as such; inevitable messiness replaced potential elegance.

Readers might note that this entire discussion of *Law* has avoided any concrete reference to Nancy Law herself. This brings us to the third and final general challenge for law illustrated by *Law*. Conversations between judges and their critics can be traced through published texts, primarily in the form of judgments and law journal articles. Conversations in law classrooms in which teachers and students scrutinize the structure and substance of judgments, and of the commentary provided, are carried on year after year. But the conversations between client and advocate, and specifically the stories of the person who lent her name to the eventual Supreme Court judgment in *Law*, tend to get submerged along the way.

Nancy Law was a woman widowed in her 30s and denied the benefits under the Canada Pension Plan that she would have received had she been older when she lost her spouse. The lawyer who represented her focused on the obvious age differentiation in the availability of survivor pension benefits. As Canadian equality rights scholar Denise Réaume has pointed out, no room was ever made for consideration of how gender and age merge as elements of the way in which Nancy Law lived through her bereavement.[105]

The very nature of an appellate judgment, focused on the contours of the legal issues at hand, is such that the details of a claimant's story fade into the background. It can take the powerful words of American legal scholar Robert Cover to remind us that the words and decision of a judge have real and potentially irreversible impact on actual human beings. Cover insists that "legal interpretation takes place in a field of pain and death. [...] A judge articulates her understanding of a text, and as a result, somebody loses his freedom, his property, his children, even his life. [...] When interpreters have finished their work, they frequently leave behind victims whose lives have been torn apart by these organized, social practices of violence."[106]

Nancy Law's story followed on the heels of death: a story in which, after losing her life partner, she was denied the benefits designed by government to help surviving spouses in the wake of such loss. The message was that, at her age, she didn't need that extra help; she could adjust and manage on her own. It might well be that limiting benefit payments to surviving spouses is appropriate given economic realities of young adults in Canada. The fact that Nancy Law's experience was interpreted as not affecting her sense of dignity meant that arguments justifying those limits never had to be made.

The Supreme Court judgment articulated the questions to be addressed as follows:

"Do the impugned Canada Pension Plan provisions, in purpose or effect, violate essential human dignity and freedom through the imposition of

disadvantage, stereotyping, or political or social prejudice? Does the law, in purpose or effect, conform to a society in which all persons enjoy equal recognition as human beings or as members of Canadian society, equally capable and equally deserving of concern, respect, and consideration? Does the law, in purpose or effect, perpetuate the view that people under 45 are less capable or less worthy of recognition or value as human beings or as members of Canadian society?"[107]

Nancy Law couldn't convince decision-makers in law that her dignity was at stake in the age-based differential treatment. Given the fact that the test changed as a result of her own appeal, she never knew she had to. An alternative way of framing the place of dignity in a claim might have been to ask whether the state, in treating the claimant in a potentially discriminatory way, could justify its actions and maintain appropriate respect for the human dignity of affected individuals. The outcome of the *Charter* complaint might have been the same. But the impact of the litigation on Nancy Law herself might have been different.

It is somewhat ironic that a judgment that stands for the importance of individual human dignity as a key element in determining equality rights violations carries a name that loses its meaning as the name of the claimant herself. "*Law*" becomes the name of the judgment; "law" refers to an entire enterprise of thinking about human relations, norms, and institutions. It is easy to forget that it is also the name of a real person who participated in the development of case law and commentary related to the Canadian *Charter*. What started out as a complaint about unfair treatment on the basis of age turns into a judgment that sets a new dignity-incorporating standard for equality jurisprudence. That transformation, and the attached failure of our protagonist's claim, may well have been experienced by Nancy Law as a blow to her own human dignity.

Back to Indigenous Justice

In introducing the judgments explored above – *Gladue, M v H, Law*, all decided in 1999 – I suggested that they presented three kinds of challenges or responsibilities for the Supreme Court of Canada: informed engagement with Canada's Indigenous peoples, innovative responsiveness to claims for inclusiveness and visibility, and careful articulation of interpretive structures. We have seen that they are also examples of Frank's contributions to ongoing conversations on justice, diversity, and equality. Another unanimous Supreme Court judgment, signed by Frank in 2000, mixes together elements of the earlier cases and the conversations to which they belonged.

In *Lovelace v Ontario*,[108] a number of First Nations and Métis communities, none of which were registered as bands under the Indian Act, brought a claim against the Chiefs of Ontario, complaining of discriminatory exclusion from a First Nations Fund associated with a pilot commercial gaming (casino) project and specifically available only to band communities.

Frank followed the test he had designed in *Law* to find that the non-band groups were not considered "less Aboriginal" than their band counterparts: a "*broad and fully contextual s. 15(1) analysis transcends the superficiality of a simple balancing of relative disadvantage.*"[109] While all Aboriginal communities in Canada share a general history of disadvantage and discriminatory treatment, there are nevertheless differences among these communities, and this was a program meant to ameliorate socio-economic conditions for a particular segment of Canadian Aboriginal society. Further, rather than constituting a general, benefit-conferring regime, it was explicitly limited and targeted, having arisen from partnerships between federal/provincial governments and First Nations bands.[110] According to Frank, "*the appellant aboriginal communities have very different relations with respect to the land, government, and gaming from those anticipated by the casino program.*"[111] The distinction made by the First Nations Fund and those responsible for its disbursement therefore did not constitute a violation of section 15 of the *Charter*.

Lovelace, like *Gladue*, is a case that demands engagement with Indigenous peoples, history, and contemporary reality in Canada. It invites the court to do what it did in *M v H* – to extend equality protection to individuals and groups not specifically listed in the *Charter* – an invitation declined in this context via application of the guidelines articulated in *Law*. It underscores the importance of community, in a way that recalls *Delisle*. Further, it acknowledges the importance of interaction between decision makers, as set out in *Southam* and *Ryan*: here in the form of dialogue between courts and internal First Nations governance norms and mechanisms.

Above, we moved from Frank's approach to Aboriginal offenders to his recognition of sexual orientation as a prohibited ground of discrimination and then to his insistence on integrating human dignity into the promise of equality. *Lovelace* combines his commitment to dignity and equality with his respect for the sites and substance of Indigenous justice. That combination doesn't mean that Aboriginal claimants win their case every time; it all depends on getting the mix of factors right in the particular context.

One of Frank's law clerks, James Hickling, traces in a compelling way the connections between Frank's judgments at the Supreme Court and his post-Supreme Court negotiation and reconciliation work with Canada's Indigenous Peoples. As a lawyer whose practice focuses on Aboriginal rights and claims, he sees Frank's turn to principles of equality and dignity as a crucial piece of ongoing reconciliation.

"Reconciliation. Where does one begin? The problem is so complex, the layers are so deep, the history is so painful, the challenges are so varied, the attitudes are so ingrained, and the economic costs are so enormous. To renovate the full range of relevant factors – social, political, cultural, institutional, legal, economic, physical, and psychological – is so daunting that we shrink from the task.

"One method for resolving highly complex, multivariate problems is to step back and regard the whole of the problem from the perspective of first principles. This is as true in law and politics as it is in physics and chemistry. The application of first principles helps us to separate the data from the noise, to identify and focus on the key issues and obstacles, and to develop a coherent understanding of what at first appears to be a confused and tangled knot ... I suggest that the technique of returning to first principles is one of the secrets of Frank's success in his work on reconciliation.

In particular, I suggest that Frank's approach to reconciliation is informed by his commitment to one fundamental idea: that the recognition and protection of human dignity is an essential feature of a just society.

"In 1999, the court decided to use *Law v Canada (Minister of Immigration and Employment)* to consolidate its views on the right to equality. Frank took on the task of writing the unanimous reasons for judgment. His review of many prior equality cases emphasized that the court had often put human dignity at the centre of its analysis of fundamental rights. Indeed, he noted that the court had expressed the purpose of the right to equality variously as: the promotion of human dignity; the protection of human dignity; the recognition of the innate dignity of individuals; and the prevention of violations of human dignity.

"But Frank didn't just provide a synthesis of past reasons for judgment; he went on to make what I think are two significant additional contributions to the law on equality. First, he explained the meaning of 'human dignity' in a way that highlights the importance of self-respect, well-being, empowerment, and valued participation in society. He wrote:

> *Human dignity means that an individual or group feels self-respect and self-worth. It is concerned with physical and psychological integrity and empowerment. ... Human dignity is harmed when individuals and groups are marginalized, ignored, or devalued, and is enhanced when laws recognize the full place of all individuals and groups within Canadian society.*

"Second, in *Vriend v Alberta*, Frank recognized that movement towards greater equality in society can cause some anxiety and discomfort when equality calls for a re-examination of long accepted prejudices and privileges. Yet he insisted that, wherever and whenever human dignity is threatened, the law will not wait for politics to catch up. He wrote:

> *In my opinion, groups that have historically been the target of discrimination cannot be expected to wait patiently for the protection of their human dignity*

and equal rights while governments move toward reform one step at a time. If the infringement of the rights and freedoms of these groups is permitted to persist while governments fail to pursue equality diligently, then the guarantees of the Charter will be reduced to little more than empty words.

"I have to admit that it is only now, after twenty years of study and practice, that it is finally starting to dawn on me that this idea – that human dignity must be closely guarded – underpins every area of law, and the practice of law, often in ways that are not immediately visible. I credit Frank for helping me to understand that the protection of human dignity is one of the foundation stones that give the law its structure and its unity, and that when we honour that idea, our legal systems can function in ways that help to ensure that individuals and communities have the freedom and self-confidence required to develop, progress, contribute, and reach their highest potentials." (James Hickling)

Hickling connects the principles articulated in Frank's equality jurisprudence to the approach taken to Aboriginal offenders in *Gladue*. In his words, it seemed by the late 1990s that "the inevitability of prison for many young Aboriginals, and all the indignities that go with incarceration, had become the contemporary equivalent of what previous generations experienced at residential schools.

"In *R. v Gladue*, Frank and Justice Cory cited statistics showing just how disproportionate incarceration rates were then for Aboriginal people. For example, in Manitoba and Saskatchewan, Aboriginal people constituted around 6 per cent of the population but made up 55 per cent and 72 per cent of admissions to provincial prisons, respectively. A similar (albeit less drastic) situation also existed in Alberta and British Columbia. *These findings cry out for recognition of the magnitude and gravity of the problem, and for responses to alleviate it. The figures are stark and reflect what may fairly be termed a crisis in the Canadian criminal justice system…*"

Hickling reflects on the significance of the court's acknowledgment of the unique circumstances of Aboriginal individuals and communities: "We have the highest court in the land stating unanimously that racial discrimination against Aboriginal people is widespread in Canada and has reached 'crisis' levels in our criminal justice system. Moreover, the court found that the crisis is deeply rooted in the disruption of Aboriginal communities and the long history of imposing various other indignities on Aboriginal people. It is therefore unacceptable for our justice system to compound those indignities by continuing to tolerate racial bias in trial and sentencing processes. I am reminded that minds and institutions can change, and I am hopeful that we are moving towards a more just and dignified society." (James Hickling)

In framing his own reflections on the legacy and continued significance of Frank's judgments, James Hickling quotes Frank's address to the 2016 Pathways to Reconciliation Conference in Winnipeg:[112]

In my 55 years of the law, I've never encountered a more complex set of issues than that which deal with Canada and Indigenous peoples. Having said that, I can also say that the establishment of a new relationship between Canada and first peoples is the most important societal issue facing our country. There's nothing more important, in my view.

Portrait of the Person – Complex Conversations

John Helliwell, professor emeritus at the University of British Columbia's Vancouver School of Economics, and Frank's friend dating back to the time they spent together as teaching assistants for Professor Tadek Matuszewski's Statistics course at UBC, notes:

"One long-standing thread in our discussions, especially since the *Charter* has come to shape Canadian democracy in all its aspects – legislative, political, legal, personal and institutional – is the risk we both see that emphasis on individual rights and freedoms should come to redefine society in ways that permit people to forget their matching responsibilities."

Helliwell draws on a lecture given by Frank at UBC in 1991[113] in which Frank asserted:

The Charter is not just about rights, but also about the shared values and principles which underlie our shared historical, social, and political experiences. These values and principles manifest themselves in legal discourse as various rights claims. But we must never forget that these values and principles also give meaning to other claims that sound in the judicial context. Charter values like freedom of expression, equality, and multiculturalism also signify some of the civil duties that we owe to one another as members of this free and democratic society.

"Thus," says Helliwell, "a collateral benefit of the *Charter* is the necessity for the courts to re-assert the importance of principles, without which contested and conflicting rights cannot be sensibly adjudicated. But the proper role for principles is much larger than that. I suspect that Frank, like me, would like to see the decades-long shift from principles to rules in the legal and accounting professions, public administration, taxation, management and finance be halted, and in many places reversed. If I have learned anything from studying the sources and consequences of happiness, it is that people are happy doing the right thing, especially when guided by shared principles rather than rules and regulations. Social trust is a key indicator of people's confidence in each other's benevolence and good sense." (John Helliwell)

We have already seen some of the ways in which Frank insisted upon, articulated, interpreted, and shaped principles he understood to be key to legal process and substance. Here I round out an exploration of principles in Frank's Supreme Court jurisprudence with an explicit focus on the links among rights, responsibilities, and communities. Whether in addressing the parameters of free expression or the contours of religious belief and practice, Frank as judge had to confront the complexities of human beings and the ways in which we live together.

Expression – Human Voice(s)

The power of individual voice and the importance of participation in public discourse are good examples of principles tied up with both rights and responsibilities. While freedom of expression is a fundamental human right, its exercise is neither obvious in scope nor unfettered in practice. Ensuring meaningful opportunities for contributions to public discourse is part of what guaranteeing the right entails; so is the design and justification of limits on truly harmful words. In an essay on free speech and privacy, published a little more than halfway through his time on the court, Frank wrote that "*sufficient flexibility exists for governments and courts to subject individual freedom of speech to such limitations as are thought necessary in democratic society to protect the rights and freedoms of others.*" He continued:

"*Accordingly, the permissible limitations on freedom of speech is a familiar issue in most legal systems. Legislatures and courts are faced with the difficult task of attempting to balance competing interests, namely the right to free expression, and the right not to be exposed to harmful or degrading expression which threatens inherent human dignity and equality. The advent of global communications technology, however, with its capacity for instantaneous dissemination of virtually unlimited amounts of information to a potentially universal audience poses new challenges which threaten to disrupt the delicate balance that has been achieved to date in domestic legal systems.*"[114]

Even without the challenge of global communications technology, achieving a "delicate balance" – between protecting individual speech on one hand, and protecting individuals from harmful words on the other – is not easy. Sustaining that balance in the face of constant disagreement about how and whether to do so is even harder. As Frank points out, this is a difficult if familiar task for courts. The Supreme Court of Canada had taken it on, just before he was appointed, in its judgment in *R. v Keegstra*,[115] upholding the criminalization of the willful promotion of hatred. It then revisited the task in 1992 in the *R. v Zundel* case,[116] which struck down the criminalization of the spreading of false news, and in which Frank joined with Justice Cory to write dissenting reasons.

Janine Benedet, law professor at UBC and one of Frank's law clerks, has reflected on how Frank's approach to free speech contributed to her own work on the regulation of pornography and workplace sexual harassment.

She read the dissenting judgment in *Zundel* in her final year of law school, before she headed to the Supreme Court to work for Frank; in doing so, she was struck by its insistence that limits on rights such as freedom of expression be interpreted within social context and in a manner consistent with recognition of other rights. In particular, the judgment pointed to liberty, security of the person, and equality, as well as Canada's *magnificent commitment* to multiculturalism: all relevant to the task of defining the scope of free speech.

According to Benedet, the place to start, in order to appreciate this approach, is with the 1990 Supreme Court of Canada judgment in *Keegstra*. An Alberta high school teacher of social studies, James Keegstra was an adamant Holocaust denier whose anti-Semitic teachings in the classroom led to prosecution under the Criminal Code of Canada for the willful promotion of hatred against an identifiable group. While the entire court found that the provision of the Code infringed freedom of expression explicitly protected by section 2(b) of the *Charter*, Chief Justice Dickson for the majority found that infringement to be a reasonable limit under section 1.

At the time that Keegstra arrived at the Supreme Court in December of 1989, I was one of Chief Justice Dickson's law clerks. I have kept a hard copy of the memo written to prepare him for the hearing. In a general paragraph that preceded analysis of the arguments, I said: "We are dealing with something that is intangible and emotional, and while we know it is linked to greater intolerance and racism in society, there is no clear cut way to say that the legislation is not controlling an attempt to convey a meaning. The words and acts are those which, in their very essence, are incompatible with the conditions necessary to support the exercise of rights and freedoms in a free and democratic society like Canada. The drafting of a careful response to the hard questions raised here will test this court's responsiveness to new ideas about expression."

Janine Benedet connects the dots between Keegstra and Zundel – both as individuals and as the names associated with the puzzle for

Canadian policymakers and judges of placing limits on what people can say in this country:

"At the same time that the *Keegstra* case was winding its way through the Alberta courts, another Holocaust denier had attracted public attention. Ernst Zundel, a German national who had lived in Canada since his teens, published anti-Semitic and neo-Nazi tracts. First brought before the legal system through a 1984 human rights complaint by a Holocaust survivor, this was converted into a public prosecution alleging that he 'did publish a statement or tale, namely, *Did Six Million Really Die?*, that he knows is false and that is likely to cause mischief to the public interest in social and racial tolerance, contrary to the Criminal Code." Zundel was convicted at trial, but his conviction for spreading false news was ultimately overturned by the Supreme Court, by a 4:3 majority. The majority found that the offence lacked a pressing and substantial objective sufficient to justify limiting freedom of expression, and that the term "public interest" was vague and incapable of definition in this context.

"I read Justice Iacobucci's co-authored dissent in *Zundel* in my final year of law school, when I knew that upon graduation, I would begin my clerkship in his chambers. The consensus around me seemed to be that Zundel had been charged under the wrong section, and that the outmoded false news offence could be supplanted by the willful promotion of hatred offence upheld in *Keegstra*. Indeed, the majority says as much in the opening paragraphs of Justice McLachlin's reasons:

> This appeal is not about the dissemination of hate, which was the focus of this Court's decision in *R. v Keegstra*, and the reasons of my colleagues Cory and Iacobucci JJ. here. In *Keegstra*, this Court ruled that the provisions of the *Criminal Code* which prohibit the dissemination of hate violated the guarantee of freedom of expression but were saved under s.1 of the *Charter*. This case presents the Court with the question of whether a much broader and vaguer class of speech – false statements deemed likely to injure or cause mischief to any public interest – can be saved under s.1 of the *Charter*. In

my view, the answer to this question must be in the negative. To permit the imprisonment of people, or even the threat of imprisonment, on the ground that they have made a statement which 12 of their co-citizens deem to be false and mischievous to some undefined public interest, is to stifle a whole range of speech, some of which has long been regarded as legitimate and even beneficial to our society.

"In their dissenting reasons, Justices Cory and Iacobucci consider in detail the history of the false news provision, acknowledge its relative disuse, and its application to Zundel himself during his trial. They do not shy away from outlining the content of the pamphlet or the central question of whether Zundel knew that the information in it was false. What was and is most interesting to me about their reasons, however, was the resort to the *Charter* values of racial and religious tolerance and equality as a way to narrow the definition of 'public interest' so as to deal with questions of vagueness:

> A "public interest" likely to be harmed as a result of contravention of s. 181 is the public interest in a free and democratic society that is subject to the rule of law. A free society is one built upon reasoned debate in which all its members are entitled to participate. Section 181, including its reference to "public interest," should, as this Court has emphasized, be interpreted in light of Charter values. [...]
>
> The term, as it appears in s. 181, should be confined to those rights recognized in the Charter as being fundamental to Canadian democracy. It need not be extended beyond that. As an example, the rights enacted in ss. 7, 15 and 27 of the Charter should be considered in defining a public interest.
>
> [...] If the wilful publication of statements which are known to be false seriously injures a group identifiable under s. 15, such an act would tear at the very fabric of Canadian society. It follows that the wilful publication of such lies would be contrary to the public interest. If the Crown is able to establish beyond a reasonable doubt that those fundamental rights are likely to have been seriously damaged by the wilful publication of statements known to be false, it will have fulfilled this part of its obligations under the section.

"Although the tracts and pamphlets Zundel published are now several decades old, they offer a clear reminder of the links between anti-Semitism and other kinds of discrimination. Zundel's publications claimed that the 'myth of the Holocaust' needed to be exposed so that people today could oppose the mass immigration of Asians and Africans without being accused of racism. The second pamphlet on which Zundel was tried expressed anti-Islamic sentiments that can easily be found in identical form in contemporary discourse.

"Of course, the fight for racial, religious and sex equality must strike a balance that recognizes that freedom of expression also faces its own threats. In recent years, these attacks have come from the self-styled progressive left, who have resorted not to criminal prosecutions, but to 'de-platforming' those whose views they consider discriminatory, triggering, or violent, with both conservative and feminist scholars and activists facing cancelled speaking engagements, threats to their employment, and acts of vandalism. Justice Iacobucci's thoughtful, measured and balanced approach to these questions should be remembered in these troubled times." (Janine Benedet)

Zundel was issued one year after Frank joined the Supreme Court. One year before he retired, he handed down a judgment in *Figueroa v Canada (Attorney General)*,[117] this time written for the majority. In his reasons, Frank himself recalled Chief Justice Dickson's approach to freedom of expression in the *Keegstra* case:

As this Court frequently has acknowledged, the free flow of diverse opinions and ideas is of fundamental importance in a free and democratic society. In R. v Keegstra, [1990] 3 S.C.R. 697, at pp. 763–64, Dickson C.J. described the connection between the free flow of diverse opinions and ideas and the values essential to a free and democratic society in the following terms:

The connection between freedom of expression and the political process is perhaps the linchpin of the s.2(b) guarantee, and the nature of this connection is largely derived from the Canadian commitment to democracy. Freedom of expression is a crucial aspect of the democratic commitment, not merely because it permits the best policies to be chosen from among a wide array of proffered options, but additionally because it helps to ensure that participation in the political process is open to all persons. Such open participation must involve to a substantial degree the notion that all persons are equally deserving of respect and dignity. The state therefore cannot act to hinder or condemn a political view without to some extent harming the openness of Canadian democracy and its associated tenet of equality for all"[118]

In *Figueroa*, the issue was one of effective representation and meaningful participation, and more specifically the constitutionality of specific restrictions on access to the benefits of registered political party status. While in both *Keegstra* and *Zundel*, the burden on the attorney general of Canada had been one of justifying the criminalization of hateful words, the burden in *Figueroa* was one of ensuring the possibility of real access and participation in public discourse.

"Put simply, full political debate ensures that ours is an open society with the benefit of a broad range of ideas and opinions … This, in turn, ensures not only that policy makers are aware of a broad range of options, but also that the determination of social policy is sensitive to the needs and interests of a broad range of citizens. […]

"To be certain, the electoral process is the means by which elected representatives are selected and governments formed, but it is also the primary means by which the average citizen participates in the open debate that animates the determination of social policy."[119]

Frank's reference to *Keegstra*, in what was a very different context in *Figueroa*, established a connecting thread between the majority of the court in 2003 and that of its 1990 version. He chose to link together acceptable and indeed necessary restrictions on hate speech, on one hand, with unacceptable and unnecessary restrictions on political participation, on the other. Read with that link in mind, Frank's full and generous support for rights of expression and participation comes along with a warning that respect for the freedoms and participation of others is a non-negotiable condition.

Frank had worried – as we have already seen in *Little Sisters Book and Art Emporium* – about state suppression of expression in the form of gay erotica, potentially deemed obscene by border officials. He had insisted, in the earlier case of *Haig v Canada (Chief Electoral Officer)*,[120] that the design of referendum legislation meet the purpose of uniting all Canadians of voting age in a collective act of expression. And, in *Zundel*, he had strongly supported state power to target the promotion of hatred against an identifiable group, including through the spreading of harmful lies. The combined message is a complicated one: we must pay attention to voices and ensure they can be heard; we should appreciate the power, both positive and negative, they can have; and we must take responsibility to ensure they don't drown out the participation of others.

In all of those earlier judgments, Frank's had been a dissenting voice. In *Figueroa* in 2003, finally, he wrote for the majority. He couldn't re-open the precise issues in those earlier cases, and he obviously couldn't incorporate explicit discussion of the limits on acceptable speech in Canada in a judgment on rules regarding political party status. But he could remind readers that the connections exist, and that the difficult task of defining the scope of meaningful expression in a free and democratic society is ongoing.

Dissent plays a complicated and yet crucial role in the development of law, and it seems particularly appropriate to note that role in the context of free expression. As suggested by Justices Ruth Bader Ginsburg of the United States Supreme Court and Claire L'Heureux-Dubé of the Supreme Court of Canada – both well known for their dissenting voices – dissent shakes up the meaning and impact of a judgment.[121] It can sharpen our understanding of the issues, shed light on different ways of responding to the arguments, and even provide the basis for a later majority position on the question. Appreciation of dissenting judgments can be crucial to following the direction of a particular area of law, and voicing dissent as a

Supreme Court justice in Canada can turn out to be a particularly significant contribution to the issues at hand.

Dissent is also a foundational piece of the notion of academic freedom: something that Frank had substantial experience with as a professor and as a university provost, and something on which in 2009 he was invited to offer principled guidance by the president of York University. President Mamdouh Shoukri turned to Frank as a "respected former judge of the Supreme Court of Canada and former university provost and president"[122] to review York's experience with a conference that had just taken place, and to provide advice on best practices grounded in the university's commitment to academic freedom. In his final report, Frank quoted another former university president, James Downey, on the role of the university: "Through teaching and research the university must cultivate a spirit of intellectual dissent. Not for its own sake, but in the interests of a free, tolerant, enlightened, and improving society."[123]

The backdrop to York University's decision to commission a report on academic freedom was a conference it hosted in June 2009 entitled "Israel/Palestine: Mapping Models of Statehood and Paths to Peace." As with any forum for interaction on Israeli-Palestinian relations and co-existence, dissent, disagreement, and even discord could be expected elements of the academic content of the conference. As it turned out, however, they characterized the lead-up to the event to such an extent that engaged learning and inquiry appeared to be at risk of being hijacked by accusations, fear, and suspicion. In his report, Frank referred to "The Mapping Conference" as the launching pad for a broader discussion of the promise and importance, as well as the limits and qualifications, of academic freedom. He wisely insisted that his report was not a detailed review of the running of the conference. But the fact that significant actors refused to participate in the process he oversaw served as a reminder of how hard it can be to speak with, rather than past, each other – whether in the context of peace in the Middle East or of a university campus that values diversity of people and ideas.

In his report, Frank reviewed the central importance of academic freedom and compared it to freedom of expression:

"Although there are similarities between academic freedom and freedom of expression under the Canadian Charter of Rights and Freedoms, they are not quite the same. The latter prevents governments and legislatures from unjustifiably infringing freedom of expression of the citizen. Academic freedom, on the other hand, protects scholars from interference with their freedom to pursue the 'scholar's profession' according to the standards of that profession ... Academic freedom does not protect the absolute freedom of expression of scholars, but rather protects their freedom of thought, inquiry, discussion and teaching in the context of their profession."[124]

As with freedom of expression, Frank went on to say, academic freedom is not unlimited. *"No right or freedom in a democratic society can be rigidly absolute ... In other words, the concept of academic freedom, like that of freedom of expression, entails not only rights but also responsibilities."*[125] Instead of articulating the relationship of rights to responsibilities in the university context, however, Frank handed the task back to the university itself. In the conclusion to his report, he underscored that the values and principles that govern academic debate and discourse must come from academics. The scope and shape of academic freedom, informed by commitment to civil discourse, mutual respect, and sensitivity to issues related to equality, are for academic members of the university to agree on. Having the hard discussions about the importance of both voice and constraints on voice is a crucial piece of building community and ensuring its internal functioning.

Both in his report for York University and in his judgments, Frank emphasized the importance of expression and participation, including by those in dissent. But his words are particularly passionate when he writes about the potentially far-reaching negative impact of words on individuals and groups, and the need to accept that the exercise of a right comes with the responsibility to respect the rights of others. On campus, that means protecting academic freedom while at the same time ensuring opportunities for constructive and respectful discourse. If we return to his reasons in *Zundel*, it means delineating the parameters of free speech against the backdrop of the promises, priorities, and power dynamics of a diverse country:

"Democratic pluralism assumes that members of society will not simply organize around single interests of race, class or gender but will explore and discern their commonalities, coming together around certain issues and diverging on others in constantly changing configurations. Deliberate lies which deny these commonalities divide groups which might otherwise organize around mutual interests, and instead forge loyalties based on artificial and reified racial identifications that do not permit society to perceive and pursue its various goals."[126]

"It is perhaps an indication of the genius of Canada and Canadians that the supreme law of the land would recognize the existence of multiculturalism in our country and encourage its enhancement. Our country has benefited from and has been enriched by the efforts and accomplishments of Canadians of many different races, religions and nationalities. The recognition of multiculturalism in the Charter is an attempt to achieve the epitome of democratic societies."[127]

Criminalizing the kind of expression that intentionally promotes hatred against groups indicates Canada's willingness to use the strongest legal tool available for condemnation, underlines a desire to end racism and intolerance, and appears to align with its commitment to multiculturalism. But criminal prosecution is neither the preferred way to put a stop to hateful and harmful words and actions in a society, nor the most effective. As Frank noted in his paper on challenges in the era of global communications technology, the internet constantly illustrates how tricky it is to sustain a delicate balance of rights and responsibilities: *"The Internet ... has fundamentally altered methods of accessing and disseminating information, with profound social, political and legal implications."*[128]

Back in 1990, the companion case decided along with *Keegstra* was one in which John Ross Taylor, president of the Western Guard Party, had placed hateful anti-Semitic messages on a telephone answering machine and then publicized the Toronto phone number, inviting callers to dial in and listen. Those facts now seem laughably antiquated. Modes of communication and message sending have come a long way from a time when telephone answering machines were a source of concern. And they remind us that there is a long way to go, albeit partly over well-worn paths, as we work out – whether on campuses or before courts – the messy co-existence of freedom to speak and obligation to listen.

Faith – Human Belief(s)

Frank's approach as Supreme Court justice to the interaction of law and identity – and the corresponding confluence of rights, responsibilities, and community – is perhaps most evident in his majority judgment in the *Amselem* case of 2004. In *Syndicat Northcrest v Amselem*,[129] the issue was freedom of religion, protected in the *Quebec Charter of Human Rights and Freedoms* as well as by section 2(a) of the *Canadian Charter*. In a passage that echoes the appreciation he had voiced in *Zundel* for the significance of the *Charter's* commitment to multiculturalism, Frank reflected on the implications of the diversity of faiths and cultures in Canada:

"In a multiethnic and multicultural country such as ours, which accentuates and advertises its modern record of respecting cultural diversity and human rights and of promoting tolerance of religious and ethnic minorities – and is in many ways an example thereof for other societies – the argument of the respondent that nominal, minimally intruded-upon aesthetic interests should outweigh the exercise of the appellants' religious freedom is unacceptable. Indeed, mutual tolerance is one of the cornerstones of all democratic societies. Living in a community that attempts to maximize human rights invariably requires openness to and recognition of the rights of others."[130]

The judgment is better known, however, for Frank's striking assertion of the individual and personal nature of religious freedom. In the case, Mr. Amselem's belief as an Orthodox Jew with respect to the contours of his religious obligations was central to the recognition of his guaranteed right to religious liberty. According to Frank:

"In essence, religion is about freely and deeply held personal convictions or beliefs connected to an individual's spiritual faith and integrally linked to one's self-definition and spiritual fulfilment, the practices of which allow individuals to foster a connection with the divine or with the subject or object of that spiritual faith."[131]

In the case, Moïse Amselem erected a sukkah, a temporary hut-like structure used to celebrate the eight-day Jewish harvest holiday of Sukkot, on the balcony of his apartment. The governing condominium association demanded the sukkah's removal, based on the bylaws prohibiting decorations on balconies, but offered to set up a communal sukkah in the gardens. The offer was rejected, the association applied for a permanent injunction against individual sukkah construction on condo balconies, and Mr. Amselem went all the way to the Supreme Court, claiming infringement of his religious freedom. He argued that he understood his personal religious obligations to include the building of his own sukkah at home, and thus that he should be exempted from the conditions of his condominium agreement. The majority of the court agreed.

The sincerity of the claimant's belief played a central role in Frank's reasons. Combined with the lack of any compelling countervailing factors or interests on the part of the condo association and other condominium owners, the fact that this particular Orthodox Jew felt that his faith demanded action contrary to his secular contractual obligations seemed to determine the outcome.

"[F]reedom of religion consists of the freedom to undertake practices and harbour beliefs, having a nexus with religion, in which an individual demonstrates he or she sincerely believes or is sincerely undertaking in order to connect with the divine or as a function of his or her spiritual faith, irrespective of whether a particular practice or belief is required by official religious dogma or is in conformity with the position of religious officials."[132]

Much of the scholarly discussion and litigation in the wake of *Amselem* has focused on what has come to be known as a "test" of sincerity of belief. If the test for equality offered by Frank in the *Law* case turned attention to the complexity of dignity, the test for religious freedom has provoked questions over the simplicity of sincere belief. Frank himself had been adamant in *B. (R.)*,[133] a judgment that pre-dated *Amselem* by almost a decade, that there were limits to the freedom, in particular when invoked by religious parents in a way that threatened the safety, health, or life of their children. Supreme Court jurisprudence after *Amselem* has considered the addition of "strength" of belief in working through the boundaries of protected individual religious liberty.[134] What is clear, once again, is that the framing of a test doesn't eliminate the difficulties of its application. Frank's judgment in *Amselem* has become part of the ongoing and intensifying conversation over the interactions of religion and state in Canada in the past, present, and future.[135]

One setting for that conversation is that of judicial education. Three years after *Amselem* was decided, the National Judicial Institute hosted a three-day seminar entitled "Emerging Issues: Judging in the Context of Diverse Faiths and Cultures."[136] In addition to a statistical presentation of religious diversity across the country, the program included a historical and contemporary overview of the relationship of law to religion in Canada, an opportunity for personal reflections on faith as a judge, and a day dedicated to Islamic law, Muslim communities, and Canadian courts. The content of the agenda revealed its objectives. Judges should be aware of the changing demographics of religion; they are encouraged to ask themselves how their own experience with faith might influence their approach to the analysis of religious freedom; and, in the early twenty-first century, they are expected to familiarize themselves with Islamic law in light of possible claims made by or on behalf of Muslim Canadians.

While more knowledge, understanding, and self-awareness are always good things – for all Canadians, including our judges – Frank's approach taken in *Amselem* might invite some clarification of the purposes and implications of judicial education on religion. As we have seen, his own religious background wasn't uniform or traditional; if he had attended the workshop, he would probably have been somewhat hard-pressed to come up with a clear self-narrative in the half hour of the judicial education seminar dedicated to personal reflections on judging and faith. If anything, his experience with religion underscored the fact that individuals can interact with their faith communities in surprising ways. Perhaps he serves as an example of how attitudes to religion and religious people aren't easily traceable to formal affiliation in the way seemingly assumed by the seminar program.

John B. Laskin recalls from his time as a law student the approach to religious identity taken by Frank as law professor and administrative leader: "We engaged on a variety of issues when I was a student member of Faculty Council. These included the difficult question of whether and how to accommodate students' religious beliefs in scheduling classes. Times and attitudes were different then. Some of Frank's colleagues were not at all receptive to the idea of accommodation. Frank was. As an advocate for the accommodation position, I appreciated and admired his willingness to bring to the issue an open and inquiring mind. (Much later, as a judge on the Supreme Court, he revisited the issue of accommodation of religious belief.)" (John B. Laskin)

It is striking that, rather than hand the question of the sukkah over to authorities in Jewish law, obligations, and practice, Frank had turned to Mr. Amselem himself as the person who could tell us what it meant to celebrate a religious holiday. His approach reminds judges that, even with sophisticated knowledge or firsthand appreciation of religious frameworks and communities, they are constrained when it comes to making decisions that intersect with the substance or norms of faith. They should not defer to religious experts and, even with extensive exposure to, and education about, religious traditions, they cannot try to assume that role.

As religion and law scholar Benjamin Berger points out, the vantage point of the Constitution is necessarily that of Canadian, rather than religious, law. It should thus come as no surprise that decision-makers referring to the *Canadian Charter* – including Frank on the Supreme Court – would see religion through a lens focused on the autonomous individual. Berger links together the guarantees of equality and religion via that lens:

> Just as the "identity" aspect of equality has been eclipsed by the concept of choice, the equality/identity aspect of religion is ultimately little more than a marker for a particularly valued manifestation of choice. In both cases – in equality and in religion – law's central concern is to treat the individual fairly as an autonomous choosing agent. Identity itself is valued because it is an expression of who the subject wants to be and to become [...].[137]

While he effectively illustrates law's tendency to construct religion as based in individual choice, rather than communal identity, Berger joins with other Canadian religion and law scholars to question and critique those limitations.[138] Dwight Newman, one of those scholars and a proponent of community-based rights claims, has quoted Justice Albie Sachs of the South African Constitutional Court on the significance of religious bodies: "Religious bodies play a large and important part in public life, through schools, hospitals and poverty relief programmes ... They are part of the fabric of public life ... Religious organisations constitute important sectors of national life ..."[139]

Where do faith-based communities belong in the constitutional protection of religious liberty in Canada? What happens when the vitality of a religious collective, corporate entity, institution, or group is threatened? Why and how should Canadian law support religious communities, generation after generation? When can religious norms inform the governance of an institution or determine the outcome of a dispute? When does state law override those norms? On what basis? Who decides? In the aftermath of *Amselem*, responding to these challenges appears particularly complicated whether in case law, scholarship, or legal education.

All these questions, however, have been alive throughout Canadian history – before and after the *Charter of Rights and Freedoms* – and the Supreme Court has been one of the places to look for answers. In two judgments in which Frank took part – *Adler v Ontario*[140] in 1996 and *Trinity Western University v British Columbia College of Teachers*[141] in 2001 – the connection between religion and education was at stake. In both cases, the court grappled with the existence, support for, and limitations on, faith-based schools. In *Adler*, state support exclusively for Catholic denominational schools in Ontario was upheld on the basis of a historical, political arrangement embedded within the Constitution of Canada; in *Trinity Western University* (*TWU*), the education degree granted to students in a private evangelical university was found adequate for entry into the teaching profession.

More specifically, parents who sent their children to Jewish schools and to non-Catholic Christian schools in Ontario argued in *Adler* that their schools should receive public support equal to that historically provided to Catholic schools in the province. In *TWU*, the B.C. College of Teachers refused to grant certification of Trinity Western University's Teacher Education Program based on the discriminatory practices of the university. All students at TWU signed a Covenant of Community Standards at the time of admission, undertaking to "refrain from practices that are biblically condemned" including "sexual sins including premarital sex, adultery, homosexual behaviour, and viewing of pornography." The university appealed.

Given his judgments in other cases, surely Frank could empathize with the religious parents in Ontario who argued for support for their schools equivalent to that given to their Catholic counterparts. Surely, too, he thought that public school teachers in British Columbia should appreciate the diversity of sexual orientation among their students, and should be counted on not to pass on to young people in public school classrooms the teachings of the church associated with the university they had attended. But in both contexts, for different reasons, Frank's reasons rested on principles that had the effect of recognizing and respecting the faith-based boundaries around the educational institutions at stake.

In *Adler*, Frank characterized section 93 of the *Constitution Act, 1867* as *"a comprehensive code with respect to denominational school rights."*[142] In giving responsibility for education to the provinces, the section specified the extension of rights and privileges related to education to Catholic and Protestant minorities within those provinces. There was therefore no way for the individual parents in the case (and, vicariously, their religious communities) to challenge guaranteed funding support for Catholic denominational schools on the basis of the *Charter*'s equality and religious freedom provisions. Political dialogue and reform, rather than constitutional litigation, would have to do the work of any change in public funding for religious schools.

In *TWU*, Frank wrote with his colleague, Justice Michel Bastarache, for an eight-member majority of the court. In response to the argument that graduates of TWU's program of education might go on to discriminate on the basis of sexual orientation in their work as teachers, Frank wrote: *"The freedom to hold beliefs is broader than the freedom to act on them. Absent concrete evidence that training teachers at TWU fosters discrimination in the public schools of B.C., the freedom of individuals to adhere to certain religious beliefs while at TWU should be respected. ... For better or for worse, tolerance of divergent beliefs is a hallmark of a democratic society."*[143] Changes to the university's community standards might be welcome from the perspective of equality in general, and of LGBTQ students more specifically, but denying graduates access to the teaching profession was not the way to get there.

One paragraph in *TWU* contemplates the complex mix of values and principles at play when the law interacts with religion, and connects the two judgments and their contexts:

"Consideration of human rights values in these circumstances encompasses consideration of the place of private institutions in our society and the reconciling of competing rights and values. Freedom of religion,

conscience and association coexist with the right to be free of discrimination based on sexual orientation. Even though the requirement that students and faculty adopt the Community Standards creates unfavourable differential treatment since it would probably prevent homosexual students and faculty from applying, one must consider the true nature of the undertaking and the context in which this occurs. Many Canadian universities, including St. Francis Xavier University, Queen's University, McGill University and Concordia University College of Alberta, have traditions of religious affiliations. Furthermore, s. 93 of the Constitution Act, 1867 enshrined religious public education rights into our Constitution, as part of the historic compromise which made Confederation possible." [144]

Trinity Western University returned to the Supreme Court a decade and a half later, this time with respect to the evangelical university's planned opening of a faculty of law. The wording of the covenant had changed, but it still made clear that same-sex relations – more precisely sexual intimacy outside the bounds of traditional heterosexual marriage – were proscribed as part of community or campus practice of religious belief. Three provincial Law Societies, responsible for ensuring regulation of the legal profession in line with the public interest, voted to withhold accreditation from the eventual law school, meaning that graduates would not be able to proceed to admission to the Bar in the same way as their counterparts with law degrees from public universities across the country. In its decision, the Supreme Court, for a variety of reasons, upheld the regulatory decisions of the law societies. [145]

Frank was no longer on the court when *TWU* – "Round 2" was decided. The facts, processes, actors, and arguments weren't quite the same as in the first TWU case, making it possible for the two decisions to stand side-by-side. But the court was much more clear with an 8–1 majority judgment in the first case, than it was in the second with four separate sets of reasons among the nine judges. Regardless of how he would have decided the case, of how he would react to the approaches taken by members of the 2018 court, or even of whether he read the judgment, Frank might be curious as to the implications for maintaining a diversity of educational institutions and sites of faith-based governance in Canada.

Despite its explicit emphasis on individual sincerity of belief, Frank's judgment in *Amselem* acknowledges, albeit implicitly, the collective dimensions of faith and religious identity. As we have already seen, it does so by situating religious freedom within the context of what Frank labels a multicultural and multiethnic country with a record of promoting tolerance of religious minorities. It adds to that by insisting that courts in Canada refrain from delving into the internal workings of faith communities, thus respecting what could be labeled religious jurisdiction:

"[T]he State is in no position to be, nor should it become, the arbiter of religious dogma. Accordingly, courts should avoid judicially interpreting and thus determining, either explicitly or implicitly, the content of a subjective understanding of religious requirement, "obligation," precept, "commandment," custom or ritual. Secular judicial determinations of theological or religious disputes, or of contentious matters of religious doctrine, unjustifiably entangle the court in the affairs of religion."[146]

It is perhaps far beyond the courtroom, however, that the collective dynamic of freedom of religion can be felt. Outremont, the Montreal borough in which Mr. Amselem's condominium building is situated, turns out to be a good place to look. As a resident of Outremont, and as a religion and law scholar who has written about this particular real life site both before and after *Amselem*, I have turned to the neighbourhood as a place to map religious identity and practice within mixed space: "A decision that embodies the idea of individual sincerity of belief, and purports to decide conflict in favour of religious individuals, sets the stage for ongoing interactions that make up a dynamic definition of community identity and practice."[147]

Every fall, temporary sukkahs go up on the balconies, in the tiny back yards, and along the narrow alleys of Outremont. Roughly a quarter of the population is made up of Hasidic Jews; their Yiddish-speaking communities have lived here over seven decades within a francophone, largely

Catholic-turned-secular, neighbourhood. Markers of their collective religious way of life include large families, distinctive traditional clothing, gender-segregated private schools, neighbourhood synagogues, and observance of Jewish holidays.[148]

While the religious Jews of Outremont are often characterized, and indeed characterize themselves, as living in a parallel universe to those around them, the picture is more complicated. In what I have called messy co-existence, there are all kinds of everyday interactions across communal borders.[149] The school buses have to be regulated, the parking rules enforced, and the content of school curricula scrutinized; the sidewalks and playgrounds, the pediatricians' offices and the grocery stores, are literally and figuratively shared by Outremont's Hasidic citizens and their non-Hasidic neighbours. Within the municipal borders, a multiplicity of collective ways of life not only exists but thrives. All of this happens whether or not collective religious rights are explicitly guaranteed in section 2(a) of the Canadian *Charter*.

The same is true, in vastly more complicated and diverse forms, within Canada's borders. Frank hadn't walked around Mr. Amselem's neighbourhood in order to write his decision. But his judgment is now a metaphysical landmark on the map. It sends a clear message about rights and responsibilities, the exercise of which is crucial to living with each other. Religious communities, via their leaders and spokespeople, no doubt refer to the success of Mr. Amselem in their negotiations vis-à-vis state governance. At the same time, they learn from the judgment that, from the perspective of Canadian law, their communal authority as to religious practice, whether official or unofficial, does not trump individual belief or squelch internal diversity.

The personal dimensions of religious freedom do not make collective interests disappear: communities have much at stake when individuals of faith make claims, and they clearly feel the consequences of any decision. We might say that with each sukkah that goes up in Outremont, entire communities across the country celebrate their shared faiths. This recognition of religious pluralism on the ground is not quite the same as that demanded by religious institutions in the form of collective rights. But it might hold out the potential to work out spaces for trust, respect, and even collaboration – something Frank would no doubt endorse.

Frank's "Why"

Is it possible to capture or summarize this multi-faceted part of Frank's career trajectory as a jurist? How can we characterize the footprint of his thirteen years of work, earning $5 a day in the exercise of judgment, as a Supreme Court justice?

As I promised in introducing my discussion of selections from Frank's Supreme Court repertoire, that discussion, informed by the insights and commentary provided by others, has not centred on whether the judgments were right or wrong. Nancy Iacobucci might have disagreed with Frank's decision in *Waldick v Malcolm*, thereby inadvertently producing a lovely prompt to students to recognize the complexities of the case, and others have no doubt disagreed with the outcome of many of Frank's judgments. But readers should glean the same message here as the one law students come to appreciate. Asking whether judgments are right or wrong isn't the most interesting question; labelling them as right or wrong isn't the most insightful conclusion. This is not to say that a judgment should escape critical scrutiny with respect to its substantive resolution and impact. It is rather to add that the words matter, the judges matter, the choices made to co-author or sign on matter, the place on a timeline matters, and, of course, context always matters.

Also in the introduction to the judgments, I suggested that the selected judgments from Frank's Supreme Court repertoire had two things in common. First, they shared a signature by someone whose commitments and experiences were woven into the text. Second, they never constituted the last word but rather were contributions to dynamic and ongoing conversations within which the Supreme Court is one, albeit unique, participant. The signature feature invited us to look for themes embedded in the judgments, trace the importance and development of key principles, and acknowledge connections to Frank's life experience and outlook on the world. The conversation feature reminded us to pay attention to what follows the judgments and to how they give rise to projects of further exploration, development, and change in the hands of others.

What do we find in the Justice Iacobucci "signature"? We find the importance of human choice – whether in associations that people value (*Delisle* and the context of labour unions), in actions that carry spiritual meaning (*Amselem* and the context of religious practice), and in norms of collective governance (*Blair* and the context of the corporation). We find the significance of visibility and participation (same-sex relationships in *M v H*, political party status in *Figueroa*). We find a generous reading of guaranteed rights (*Little Sisters, Adler*), combined with a readiness to impose limits in the name of other rights and values (*Zundel, Lovelace*). We find acceptance of the challenge of repair at a nation-wide level, whether in the *Secession Reference* case, or in *Gladue* vis-à-vis Indigenous justice. We find respect for institutional integrity combined with high expectations for responsible decision-making (*Southam, Ryan, TWU*). We find a willingness to intervene when people don't behave with the care required in the circumstances (*Waldick*), and to provide a how-to guide when the law seems to need clarity (*Law*).

The sound and signature of a Supreme Court justice aren't limited to the words and organization of judgments; they are found in commitments repeated over and over again in different ways and in very different contexts. When John B. Laskin says, "I couldn't help but reflect on how much the *Law* decision's focus on human dignity embodied Frank's approach to life and the law," he invites reflection on the correlation, even if not always starkly evident, between any Supreme Court judgment and its author's "approach to life and the law."

As we have seen, it is possible to trace connections between the experience that marked Frank's path to the court and the approach he took in his judgments. We have seen links between Frank's corporate and tax practice on one hand, and his corporate and tax law decisions on the other; we have connected the dots between Frank's frontline engagement with Canadian federalism and his participation in related constitutional jurisprudence, and between his university governance work and his approach to labour relations and administrative law. And, if we step further back, we can imagine the impact of growing up around Commercial Drive in Vancouver on his approach to identity and diversity.

For Frank, self-conscious commitments to dignity and dialogue seem to stitch together the wide-ranging scenarios, contexts, and issues with which he engaged as a member of the court: dignity captured the human significance of law and justice, while dialogue signalled the importance of interaction, institutional respect, and complementary responsibilities. Neither notion determined substantive outcomes, but both helped shape approach and sensibility. Frank focused on both the vulnerability and the power of individual people; he acknowledged the strength, combined with responsibility, of the institutions and communities they create, whether in the form of governments, corporations, administrative agencies, neighbourhoods, or First Nations.

At the time Frank was appointed, there was no process in which nominees filled out long questionnaires and appeared before a parliamentary committee. Unlike his counterparts three decades later, he didn't have the opportunity to reflect explicitly on how his previous $5 a day projects and positions might inform the work he would do as a Supreme Court justice. Instead, as with any appellate judge, his judgments themselves reveal what Cardozo called the "stream of tendency ... which gives coherence and direction to thought and action.... an outlook on life, a conception of social needs."[150]

If we want to trace judicial footprint, however, scrutiny of the signature on each judgment is not enough. Instead, as I have suggested, the cases are contributions to continued projects, or points of participation in ongoing conversations. Just as there is a "before" to each judgment, there is also an "after." There is always a post-judgment story touched, but never controlled, by the judge.

The Honourable Louis LeBel, Frank's colleague at the Supreme Court from 2000 to 2004, reflects on Frank's approach to the job as follows:

"I still think that Justice Iacobucci, in a certain manner, was not primarily interested in deciding cases, although this remains the essential core of the trade of a judge. He was certainly concerned about the fairness of court decisions and he fought hard for the dispositions that he thought were the most appropriate. Moreover, he did not like to lose.

"But, in my view, as a member of a final court of appeal like the Supreme Court of Canada, Justice Iacobucci was deeply interested in planning the development and application of the law. Indeed, parts of his judicial work give support to the view that judges do not only engage in interpretation and application of the law but also in its creation. He sought to develop the structure of legal analysis and the definition of the conditions of interplay between different parts of the law in the domains where a particular appeal came before the court …

"He adopted a holistic approach to legal problems beyond the specifics of a case and the need to dispose of it. He sought to organize the law and to give some guidance as to how it might be applied. Sometimes, the project might have been too ambitious, but there remained a common thread of concern about the future of the law and its development for tomorrow in his judicial work. In discussions with him, in reading the first drafts that circulated within the court and his final opinions, I felt that his contribution to the court and to Canadian law was really in building up the key structures of the law to allow judges, lawyers, and law makers to apply and develop it in the future." (Louis LeBel)

Justice LeBel suggests that Frank was often acutely aware of the "after" aspect of Supreme Court judgments. That awareness might explain his efforts to offer tests or frameworks across a spectrum, from corporate governance to *Charter* equality to criminal justice. Taking responsibility for offering such guidance goes hand in hand with accepting humility as to the scope of any given judgment. The court might settle the particular disagreement that led to litigation, but it lacks the power to put an end to uncertainty. Instead, each judgment makes way for further interpretation, application, and modification.

Frank's interest in looking to the future seems embedded in his understanding of the Supreme Court as an important site for ongoing "conversations" in the development of law in Canada. That interest explains the support he offered, after retiring from the bench, to the creation and establishment of the Supreme Court Advocacy Institute. Grégoire Webber describes Frank's influence and guidance with respect to an institution devoted to helping the court with its work by supporting high quality advocacy:

"The credibility of the Supreme Court Advocacy Institute was carried by Frank. Less visible but no less central was Frank's encouragement in shaping the success of the Institute. Owen Rees and I sought to establish an immediate, national presence for the Institute. Frank counselled starting small and building up. Owen and I aimed to diversify the Institute's activities beyond moot court advocacy sessions. Frank counseled starting with a more focused mandate and expanding with time. Time and again, Owen and I would overreach; Frank would gently suggest a sound alternative. His was the advice of someone learned in institution building.

"On Frank's recommendation, we designed the Supreme Court Advocacy Institute on a federal model, beginning with a regional presence in Quebec, Ontario, and British Columbia. Frank would serve as the Institute's inaugural chair of the national advisory committee. Owen and I would serve as the Institute's inaugural executive directors, with carriage of day-to-day activities including the coordination of moot advocacy sessions. The session panels would be staffed by counsel from the local bar with expertise in Supreme Court advocacy. Those experts would be identified by regional committees representing the civil and criminal bars, private and government practice. Frank identified and convinced Daniel Jutras, Sheila Block, and Rick Peck to chair the committees in their respective provinces. They would also join Frank, Owen, and me as members of the national advisory committee. The Institute was off to a most promising start.

"Initiated in 2004 and formally launched in 2006 with a reception at the Supreme Court of Canada, the Institute has grown from strength to strength. In its first two years of operation, it assisted counsel in 16 per cent of cases before our final court of appeal. In its next two years, it assisted counsel in 30 per cent of cases. In the 2011–2012 year, that number jumped to 47 per cent and, in the following year, the 50 per cent threshold was comfortably surpassed with a 56 per cent participation rate. Ever since, the Supreme Court Advocacy Institute has assisted counsel in one of every two cases before the Supreme Court of Canada. Frank's role in the Institute's success cannot be underplayed." (Grégoire Webber)

"You will pursue justice" serves as the title for this extended discussion of Frank Iacobucci at the Supreme Court. That should not be surprising as a directive relevant to the job of justice of the Supreme Court of Canada. That directive can be read more generally, however, as something that might be said to members of a graduating class in law, all preparing for their careers and lives as jurists. It could also, of course, be a directive to all human beings, whether or not holders of law degrees. I conclude my focus on the Supreme Court with a broad inclusive picture of the never-ending conversations in which judgments are situated, and of the spaces in which those conversations happen.

Let us return briefly to some of the selected judgments, noticing how we overheard bits of the conversations that followed. Conversations within the RCMP included *Delisle* and moved toward union certification; conversations within and with Indigenous communities included *Gladue* and have continued to work at meaningful reform of criminal justice processes and institutions. Conversations regarding awareness and justice around sexual and gender identity included *M v H* and *Little Sisters Bookstore* and continue in the contexts of education, employment, and access to justice. Promises of substantive equality, marked by *Law*, continue to evolve, to defy attempts to capture fixed tests or definitions, and to demand systemic investment of resources and commitment. The rights and responsibilities attached to free expression, addressed in *Zundel*, continue to demand our attention, whether on campuses or in social media; and the relations of individuals of faith to religious communities, and of religious communities to diverse societies, at the core of *Amselem, Adler*, and *TWU*, have lost none of their complexity. Finally, long after *Waldick*, the question of when and whether to use salt or sand on icy driveways throughout rural Canada is no doubt still open to debate!

Participants in these conversations go well beyond judges, practitioners, and policymakers. They are the people central to, and affected by, the issues at stake, and they speak in workplaces and town halls, on reserves, on campuses, and along neighbourhood sidewalks, in boardrooms and around kitchen tables. They are all engaged in shaping the law. Indeed, they could all be labelled justice-seekers, even if they don't earn $5 a day with a law degree in hand.

Awareness of this broad picture of law-making and justice-building is crucial for law students who, of course, are also active participants in the infinite conversations that include appellate court judgments. They know that the voice of a Supreme Court justice is distinctive and that the responsibility on the shoulders of any member of that court is unique to the job. Yet no judgment provides finite clarity and certainty. As law students explore the themes found in the jurisprudence discussed above, all of them building blocks of their legal education, they are invited to listen with care and to embrace the reality and noise of intersecting voices.

As we close this stage of Frank's career as a jurist, it seems appropriate to return to the observation that opened it: *I don't really see anything omnipotent or magical about courts.*

Frank at age three in between siblings Danny and Teresa. 1940

Frank, second from right, surrounded by his family (Gabriel and Rosina, parents, and Danny, Teresa, and John, in front, siblings). Vancouver 1949

Pretending to play piano in Nancy and Frank's first apartment! Brooklyn 1964

The garden work crew! Frank and the children (Edward, Catherine, Andrew, left to right). Toronto 1973

Swearing in as chief justice of the Federal Court of Canada - Frank and Nancy with their children (Edward and Andrew on the left, Catherine on the far right), together with Governor General Jeanne Sauvé and Minister of Justice Ray Hnatyshyn. Ottawa 1988

Frank and Nancy, Supreme Court of Canada swearing in ceremony. Ottawa 1991

Frank as interim president of the University of Toronto. 2004

Honoured by the Assembly of First Nations (Chief Phil Fontaine, centre),
Frank wears gifts of a coat and headdress as he receives a pipe from its maker, Mr. Kelly,
at a ceremony to mark approval of the Indian Residential Schools Settlement, 2007

Nancy and Frank at the "To Be Frank" colloquium, with author Shauna Van Praagh. Montreal 2017

5

Less than $5 a Day – Nancy Iacobucci as Lawyer

In the fall of 2019, there was a knock at my office door. A student wanted to talk with me. A few months before, she had heard me give a lecture to the entire first year class based on the stories of the Honourable Frank Iacobucci and the many paths made possible by legal education. I invited her to sit down and asked how I could help.

"I've been thinking a lot about Nancy," she replied.

Everything I have done takes a back seat to the support, guidance, and love that Nancy has given to me ... it is my spouse and offspring that dominate my universe, not the law.[151]

Frank and Nancy started their working lives as jurists together, both making "$5 a day" as practising lawyers in Manhattan. Two years later, in 1966, that shared work experience came to an end as Nancy became a mother and took a corresponding and complete pay cut. From young lawyer full of potential, she followed Frank to Toronto, settled into life as Mrs. Iacobucci, and became the person perhaps most strikingly responsible for Frank's trajectory and accomplishments – all for $0 a day.

Frank offers effusive thanks and recognition to Nancy in all of his public speeches, and there is clearly gratitude and respect in their relationship.

And yet a tough but obvious question can be asked. Did Frank's career result in the suppression of Nancy's ambition, a sacrifice of her goals, and a denial of her individual career success – even if both Frank and Nancy might characterize and experience their friendship, marriage, and partnership as principled and equal?

I always had a concern, I even felt guilty … some of her classmates called her "Nancy What a Waste" … because she chose to stay home and not to practise.

When I shared this quote in my lecture to the first-year students at McGill, there had been a collective and audible gasp. The fact that classmates could be so mean to each other was hard to digest. Upon reflection, as the student who came to my office had realized, it was even more troubling if "Nancy What a Waste" was meant to be less insult than observation.

Did Nancy waste her time in going to law school? Was it a waste for her to expend so much energy as a law student? Why bother to do the work required to succeed so spectacularly, if she wasn't going to sustain a career as a lawyer? Did Harvard waste its resources in providing a legal education to someone who became "only" a wife, mother, and grandmother?

The questions force us to scrutinize the assumption that the purpose of law school is to lead students to recognizable careers as lawyers. In his comprehensive report on legal education in Canada, Harry Arthurs convincingly demonstrated a tenacious gap between legal education and law practice.[152] Much or even most of what lawyers do on a daily basis does not require the level of sophisticated intellectual engagement associated with legal education. This realization has made it to pop culture, albeit in less thoroughly analyzed format, through the television series *Suits*: Harvard-educated lawyers in a big law firm appear to do no better a job than a newcomer who just pretends to have studied law at Harvard. If a legal education might not even be a prerequisite to working for $5 a day as a lawyer, how is it not wasted on someone who settles for "nothing"?

These questions also lead to consideration of the insights that come from focusing on "waste." The study of waste turns out to be a fruitful terrain for exploring human activity, organization, and innovation.[153]

The terms used for waste, and the approaches taken to dealing with its production, movement, and destruction are tied to the development of resource and space management, the evolution of recycling, and environmental sustainability. A reference to waste in a selected location and at a selected moment in history can open the door to deeper understanding of human behaviour, choices, and capacities through time and space. In the context of legal education, a serious consideration of waste moves us from the term's negative implications to a constructive assessment of the value of studying law.

The support has been incredible … the impact she's had on me has been greater than the impact that I've had on her. She made the home, as my mother used to say … and I participated. But she's the one responsible for raising three terrific kids, good people with good values, good citizens. How can you beat that? How can you top that?

Nancy gives a little more detail, with a sense of humour, about their partnership in bringing up the three kids. Dads didn't do too much in those days. Frank read to them when they were small, but he probably didn't give so many baths. He did coach them in soccer and hockey, and he usually made it to practices and games on time! Once he had retired from the court and they had moved back to Toronto, he started to help with the grocery shopping.

When Frank was a judge, Nancy says, she enjoyed talking with him about his thoughts on issues that he was grappling with. In every one of his roles, in fact, she was ready to offer advice on how to express himself as clearly as possible. She remembers keeping up with what was going on in the legal community by reading *Lawyers' Weekly* and the *Law Times*, and she enjoyed hosting parties for the first-year law students at U of T with the women's group of professors' wives.

All of this explains the presence in my office of a young woman starting the second year of her studies in law. Of course, she was thinking about Nancy. Like Nancy Iacobucci, she was someone strikingly adept at studying law, someone who enjoyed doing well on her exams and papers. But she had noticed that her male counterparts at the top of the class seemed to have more confidence and certainty about where they were headed. They seemed to receive more recognition from their classmates as smart students certain to succeed in whatever they did. And they didn't worry so much, at least not explicitly, about potential parental responsibility.

Frank refers to the increase in enrolment of women at law school over the time of his deanship as the biggest and most important shake-up of the Canadian legal landscape. More women were choosing law as a field of study, women were starting to join the academy as law professors, and women were participating fully in the practice of law. Frank also makes a point of the fact that he followed women both at the University of Toronto in the office of the vice-president of Internal Affairs (Jill Conway), and at the Supreme Court of Canada (Bertha Wilson). For him, women played significant roles in shaping his life and work: they came before him and after him, they supported him and benefited from his support, they went from unusual newcomers to full participants.

The increased participation of women is the number one change in my life-time in the law – in all components, that is the academy, the profession, and the judiciary. To have the study of law, the teaching of law, the practising of law, the judging of law, not involving women is just nuts … It doesn't make any sense. Because so much of the law relates to people, then having women in all sectors is important. I make the same point for minorities … If we want to participate in a democratic society, there's no closed shop for anything that you wish to be.

It is tempting to read the narrative of Nancy's supporting role as one of sacrifice and even unarticulated regret. It is easy to interrogate the point of a legal education for Nancy and other women students like her if they weren't going to hold onto their careers as lawyers. But nothing about Nancy suggests that she somehow feels one step behind, or that she has missed out on doing important things with her life or for society. That observation raises the possibility of a more subtle and complicated explora-tion of the choices made by law graduates, law degrees in hand, at the time of convocation and then over and over again.

What is the value of a law degree? The fact that much of the practice of law might not require a formal legal education at all, combined with Nancy's story of learning law but not pursuing a lifelong career in practice, prompts a renewed and revitalized understanding of where a legal education can lead. There is no clear-cut choice between, on the one hand, a job clearly recognized as that of a lawyer and, on the other, a life spent doing nothing law-related. If we adopt a broad concept of law as the way in which human beings create and sustain communities, then studying it informs an extensive panoply of life options – options that include, and can go well beyond, the concrete $5 a day job titles held by someone like Frank.

Maybe Nancy reminds us that all law school graduates will be lawyers for the rest of their lives; all of their projects, whether in the work force or not, will be infused by the legal education they received. She acknowledges, for example, that she explicitly used her legal background for her volunteer job as public member of the national examining board of the Canadian Veterinarian Medical Association. She definitely stood by Frank as a lawyer and legal adviser – not as someone who threw away her knowledge of law's approach to human relations and problems, but rather as someone who put all of that to use within the framework of a marriage that doubled as a dynamic legal partnership.

We have already seen that Nancy was a commentator and constructive critic. If that was true with respect to the *Waldick* case, and its central issue of reasonable care in the context of rural Ontario, there is no reason it wasn't with respect to any other piece of work done by Frank, whether written or not. Frank acknowledges her contributions, and we can assume that, as a past student editor of the *Harvard Law Review*, Nancy shared her gifts in both language and law.

"Nancy never wrote anything that I had to write as an academic, but she was a gifted editor of virtually everything that I wrote. She also never wrote any opinions I did or have done as a lawyer, but she would have improved on them; and the same could have been said about my work as a judge."[154]

But why not reach beyond the obvious, if unpaid, work enriched by Nancy's legal education? Why not insist that Nancy raised her children *as a lawyer*, volunteered with the Girl Guides *as a lawyer*, even sang in her Church and community choirs *as a lawyer*? In every one of these contexts, she would have brought the abilities and sensibilities of someone who had studied the complexity of rules, the fairness of process, and the functioning of institutions. Thinking about Nancy's contributions in this broader way pushes us to enlarge our understanding of what the point of a legal education might be, what holders of law degrees are prepared to do in the world, and how they think about and respond to the people and problems they come across in their lives.

My student and I talked about all these things. We talked about how titles and prestige associated with particular ways of making $5 a day as a jurist don't necessarily coincide with how well someone thinks as a lawyer, or even with the kinds of valuable contributions that person can make in law. I told her how another one of my past students, who had worked as a research assistant for me, had suggested that, while Frank might be nominated in the best actor category, Nancy might win as best supporting actress. Neither of us is sure which is better.

Even for jurists who do join the legal profession in easily recognized jobs, maybe the work they do for $0 a day enriches what they do for $5. This is an insight perhaps especially obvious for law professors.[155] Those of us who raise children at the same time we teach first-year law courses in torts or contracts can't help but refer to examples and challenges tied up in our parenting roles. Family law, wills and estates, trusts: all are areas of law where parenting experience is clearly relevant to analysis and teaching. There are less obvious candidates as well; constitutional law, international law, property law, taxation law, corporate law may not appear on the surface to invite insights from family life, but they too are all about the construction of social relations. And for law teachers who take on administrative roles, there is constant and constructive analogizing from family to institution and back again.

I don't know what my student will go on to do after graduation. Neither does she. Like her peers, she will likely take on a number of different roles as a jurist over the path of her career, and one of them might well be that of mother. When she gets to convocation and listens to what the honorary doctorate recipient has to say to the graduating class, perhaps she will remember bits of our conversation. Thinking about Nancy might help her question what can feel like an inexorable hierarchy of ways to work as a jurist. Thinking about Nancy might remind her that a legal education hands her a broad range of possibilities for living a life, not simply earning a living, as a jurist. Finally, thinking about Nancy helps us move past the notion of the Supreme Court as the most impressive or important way of making $5 a day.

6

Beyond the Court

I arrived at the apartment of Aharon and Elika Barak at 5:00 on a Wednesday afternoon – having walked from my hotel along busy Tel Aviv streets, already hot and humid in early June of 2016. Originally scheduled at Justice Barak's office at the Interdisciplinary Center in Herzliya, the meeting had been switched to his home so that he could fit in a later appointment at 7 that evening. Justice Barak met me at the door and invited me in, taking the flowers I had bought that morning at the Carmel market for his wife. Elika came through the hall and offered me cheesecake and green tea, along with a big bowl of cherries balanced on a little table in front of me. The three of us sat down in the modest living/dining room with a small open kitchen at one end.

Here I was with the most famous judge of Israel, the man who left the deanship of Hebrew University Law School after one year to become attorney general of the country at the age of 38 and joined the Supreme Court four years later in 1978. After serving as president of the court, or chief justice, from 1995–2006, he returned to being Professor Barak or more accurately law scholar Barak. Israel is a country with a mixed legal system, and Aharon Barak might be said to embody that mix – in his own experience as a student of law, in his enjoyment of private, public, and constitutional layers of legal thinking, and in his impact on teaching and advocacy and judging.

Frank Iacobucci always speaks of Aharon Barak with great warmth. The personal and professional friendship of these two 80-year-old men – Barak turned 80 in September 2016, Iacobucci nine months later – has informed their respective paths as jurists; they have been co-teachers as well as fellow high court justices. Frank knows Elika well too. A retired vice-president of the National Labour Court of Israel, Elisheva (Elika) Ososkin is a well-respected jurist and judge, and it is clear that she and Aharon are partners in life and law. Their four children have all studied law, and I had met their daughter, Michal, only a couple of weeks earlier at the Centre for Multiculturalism and Diversity at Hebrew University where she was serving as executive director.

There are some obvious parallels between the trajectories of Barak and Iacobucci. Both grew up in difficult circumstances – Frank as the son of poor immigrants, Aharon as a Holocaust survivor – something they connect to their dedication to public service. Both have participated actively in the development of the constitutional framework of their respective countries; both have engaged with the notion of human dignity and the consequences of giving it full recognition in law; and both have led active careers post-retirement from the Supreme Court and the particular burden and power that judging entails. But their paths after leaving the judiciary diverged.

Aharon Barak, as was evident from his enthusiasm about the book he was working on, had immersed himself in writing and intellectual puzzle-solving. He told me that he left lawyering behind when he retired, meaning that legal practice, arbitration, and mediation were all off the table. We talked about dignity, the ongoing focus of his analysis and writing, and he explained his wide concept of dignity, something he described as the "right to write one's own story." While he admitted to disagreeing (in the form of what he called an interesting fight) with Frank over the years about some aspects of methodology in constitutional analysis, he asserted that it was a "very great thing" to have Frank on the Supreme Court.

And then, Aharon Barak asked his question. "Why did Frank leave when he did?" Barak had waited until he hit mandatory retirement age; why didn't Frank do the same thing? "I told him at the time he was thinking about leaving that I would fly to Canada to talk to him 'judge to judge,'" Barak told me. But Frank went ahead and made the announcement, and then it was too late.

Barak's question was not to suggest that it wasn't possible to make important contributions after leaving the judiciary. He was acutely aware and proud of the fact that post-court retirement could open new paths for significant work and reflection. Instead, it came from his insistence that the court had unnecessarily lost him too early. He acknowledged that Frank had gone on to use lawyering "as a tool for his country." But it was very clear that he was disappointed and still perturbed by the fact that Frank had left before he had to.

Why did Frank retire from the Supreme Court when he did? At the time, he said he wanted to spend more time with his grandchildren. Maybe he got tired of doing the same job for 13 years, and realized he was never going to take on the different challenge of being Chief Justice of the Court. Maybe, after so many years in intensely community-grounded workplaces, working and writing at the Supreme Court was a uniquely lonely experience for Frank. Maybe he thought it was time to make a lot more than $5 a day, something only possible if he left public service.

I don't know the answer. I don't know if there exists a clear answer. The answer at the time Frank made the decision might be very different from the answer he would give years later. I am not sure that it matters. As explored in the coming pages, leaving behind the task of issuing Supreme Court of Canada judgments was far from synonymous with slowing down on making important contributions. Perhaps, without acknowledging or anticipating it, Frank was looking not so much for new modes of earning a living as for renewed ways of building a cathedral.

PART III

Building a Cathedral – Called to Action

1

The Third Worker

Three workers describe what they are doing. The first says, "I'm cutting stone." The second says, "I'm making $5 a day." The third says, "I'm building a cathedral."

In the Law convocation address Frank Iacobucci delivered to McGill's graduating class in 2003, he told the students, *"For me personally, hardly a day goes by without my thinking of that story of the three workers."*

When Frank tells the story – and when people who have heard him tell the story decide to retell it – it typically serves as a compelling reminder or directive as to attitude. Even a job that appears menial is crucial to the construction of the larger, and greater, whole. The description of the task is not what really matters, nor is it how well remunerated that task might be. We are encouraged to think, act, and speak like the third worker at all times, to reflect on the contributions we make, and the connections we forge with others.

The third worker's self-narrative is infused with a sense of dignity: presenting one's work as that of a cathedral builder conveys self-worth in a way that identifying oneself as a stonecutter or a wage earner doesn't. The cathedral builder acknowledges the importance of teamwork: after all, a cathedral is never the project of only one person. And the third worker accepts the timeline for building a cathedral: one person's contributions are unlikely to stretch all the way from the beginning to the end of the construction calendar for such a huge undertaking.

We could also take the third worker's words as an invitation to think about cathedral building a little bit differently. We can start with what comes to mind in those who listen to the story, and then subject that image to questioning and modification. The *Cathedrals of the World* colouring book[1] provides pictures of forty famous cathedrals across a geographical, historical, and architectural spectrum; included are Chartres, Hagia Sophia, St. Paul's, St. Peter's, and St. John the Divine. Even if not familiar with the colouring book, people who hear the three workers story probably have one of these cathedrals – or some approximation of one or a mix of them – in mind. All display dimensions of grandeur, all form part of our human heritage, and all possess unique features even as they share fundamental elements of Christian worship.

It seems obvious that, for the third worker, the eventual finished cathedral will be great and everlasting. Yet the Notre Dame de Paris fire of 2018 reminds us not to be certain of the durability of even the grandest cathedral. And Sagrada Familia in Barcelona, under construction for over a century, reminds us not to be certain that the work of building a cathedral is ever done. Those reminders suggest that the image of a cathedral can incorporate vulnerability, that it can be always evolving rather than fixed. The image is necessarily complicated. Not only is it not one person's sole responsibility to bring the cathedral to completion, but finishing it at all might not be possible.

Along with images of cathedrals come their stories. Historians remind us to pay attention to context of time and place in which labourers carried blocks of stone, or in which apprentices learned their trade. The building of a particular cathedral might be driven by political ideology or conflict in the Church; its rebuilding might follow destruction by fire, water, or war. The use, significance, and narratives attached to the land on which a cathedral is built might be effaced and forgotten; the people and traditions in place as a cathedral is designed might be displaced or even destroyed by the time the bell tower goes up. The message is necessarily complicated. Building what becomes a celebrated, beautiful, and awe-inspiring structure may be the result of actions that are far from any of those things.

Yet another way of hearing the third worker is by focusing on the cathedral as congregation rather than physical structure. Building a cathedral might mean making space for the soul, bringing people together in gratitude and humility, opening possibilities for inspiration and good deeds. Here, the walls and wings of the cathedral aren't observed for their architectural brilliance; instead the emphasis is on what people are doing within those walls and in those wings, and how the impact goes far beyond the constraints imposed by the construction. In this sense, too, cathedral building is never completed.

Given the complexities of cathedral building – its unfinished character, its stories of loss and hardship, its dependence on human congregation – the third worker's pride is infused with humility. The story does not suggest that we follow the third worker's example by presenting ourselves to the world as more important than the workers beside us. It does invite us to consider how dedicating time and energy to building a cathedral is neither easy to do nor easy to articulate.

When friends of Frank Iacobucci share his story of the three workers, they and their listeners are no doubt encouraged to make connections to Frank's own trajectory and contributions. Like cathedrals, the Canadian academy, Canadian federalism, or the shape of corporate responsibility could all be characterized as complex projects that demand dedication by many participants, rely on strong foundations, and display impressive architectural detail. Most obviously, one might think of the Supreme Court – or the collection of its jurisprudence – as a grand cathedral for which Frank was indeed a builder. We have instead explored all of these as ways, albeit significant and impressive ways, to make $5 a day, and have left for this final part a different account of Frank in cathedral-building mode.

As we will see, figuring out the contours of the cathedral is not so straight-forward or concrete, whether for Frank or for jurists in general. What does it mean for jurists in particular to build a cathedral, or to acknowledge that that is what they are doing? While the fact that they have gone through a legal education is something they have in common, it is far from clear how that experience connects to the contributions or responsibilities that they value most highly. In what follows, I will point to less expected and perhaps less tangible forms of Frank Iacobucci's cathedral building, and will draw on those to trace the links between learning law and becoming specialized "jurist cathedral builders." The lines may not be as clear as those of the cathedral drawings in the colouring book. But the task may be more rewarding than that of simply colouring inside the lines.

Part I opened with the dean's welcome to the study of law and went on to acknowledge that individuals take many paths – marked by experience and the development of identity – to prepare to "cut stone." Part II began with the messages and hopes of a convocation address, delivered to new lawyers as they set off on their many paths in the practice of law and in their many ways of "making $5 a day." Part III shifts to a law class reunion, decades after graduation, as people come together to share memories, offer updates on what they have been up to, and reflect on the ways they might have made some small contribution to a collective cathedral.

2

The Law Class Reunion

I went to the class of '79 reunion and said a few words. As I was saying goodbye, one woman said that she and others had just been remarking, "Iac hasn't changed since he was our Business Organizations professor." I took it as a great compliment. If my epitaph is: 'He remained the same person in the values that he represented, or the beliefs that defined him as a human being,' that wouldn't be bad. I was part of their journey to where they are going in life.

To Frank Iacobucci's past law students, gathered together at their 30th reunion, he was still essentially their teacher. In the intervening time, he had gone on to do other things. So had they. But this was a moment of memory, of recalling the relationship between professor and students. It is unlikely that anyone in attendance could remember in precise detail the substance of any specific lecture from their Business Organizations Law course decades ago. And yet the quote suggests that many were influenced in some way by the interactions in the classroom. As acknowledged by Frank, he was part of the journey of his law students. He was one of the people who supported their trajectory from the first day of law school to graduation and beyond. The encounter with his past students served to remind him of perhaps the most important aspect of the legacy any one person can hope to leave.

In the same fall term that I looked back 35 years to Provost Iacobucci's suggestion that I study law, I attended a McGill class reunion dinner as one of the past professors in the room. I sat with law students I taught a quarter of a century ago, surprised them with the fact that I could still remember where they sat in the classroom, and recalled questions they posed or term papers they wrote. At about the same time, I offered to speak at the 30th reunion of my own graduating class at the University of Toronto. In my short address, I reflected on uncertainty and change in legal education, asked whether and why studying law is worthwhile, and initiated a conversation of what, how, and why we learned together before going on our different ways. All of my old classmates could contribute to the conversation, regardless of the fact that only a small handful of them have spent most of the intervening time, as I have, in law school.

What is it that prepares graduates of university law faculties to contribute to and enrich the world around them through law? In the same way that individuals contemplate their own past and try to make sense of their life projects and contributions, legal education is confronted with the need to scrutinize what it is, how it got there, and how it sees itself going forward. What does legal education stand for? In what ways can it be flexible and innovative? To what extent would remaining the same, celebrated with respect to Professor Iacobucci, be seen in a positive light about Canadian legal education?

With the passing of years, a reunion serves as more than an occasion to challenge our powers of recognition or take stock of achievements and titles. "What have you done?" is a question not so hard to answer. "What have you been?" is trickier. Whether they realize it explicitly or not, alumni confront the message of the third worker. What has it meant to be jurists?[2] What impact have we had? Is there something about our law degrees that not only brings us together years after graduation, but also prepared us for the task of cathedral building? Indeed, at a moment of reunion, the cathedral building description of what we do with our lives has particular resonance: time and experience help the cathedral come into view and permit us to acknowledge and even try to articulate the role we might have played in its design and execution.

One way to express this idea is to imagine Frank and Nancy attending a class reunion at Cambridge together after 2004. To the question "What have you done?" Frank might answer, "I've retired from the Supreme Court of Canada," while Nancy might say, "I've stayed home." Both answers – neither one typical or obvious – push us to think differently about where a law degree takes you. Both have the potential for disrupting the narrative of ascendancy, one job at a time, to the highest position a jurist can hold and the most valuable contribution that a jurist can make. And both might prompt reunion attendees to reflect on how they have put justice into practice and how they have had a positive impact on the people around them: questions to which there aren't easy-to-articulate answers.

In what follows, I trace three alternative, yet intersecting, modes of cathedral building. The first – cathedral as project – focuses on Frank's contributions to reconciliation between Indigenous and non-Indigenous Canadians. It suggests that the most significant cathedral to which Frank added pieces might be one that comes after the Supreme Court on his timeline as jurist. The second – cathedral as congregation – focuses on Frank's contributions as mentor. Perhaps most obvious in the relationship between Frank and his law clerks, this cathedral stretches from before, to during, to after his time at the court. The third – cathedral as identity – focuses on Frank's connections and overlapping communities. It reminds us of the individual signature of every builder, a signature that retains its unique character even as it undergoes variations over time.

3

Cathedral as Project – Residential Schools and Reconciliation

Residential Schools: A Mandate for Settlement

Frank and Nancy moved back to their house in Toronto in the summer of 2004 – with Frank settling not into true retirement, but rather into the role of interim president of the University of Toronto. It seemed that, at the age of 67, he had walked back into his past life, albeit with a different office at Simcoe Hall, commuting from the Old Mill subway station in Toronto's west end to the St. George stop at the university. In a way, this was the sabbatical year that Frank had never enjoyed while in academia: instead of leaving the campus for a year of reflection and renewal, however, he enthusiastically returned to the university setting. After 13 years of intensive judicial service, Frank chose not so much to stop and observe what he had created, as to immerse himself in a community he knew well and within which he could prepare for what came next. Within a year, he got a call from Ottawa.

This time, the call came from Irwin Cotler, minister of Justice in Prime Minister Paul Martin's cabinet. Cotler invited Frank to act as representative of the federal government to negotiate a fair and lasting resolution of the legacy of Indian residential schools. At the end of May 2005, the deputy prime minister, Anne McLellan, and the National Chief of the Assembly of First Nations, Phil Fontaine, had signed an agreement setting out guiding principles for the settlement process. Frank Iacobucci's appointment as the person who would negotiate on behalf of the Federal Government was announced the next day.

Frank's mandate was to reach a settlement by the following spring. In satisfaction of that mandate, on 8 May 2006, the Indian Residential Schools Settlement Agreement was finalized, signed by the federal government, the churches, and the residential school plaintiffs.[3] Once approved by the provinces, the agreement went into effect in the fall of 2007: survivors could receive one payment based on how long they attended a residential school, and another based on the kinds of abuse they experienced as individual students. The following spring, newly elected Prime Minister Stephen Harper issued an official apology from the Canadian government for the abuse suffered by Aboriginal children at the government-funded residential schools they had been compelled to attend. At the same time, the Truth and Reconciliation Commission, the establishment of which was provided for in the Agreement, began its work of hearing the voices of survivors across the country, and gathering together their individual stories in anticipation of issuing a Report and Calls to Action in 2015.

Frank Iacobucci describes his contribution to what is an ongoing project of justice, building of trust, and reconciliation with Canada's Indigenous peoples as *the most satisfying task I have ever had as a lawyer.* He was understandably proud of reaching a solid settlement, and of tying that settlement to other connected pieces of a meaningful response to the harms inflicted on individuals, families, and communities by this country's residential school legacy. *"Without a doubt, I have never encountered a series of more challenging or difficult issues than those relating to aboriginal people. When one adds to the legal complexity the immensely serious social, economic, political science, and historical aspects it is an amazing constellation of what appear to be insurmountable and irreconcilable interdependent problems."*[4]

A brief review of the history and timeline of residential schools helps to situate the task entrusted to Frank and to appreciate the significance of the settlement. Initially established and operated by churches starting in 1880, residential schools became a central piece of federal government policy run through the Department of Indian Affairs. By 1930, three quarters of Indigenous children aged 7–16 were in 80 residential schools across Canada; approximately 150,000 First Nation, Métis, and Inuit children attended residential schools during the more than a century in which they were in operation. The last federally run residential school, located in Saskatchewan, closed in 1996.

In justifying the government's residential school policy, Canada's first prime minister, Sir John A. Macdonald, told the House of Commons in 1883:

> When the school is on the reserve the child lives with its parents, who are savages; he is surrounded by savages, and though he may learn to read and write his habits, and training and mode of thought are Indian. He is simply a savage who can read and write. It has been strongly pressed on myself, as the head of the Department, that Indian children should be withdrawn as much as possible from the parental influence, and the only way to do that would be to put them in central training industrial schools where they will acquire the habits and modes of thought of white men.[5]

Residential schools were total institutional settings. Children were removed from their families and home communities; as students, they were subjected to the disconnection, powerlessness, and isolation associated with institutional life. Their psychological, emotional, and spiritual suffering was often combined with physical and sexual abuse. Woven into the harm suffered by residential school students was the degradation of their identity through the severing of connection to their native languages, cultural frameworks, and faith traditions. The impact of the residential school system extended beyond the thousands of individual children who survived, or didn't, within it, to their families and entire communities. The harmful policies and practices implemented and sustained by the Canadian state called out for meaningful remedies and responses across Canadian society.

The formulation of those responses, accompanied by collective acceptance of responsibility, began over a century after the first residential schools had opened. Starting in the 1980's, official apologies were issued by the churches which ran residential schools: the United Church in 1986, followed by the Oblates of Mary Immaculate (an order of the Roman Catholic Church), the Anglican Church, and the Presbyterian Church in 1994. Public sharing of experiences in residential schools was initiated in the 1990's, with National Chief Phil Fontaine leading the way as the first Aboriginal leader to disclose the abuse he suffered as a student.

The Royal Commission on Aboriginal Peoples issued its Final Report in 1996,[6] including a significant chapter dedicated to shedding light on the history of the residential school system, and condemning the treatment of the children subjected to that system. The Assembly of First Nations followed that report with a multi-pronged healing strategy, calling for full apology, endowed funds, counselling, language revival, and community healing. In 1998, the Law Commission of Canada sent a report to Anne McLellan, minister of Justice at the time, focused on the harms inflicted on the young residents of total institutions, the needs generated by that experience, and the multiple, co-existing ways in which Canadian law and society could acknowledge and answer those needs.

At the same time, pressure was mounting through the courts. Some individual teachers and school directors were subject to criminal charges, and survivors were bringing claims for compensation against churches and the Canadian government: in the early 2000s, the number of lawsuits rose from 8,000 to 18,000. Churches feared for their solvency and sustainability, even as the Federal government agreed to cover a major proportion of the awarded damages and implemented what quickly turned out to be an inadequate alternative dispute resolution process.

Class actions were developing as effective procedural vehicles for addressing collective harms in Canada. In 2000, the Supreme Court of Canada formally opened the door to residential school survivors to combine their claims.

Given the convergence of all these factors, it was time for the Canadian government to act. On 31 May 2005, it announced an accord with the Assembly of First Nations, the key principles of which were the following:

1. Canada recognizes the need to continue to involve the Assembly of First Nations (AFN) in a key and central way for the purpose of achieving a lasting resolution of the Indian Residential School (IRS) legacy, and commits to do so. The Government of Canada and the Assembly of First Nations firmly believe that reconciliation will only be achieved if they continue to work together;
2. That they are committed to achieving a just and fair resolution of the Indian Residential School legacy;
3. That the main element of a broad reconciliation package will be a payment to former students along the lines referred to in the Assembly of First Nations Report [the AFN report on the Alternative Dispute Resolution process];
4. That the proportion of any settlement allocated for legal fees will be restricted;
5. That the Federal Representative will have the flexibility to explore collective and programmatic elements to a broad reconciliation package as recommended by the AFN;
6. That the Federal Representative will ensure that the sick and elderly receive their payments as soon as possible; and
7. That the Federal Representative will work and consult with the AFN to ensure the acceptability of the comprehensive resolution, to develop truth and reconciliation processes, commemoration, and healing elements and to look at improvements to the Alternative Dispute Resolution Process.

The federal representative, referred to in the agreement, was Frank Iacobucci. Bob Rae, political leader, diplomat, and one of Frank's past law students, offers a snapshot account: "Frank was quickly asked by the federal government to try and resolve the class actions that had been brought across the country on the residential school issue. His deep humanity and sense of the profound need for reconciliation led to a historic, multi-billion-dollar settlement, and to the establishment of the Commission on Truth and Reconciliation." (Bob Rae)

Why was Frank the right person for the job? Complementing Bob Rae's reference to Frank's "deep humanity," James Hickling casts the connection between the judge he had clerked for and this new role at a high level: "It is fitting that the person chosen to serve in that capacity would be someone with a longstanding and determined dedication to the protection of human dignity, since residential schools were one of the primary ways in which the State attacked the dignity of Aboriginal people." (James Hickling)

Frank answers a little differently: *I think my qualifications for doing the federal representative job were first, you had to have someone outside the government, because there was a lot of mistrust, suspicion and so on. Second, you needed someone who knew a little about government. And I suppose, third, it was useful to have someone with a skill set that could deal with lawyers and their clients from experience. If there were other things like credibility and all that, I leave that to others.*

It is probable that Frank was selected for the mix of his pragmatic capacities and personal qualities. The legal questions at stake were, in Frank's words, *intractably difficult;* they were as complex or more so than any question that had reached either the Federal or Supreme Court. An experienced judge was clearly needed. This was a class action in nine jurisdictions – six provinces and three territories – for harms reaching back over 100 years. The fact that it was a class action meant that, not unlike the case with many appellate judgments, its resolution would have an impact on the rights of people not involved in or even aware of the litigation. In general, members of the affected group or class in a class action may opt out individually; anyone who does not opt out is bound automatically by the final settlement or decision. To negotiate a representative and fair settlement, Frank would need to be aware not only of who joined him at the table, but of those who stayed away.

They also needed an experienced judge because of the immense theoretical complexities surrounding harm and evidence of harm in the context of the residential schools. Some of the injuries suffered by students came in the form of physical or sexual abuse; claims on this basis, while painful for victims to recount, were easy enough for the law to recognize. Frank understood that the broader, distinctive, and ongoing harm – what he referred to as *the real tort* – was the loss of language and culture, paired with the intergenerational suffering on the part of the children of survivors. All of this was impossible to fit into existing frameworks of damage or injury. Moreover, even if the law came to accept these harms within the assessment of accountability and compensation, how could you go about establishing them? These challenges required creative, judicious thinking. *One thing being a judge teaches you is to be a listener, to be open, and not to have a closed mind.* The process of listening and, beyond that, believing would need to be played out thousands of times, against a backdrop of thousands of highly unique circumstances, in order to get the full picture.

In addition, they needed a negotiator. As a corporate lawyer, Frank was well aware of the risks and costs associated with litigation. Court processes are expensive and lawyers need to be paid. Hurdles in meeting all the requirements of a successful civil action, combined with likely delays and unforeseen complexities, could prevent aging survivors from receiving justice within their lifetimes. The viability of Canada's major churches was also at stake; they needed to be included in the settlement while continuing to serve *the present and future generations of adherents of major faiths in our country.* The settlement process required a holistic appreciation of all the factors and actors involved. More like a corporate deal than a litigated settlement, it took on the form of private ordering and demanded the creation of a tailor-made solution.

John Terry, a lawyer at the law firm Torys LLP, first met Frank in June 2005. Asked by Frank to join him on his new project of moving toward settlement on the Indian Residential Schools, John agreed: "I'm not sure either of us realized at the time how profoundly that project would shape our respective career paths and, eventually, the country itself." Based on close and sustained observation, John points to some of the traits that made Frank so effective in his role in addressing complex Indigenous issues:

"Frank as scholar and judge. I have seen this in two ways in particular. First, Frank tries wherever possible to build the negotiations in which he is involved on a foundation of sound principles. Early in any negotiations, Frank will take steps to ensure that both sides agree to a set of principles to govern the negotiations. The principles will vary depending on the circumstances, but will typically emphasize such principles as mutual respect, recognition of the government-to-government relationship between the parties, a willingness and commitment to understand each other's cultures, responsibilities, and limitations, and consideration for the interests of third parties. Enunciating these up front builds trust and provides a core set of principles and themes that the parties can return to again and again through the negotiations.

"Second, there is Frank's linguistic dexterity. He is never at a loss – even when all the rest of us are – to find the nuanced wording that will bridge a gap between the parties. This might be a sentence, a phrase, or just an adverb or adjective. It is the skill of the closer – the final touch to end the day and get the settlement. I don't know whether it is a gift more of intuition or the product of many years of practice, or a combination of both. But it works – beautifully.

"Frank's unique stature. There are very few people in this country that have the relationship with senior government officials that Frank has earned through his years of service. This is particularly important when he is appointed by a government as its representative, as he was when appointed federal representative for the residential schools negotiations. The non-governmental parties to these negotiations properly see this as a sign of the seriousness with which the government views these issues, and its willingness to take wise counsel from Frank as its representative during the negotiations, even when the government may initially disagree with a perspective put forward by the other side.

"Frank as strategist/consensus builder. Frank was a consensus builder on the court, and he remains one in Indigenous negotiations, whether acting as mediator or as representative of one side or the other. He achieves consensus through some of the skills described above. But he is also a strategist, with a keen sense of how process and substance interact to put pressure on the parties to agree. Discretion restrains me from providing examples. Most come down to showing the parties that settlement is better than non-settlement and that, as Frank often says, 'we all have to take a little water in our wine.'" (John Terry)

Frank came to the table as a jurist with exceptional abilities to understand, listen, communicate, strategize, and offer wise counsel. He was the right person for the job because of who he was, what he could do, what knowledge he had, and how he was perceived.

I didn't have a blank cheque (and I shouldn't have had a blank cheque), but I was prepared to listen. And I said that. That was my approach. If I found there were convincing arguments to go beyond the mandate that I was given, I wasn't going to be shy about going back to government ... I made my involvement conditional on everyone being committed to trying to make a deal. I don't mean that you've got to guarantee a deal – that's not what I was saying to either party, but I wanted that assurance before.

From the outset of the negotiations, Frank made two things clear to all sides. Listening was fundamental, but any resolution would have to include accountability for the money spent. And the process had to be serious and meaningful, neither tied to political optics nor unreasonably constrained by the initial scope of the mandate. Over the course of the negotiations, Frank met individual survivors as well as organizations including the British Columbia Survivors' Society, the Aboriginal Healing Foundation, the Native Women's Association of Canada, and the Grand Council of Crees.[7]

Time spent listening was crucial to the building and reaching of agreement over four principal issues: first, the implementation of a settlement procedure (including confidentiality of claims); second, the goals of healing and reconciliation; third, the determination of eligible schools and institutions; and, fourth, legal fees.

In November 2005, the parties – including the Assembly of First Nations, the federal government, the Anglican, United, and Presbyterian Churches, and various Catholic entities (reflecting the absence of a unified Catholic Church of Canada) – reached an agreement in principle. At this point, Iacobucci formally recommended the settlement to the federal government. The final arrangement was made up of five foundational pillars:

1. The Common Experience Payment (CEP)
2. Independent Assessment Process (IAP)
3. Truth and Reconciliation Commission
4. Aboriginal Healing Foundation
5. Commemoration Initiatives

Funds would go to survivors through five distinctive pathways. For individuals, the Common Experience Payment provided that each claimant who had spent any time in a residential school, down to a single day, would be eligible for a single payment of $10,000, plus $3,000 per year in the school. As the name suggests, this payment was intended to address the shared experience of all residential school survivors; it addressed the historical fact of residential schooling and the generalized loss of culture, language, and family and community relationships.

In addition, individual survivors could make specific claims of physical and sexual abuse via the Independent Assessment Process (IAP). Supervised by an Oversight Committee and chief adjudicator, the IAP provided for individual claims to be heard by adjudicators in closed sessions, in which the parties were permitted to be represented by counsel. The IAP operated on a points system, ranging from "serious dysfunction" to "modest detrimental impact," with dollar values attached to the kinds and timelines of abuse suffered. Further funds were allocated to initiatives dedicated to healing, to commemoration, to the sharing and safeguarding of stories, and to the building and repair of respectful relationships – all of which were meant to have an intergenerational and collective impact.

James Hickling synthesizes Frank's accomplishment as follows:

"By 2006, Frank had guided the parties to a settlement agreement that provided for the establishment of new institutions and processes, healing and commemoration initiatives, compensation for survivors, and for the work of the Truth and Reconciliation Commission (because as Frank has said, there can be no reconciliation without truth). By most measures, the settlement ranks as the largest ever achieved in Canada; the total funding made available under the agreement and related initiatives will likely top six billion dollars once implementation is complete. It resulted in the settlement of 23 class actions and around 30,000 individual actions, and provided a measure of justice for all of the approximately 80,000 survivors who were alive at around the time of the settlement.

"To get there, Frank was aided by various reports and studies that presaged the settlement package, but still he had to corral multiple government agencies, more than a dozen law firms, over fifty church-related entities, several Aboriginal organizations, and many other interested parties – and he had to get them all in the same room, working towards the same goal. The negotiations were intense, emotional, and unwieldy; some sessions included up to 80 lawyers and other representatives in one room. Then, the proposed settlement had to be approved by the cooperative efforts of the courts of nine jurisdictions. This was an enormous and enormously complicated task by any measure." (James Hickling)

The agreement required authorization from the nine provinces in which the national class action had been filed. In BC, Justice Brenner remarked upon the innovative character of the agreement as he authorized the settlement for the province[8]:

> A repeated theme in these cases is the effect that attendance at Indian Residential Schools had on the language and culture of Indian children. These were largely destroyed. However, no court has yet recognized the loss of language and culture as a recoverable tort. Even if such a loss was actionable, most claims would now be statute barred.

The parties had succeeded in crafting a principled deal that overcame many of the legalistic barriers to compensation and support for healing. By 22 March 2007 the class action had been certified across Canada and an opt-out period began. The Settlement Agreement stated that if 5,000 people opted out of the Settlement class, the Settlement would be abandoned. Only 1,074 opted out, and the Settlement took effect on 19 September 2007. Ten years later, close to $1.7 billion had been distributed to residential school survivors.

Truth and Reconciliation: Lessons for Legal Education

In the fall of 2001, my first-year students began their study of law by learning about the experiences and claims of survivors of Canada's Indian Residential Schools. This was their course in Torts, the area of law concerned with individual responsibility for repairing the harmful consequences of wrongful action. I invited them to reflect on the range of human needs that may result from wrongfully caused injury by reading excerpts of the Law Commission of Canada's report to the minister of Justice, entitled "Restoring Dignity: Responding to Child Abuse in Canadian Institutions" and published in 2000.[9] For most of the students, this was the first time they had heard anything about residential schools.

In every September since, I have started the course in the same way. Very little has changed in terms of the purpose, structure, and scope of an introductory unit focused on the needs of injured individuals and the co-existing responses offered by Canadian law and society. The Law Commission lists eight primary types of survivors' needs: establishing an historical record (remembrance); acknowledgement; apology; accountability; access to therapy or counselling; access to education or training; financial compensation; prevention and public awareness. I divide the class into five groups, assign each one a distinct form of response, and then ask how well the students think that their assigned form meets the eight listed needs. We start with community-based initiatives, then truth and reconciliation, then formal institutional apology, followed by criminal justice, and finally civil liability. By the time we get to the last form of response – and the focus of the year-long course in front of us – the students have an appreciation of how these responses can, and indeed must, co-exist rather than compete with each other, and of how the shape of each one gives it a particular character and role to play.

Some things indeed have changed. Most obvious have been the changes in the contours of the legal landscape. In 2001, the students had to imagine individual claims for civil liability on the part of survivors, and the discussion provided a preliminary glimpse of the hurdles that exist in the path of any tort claimant: hurdles that would constitute the basic content of the course. They also had to draw on their awareness of truth and reconciliation processes in other parts of the world – in South Africa, in Cambodia – in order to imagine what such a process might look like in Canada. In 2007, students read key features of the settlement agreement and the details of the common experience payment combined with an individual assessment process; together, we examined the information provided to all survivors regarding their options as claimants, and discussed the pros and cons of joining in or opting out. In 2008, they could read and watch Prime Minister Harper's apology on the part of Canada's government to the former residents of Indian Residential Schools.[10] In the fall of 2015, I added to the class materials excerpts from the newly released Report of the Truth and Reconciliation Commission; students could finally ground their assessment of the truth and reconciliation approach within the distinctive Canadian context.

The other obvious change has been in the quantity and quality of background understanding with which students arrive in law. Since 2001, the collective knowledge of the students in my first-year class about Canada's policy and practice of sending Indigenous children to residential schools, and about the harms and long-lasting damage inflicted on individuals, families, and communities has broadened and deepened. They often have considerably detailed appreciation of the history and legacy of the residential school system. Individual students over the years have shared stories that range from having a grandparent who went to residential school, to working on reserves as a nurse, to processing applications for individual assessment and compensation for physical and sexual abuse. In various ways, students often have already "heard" the voices and stories of residential school survivors in this country. They arrive open to integrating continued listening into their legal education.

That experience of listening is the final major change in this introductory unit. As residential school survivors have shared their stories, and have had those stories relayed and archived, their voices can be introduced to law classrooms like mine. Before my students begin their discussion of what they know – or think they know – about criminal prosecution, or about lawsuits for monetary damages, or about pathways to healing and reconciliation – they listen. I distribute small pieces of paper around the classroom, each one with a numbered quote from a survivor, and I ask them to read out loud in turn. As I tell them, we fill our collective learning space with words from real people – in unique detail, reflecting unique perspectives and pasts – and then try to keep in mind that real people are at the heart of the study of human wrongs and harms, acts and injuries, responsibility and suffering. Here are some of the voices we listen to together[11]:

• "We were called by number all the time. The nuns used to call, '39, 3 where are you?' Or '25, come here right now!' I was number 116.

I was trying to find myself; I was lost. I felt like I had been placed in a black garbage bag that was sealed."

- "I remember seeing my brother in the back of the class. I went to talk to him and he was really nervous. He said, 'Don't come over and talk to me.' I asked, 'Why, I want to talk to you.' And he was saying, 'You're not supposed to.' I told him. 'Why, you are my brother.' And right away I was taken to the front of the class and I was given the ruler on the palm of my hands."

- "Hunger is both the first and the last thing I can remember about that school … Every Indian student smelled of hunger … We were hungry all the time. The mainstay of our diet was a porridge which was actually cracked wheat that sat on the back of the stove all night, ended up with a bunch of lumps and kind of slimy."

- "We cut wood, picked stones – all the worst jobs. We didn't learn anything. We didn't know anything. I read only a little now."

- "I started wetting the bed. What was really bad about it was I couldn't stop. I wanted to. I tried everything. They would take our sheets and wrap them around our heads and make us walk past all the other kids."

- "At Fort Alexander in the 1950s, younger boys were sent to one of the priests for what was termed ménage, during which he would wash their genitals. One recalled that the practice did not end until 'we became older and bigger, and our determination to threaten, maim, hurt or even kill our tormentors gave us the power to refuse the treatment.'"

- "At the residential school, if it wasn't for hockey, I would have gone crazy. Sport became my support. Until I was thirty years old, I played and when I was on the ice, I would let it all out."

- "Through my experience with Kamloops Indian Residential School Dancers, I learned some assertiveness skills. I learned to smile even when I wasn't happy. I learned to get along and talk with people and that was good."

- "As much as that particular teacher used to call us bloody dodos and no good for nothing, a bunch of hounds of iniquity, he taught us pretty good in terms of English."
- "I knew the strap, because a man strapped me with the same one across my bare buttocks ten times because I made a noise after the lights were out."
- "I remember my head being shaved and all my long hair falling on the floor, and the way they dealt with the crying and the hurtful feeling was with a bowl of ice cream."

Why ensure that law students hear pieces of stories told in the first person? Because they reveal the complexities of human experience, the range of individual harms and the range of individual perspectives, and the strength and determination of people too easily reduced by the simplistic label of victims. And because they place a weight on the students' shoulders, a burden of constant critical examination of the potential and limits of law.

Lessons from this way of introducing law students to the law of civil wrongs coincide with key features of Frank Iacobucci's contribution to addressing the legacy of residential schools. Frank recognized that the compensation scheme central to the settlement was only one, albeit important, piece; it needed other complementary pieces in place in order to be meaningful and effective. In particular, the promised establishment of a Truth and Reconciliation Commission was a key part of the agreement. Instead of adopting the same model as that found in South Africa, complete with subpoena power and the authority to compel witnesses, Frank wanted to avoid an overly legalistic approach to what he saw as fundamentally a process for education and healing. He had agreement from Phil Fontaine, keen that the Commission should help move the experience of residential schools from living history into fully documented history.

Hearing stories and listening to voices was crucial – to ensure that those stories and voices were not lost, but rather remembered and indeed woven into ongoing teaching and learning. That commitment underscores the other principal feature of Frank's work as federal representative: able and eager to meet individuals, to listen to what they had to say, and to learn with curiosity and openness, Frank modelled how to act as a responsible jurist.

Quoted by the Truth and Reconciliation Commission, two speakers remind law students of the particular features and limits of an area of law in which compensation of victim by wrongdoer is typically understood to "close a chapter." In contrast to civil liability, reconciliation opens pathways, and often expands responsibility. In the words of Anishinaabe elder Mary Deleary: "I'm so filled with belief and hope because when I hear your voices at the table, I hear and know that the responsibilities that our ancestors carried ... are still being carried ... even through all of the struggles, even through all of what has been disrupted ... We have work to do ... [to] reconcile with this land and everything that has happened, there is much work to be done ... in order to create balance." Insistence on the shared task is echoed by Reverend Stan McKay: "[We cannot] perpetuate the paternalistic concept that only Aboriginal peoples are in need of healing ... The perpetrators are wounded and marked by history in ways that are different from the victims, but both groups require healing ... How can a conversation about reconciliation take place if all involved do not adopt an attitude of humility and respect?"[12]

Significant implications for education of the legacy of residential schools are included in the Calls to Action issued in 2015 by the Truth and Reconciliation Commission. As had been envisaged from the start, the Commission's work incorporated a strong teaching and learning component, and the scope of its recommendations reflected an emphasis on education. In particular, they explicitly invited those of us involved in Canadian legal education to reconsider curriculum and pedagogy, and more broadly to reflect on the responsiveness, inclusiveness, and impact of the teaching, learning, and practice of law.

Call to Action # 28 reads as follows: "We call upon law schools in Canada to require all law students to take a course in Aboriginal people and the law, which includes the history and legacy of residential schools, the United Nations Declaration on the Rights of Indigenous Peoples, Treaties and Aboriginal rights, Indigenous law, and Aboriginal-Crown relations. This will require skills-based training in intercultural competency, conflict resolution, human rights, and anti-racism."[13]

Projects for change in legal education are often designed at an institutional and structural level: which courses should be mandatory, how many credit hours should be devoted to a particular area of law, what is the desirable proportion of theory to practice or knowledge to skills? Along these lines, faculties of law might respond to recommendations of the TRC by incorporating learning about Canada's history of residential schools in substantive courses, creating a specific course on Aboriginal Peoples and Law, and adding cross-cultural competency skills training to the already mandatory Ethics course. Taking those steps would directly correspond to the Commission's specific recommendation. But there is room for going beyond, or modifying, the particular form and substance suggested by the Commission. Many members of Canadian law faculties have taken the Call to Action as an opportunity to implement a striking range of initiatives to incorporate into legal education Indigenous legal traditions, histories, claims, and insights. By 2018, Canadian Law deans were sharing those initiatives with each other and working within their own institutions to develop distinctive responses.

As we collectively imagine the future of legal education, there are lessons we can learn from Frank Iacobucci's part in the Canadian story that unfolded from 2005 to 2015 and stretched from before to beyond. Of course, as we have seen, Frank had a significant and leading role to play in reaching the settlement of a class action of incredible scope and significance, and in ensuring the inclusion in the agreement of interlocking pieces including a truth and reconciliation process. His example serves in another, more foundational, way. It forces us to confront the fact that preparation to do the kind of work he did is not contingent on taking a particular course. It is impossible to identify some precise component of

Frank Iacobucci's own formal legal education that explicitly provided the knowledge and lawyering skills required for leadership and engagement with Indigenous individuals and communities.

That doesn't mean that Frank's experience of studying and practising law wasn't implicitly crucial to that leadership role. We know that the various hats he had worn as a jurist meant he had developed capacities necessary for the task. But his path suggests that legal education that equips jurists for a lifetime's varied and unique work in law can't be boiled down to a list of content, courses, and competencies. More specifically, the work of reconciliation demands more than checking off requirements linked to knowledge and ability. We can read Call to Action #28 as a directive to introduce a course named Aboriginal Peoples and Law into the mandatory curriculum. Beyond answering the Call in this literal and limited way, however, we might take it as a rich opportunity to identify and articulate elements of learning in law that lead to innovative, responsive, and justice-driven lawyering.

What are those elements? There isn't a magical set, of course, but we can glean several from Frank's participation in finding a way forward in the wake of the Residential Schools. Below, I suggest three: humility, self-knowledge, and responsibility. Humility goes hand in hand with a heightened capacity for listening; self-knowledge demands awareness of law's power; and responsibility translates into the acceptance of particular obligations as lawyers.

First, humility:

There's no question that I had to be very candid. I had only peripheral knowledge of Indian residential schools. I'd heard things and actually experienced visiting one when I was a kid but I didn't know it was an Indian residential school.

Frank had much – indeed everything – to learn. The first step in his task of negotiating a nationwide settlement scheme was to realize how little he knew, to turn to those who had experience and stories to tell, and to listen. The need to start from a position of substantive ignorance was no doubt difficult, especially for someone with so much expertise in a wide range of issues in Canadian law, history, politics, and social relations. An appropriate level of humility, a willingness to listen intensely to painful and provocative stories and claims, was crucial.

We need "legal ears"[14] that can hear previously unheard stories: stories told by people whose histories, lives, and attachment to the land don't take on the form of easily recognizable documents and agreements. This is particularly apt to describe the way Frank, as someone without any firsthand experience or specialized knowledge of residential schools, had to prepare for his role as federal government negotiator.

Humility also captures a crucial aspect of a legal education that prepares jurists to confront complex human stories, needs, experiences, and modes of communication. Law students, including Frank almost fifty years before taking on this particular role, practise the specialized listening skills required to think, and write, and speak as lawyers. Whose voices do they hear? Through the texts they read, they listen to judges, legislators, and scholars: the authors of judgments, codes, statutes, charters, and critical commentary. Behind that formal legal language, they can hear the voices of advocates and litigants, of intervenors, of collectives, of institutions. Beyond the texts, however, perhaps the most significant practise in listening with humility can come in a classroom where, with the guidance of engaged teachers, students practise listening to and learning from peers able to bring a diversity of experiences, perspectives, families, and communities to every discussion.

Second, self-knowledge:

It was so moving when I went to Kenora to visit a reserve and met with some of the leaders. One of the Chiefs told me that his parents were both residential school attendees and on his father's deathbed, his father looked at him and said, "I'm sorry that I never really told you I loved you and I have to say that I don't think I ever learned how to say that because I never really saw my parents. I never learned how to be a parent." And that was to me just so dramatically striking and touching.

Self-knowledge as a jurist demands awareness of the particular contours and scope of personal and professional identity. It signals the importance of individual background, shaped by relations within families, communities, neighbourhoods, schools, workplaces, and an appreciation of the potential and limits of law. When confronted by broken relations across generations, Frank's awareness and experience of building and nourishing relationships in his own life guided his personal reactions. In addition, as a jurist, he brought sophisticated understanding of the ways in which the state can exercise its power to target and even destroy human connections and identities. He was determined to find ways in which the state could instead divert its power to support and strengthen those same connections and identities.

In this double sense of knowing where one comes from, self-knowledge operates throughout the learning and practice of law. Jurists constantly grapple with the connections between the projects they take on and their own convictions, backgrounds, and perspectives; they start that grappling as law students. Frank's account of being touched by the stories he heard reminds us of something that any law student knows: emotions are often and necessarily entangled with our learning of principles and policies.[15] Students hear stories that are dramatically striking and touching throughout their legal education, whether in discussing child custody, compensation for grief, language rights in primary school, the consequences of opioid addiction, or the elements necessary to establish sexual assault. Their reactions at a personal and emotional level are valid and even necessary, even if those reactions cannot constitute in themselves complete responses to the issues at stake and the people involved.

Frank's account reminds us that the personal never disappears in practice. It is crucial to the human dimension of work as a jurist; we might say that the personal is "legal." Self-knowledge as jurists thus includes individual sensibilities and personal engagement, even as it requires immersion in law. Literacy in the substance, method, and language of law obviously shaped Frank's approach to the work of envisaging a settlement and negotiating its features. But his story from Kenora illustrates the constant presence of emotional connection intertwined with that literacy. The challenge in legal education is that of supporting students in their own work of combining empathy, personal connection, and self-awareness as developing experts in the reach and limits of law.

Third, responsibility:

A meaningful response in Canada to our history of residential schools includes everything from compensation payments to funding for healing, commemorative projects and (the one I like by far the most) a truth and reconciliation process ... Canadians should learn from, not just about, the tragedy.

Frank's answer to the question of what constituted the key components in acknowledging and accepting accountability for the residential schools underscores the multi-pronged character of the settlement he negotiated. Read more generally, however, it offers a broad and rich picture of the particular kind of obligations that jurists take on, and for which their formal legal education offers a foundation. Legal educators often talk about leading their students to learn how to act as problem solvers. But Frank's role in the larger project of reconciliation between Canada's Indigenous and non-Indigenous peoples points to a more textured and varied description of what law students should prepare for. As jurists, they will often act not as problem solvers but rather as participants, builders, team members, dreamers, and burden carriers.

This last label – as carriers of a burden – is one that reflects the striking magnitude of what Frank took on, and of what current law students in Canada take on in trying to understand the unfinished puzzle of *meaningful response to our history of residential schools*. Along with the stories come formal inquiries and reports, compensation guidelines, government and church apologies, community rebuilding initiatives, judgments, and calls to action. Along with critical reading and analysis comes appreciation of the challenges of cooperation among Indigenous representatives, individuals, and communities, and their non-Indigenous counterparts. Along with working with words comes exploration of human expression and participation in the form of ceremonies, rituals, symbols, practices of mourning and celebration.

Taken together, all of this results in a sense of being submerged in inquiry and burdened with responsibility. The range of sources, mechanisms, and institutions with which law students and jurists must be familiar should feel daunting; even more daunting is the heavy obligation to work with all of these in as serious, open, and ethical a way possible. As suggested by James Boyd White, American law professor and scholar of legal education, "[t]he heart of this education is learning to be responsible in a new way for what one thinks and says."[16] The learning of law leads to ongoing learning accompanied by never-ending responsibility.

The introduction of "Honouring the Truth, Reconciling for the Future," the summary volume of the Final Report of the Truth and Reconciliation Commission, includes a photo of the residential school in Mission, British Columbia, in operation from the early 1860s to 1984. This was the school, operated by the Missionary Oblates of Mary Immaculate in partnership with the Canadian federal government, that a 12-year-old Frank Iacobucci had travelled to for a soccer match in 1949. *When I got into this, I looked back and thought, "Oh my God, I went to visit that school that was on the list."* A year earlier, students at the school had lost the right to visit the nearby town of Mission, making their sense of isolation even more profound. Frank and his teammates, like most Canadians, would not have had any concrete or detailed picture of what life was like for the students at the Mission school. It would be decades before that sense of isolation began to lift.

The combination of Frank's example and the inclusion of a Call to Action focused on law schools turns our attention to all of the sites in legal education at which the capacities for humility, self-knowledge, and specialized responsibility can be developed. By imagining ways to enrich these elements and capacities, our energies shift away from the particular courses and credits that make up a curriculum. Instead, we confront a much harder task: that of sustaining and enriching the components of legal education that ensure law students graduate ready for continued learning as jurists, adaptability to a necessarily dynamic professional landscape, and significant justice-related challenges such as that of meaningful reconciliation.

If it were the case that a lawyer who hadn't taken a course in Aboriginal law couldn't work in a constructive and important way on a project involving Indigenous perspectives, people, and preoccupations, then Frank Iacobucci's contributions to a comprehensive response to residential schools would not have been possible. This isn't to say that such a course couldn't or wouldn't be a valuable component of any program of legal education. But Frank implicitly reminds us that any one substantive course in law school does not, on its own, prepare a law student for practice, even practice related to that area of law. The capabilities needed to face new and complex questions in any area of law are forged and refined across legal education, rather than in any particular classroom.[17]

The general lessons for legal education leave room for specific assessment of Frank's role and accomplishment. James Hickling reflects on the ways in which Frank served both as team player and as leader:

"Frank is the first to give credit to others: the previous commissions, the Aboriginal organizations, the churches, the lawyers, law societies, and bar associations. He singles out for particular praise former National Chief Phil Fontaine, former Ministers Cotler and McLennan, and Senator Murray Sinclair. And he gives the greatest credit to the survivors of residential schools themselves, whose courage, patience and persistence in the pursuit of a restoration of their dignity he found humbling and inspiring ... But there is another truth that must also be spoken, and that is that there could not have been a negotiated settlement of this kind without Frank Iacobucci. The terrible legacy of residential schools was so steeped in pain, shame, and distrust that only someone whom all others recognized as having a deep, abiding commitment to equality and dignity as first principles could have bridged the divisions and brought the parties together to find workable solutions." (James Hickling)

Beyond Residential Schools: An Ongoing Project

It is not difficult to see reconciliation between the Indigenous peoples of Canada and their non-Indigenous neighbours as an obvious cathedral, the building of which requires workers like Frank. This is a cathedral with neither a clear architectural blueprint nor a defined timeline for construction. It is a cathedral in constant progress. Some of its features are beautiful to behold, others are difficult to see with certainty; some are breathtakingly bold, others quiet and peaceful. Perhaps the most significant aspect of the cathedral of reconciliation is the congregation, the people who trust each other and come together to imagine and implement ways to move forward.

It may seem ironic to turn to an image associated with the very churches that collaborated with the Canadian government to set up residential schools and are still coming to terms with the harms they inflicted on young students. The cathedral image is all wrong if it conjures up an imposing building associated with one faith and the imposition of a monolithic mode of belonging. But if we see the cathedral as sacred and symbolic space, as place of belief and trust, as site of connection and forgiveness, then it works pretty well as metaphor for the project of reconciliation. In particular, a cathedral retains its meaning for people if it combines grandness and the everyday; if it inspires with its architecture, art, and music, while opening its doors to anyone who arrives in need. Cathedral builders need not have all of this in mind as they go about their job, and yet the promise of the cathedral cannot be realized without them.

Frank couldn't have known, when he left the Supreme Court, that he was moving to the building site of this particular cathedral and, arguably, to the most important file that had ever landed on his desk. In 2017, he was invited to Jerusalem, this time by the Halbert Centre for Canadian Studies at Hebrew University, where he gave a lecture as visiting holder of The James R. Bullock Chair. He spoke about the Residential Schools of Canada, about his responsibility as federal representative on the most significant class action in Canadian litigation history, and about the forward-looking Calls to Action issued by the Truth and Reconciliation Commission. Perhaps Aharon Barak asked Frank yet again why he retired from the court when he did. Perhaps the subject of the lecture provided the answer.

Frank's own work on the cathedral didn't end in 2006. The expertise, experience, and, most importantly, trust that he had developed on the

Indian Residential Schools settlement led him to other projects. On behalf of Ontario in the mid-2010s under a provincial Liberal government, he negotiated with the nine Matawa First Nations to reach a regional framework for development of the Ring of Fire mineral belt in Northwestern Ontario. Cancelled in 2019 and replaced by bilateral talks, the proposed framework proved unsuccessful, and yet the project was still one of building, albeit followed by significant renovation and rework. In addition, and as we have already seen in discussing the aftermath of the Supreme Court's judgment in *Gladue*, Frank authored the report on First Nations Representation on Ontario Juries, submitted in February of 2013.[18]

In the approach, style, and form of the report, in the visits and meetings and long conversations, in the physical closeness associated with the sharing of space, in his promise to incorporate what he heard and saw and felt into the review and its recommendations, Frank set an example for building a foundation of mutual respect and mutual trust. *"It is my sincere hope,"* he wrote, *"that the trust that First Nations people have invested in this Independent Review process will be rewarded with prompt response and action by the Government of Ontario."*[19] He cherished the ongoing opportunities to make connections, to listen to stories, and to serve as conduit in a relationship of co-existence. This kind of work, perhaps more strikingly than any other, demanded a jurist who could act as translator and trustee, dreamer and do-er.

In October 2018, it was Prime Minister Justin Trudeau's turn to ask Frank for assistance. The federal government's Trans Mountain Pipeline project had been scrutinized by the Federal Court of Appeal at the behest of the Tsleil-Waututh Nation;[20] according to the court, the framework for consultations with affected First Nations was adequate but its implementation was flawed. The National Energy Board had reviewed the project, but the government had been wrong to reject the possibility of modification during the period of consultation. A year before Canada was due to head into a federal election, the prime minister had to find a way to meet the requirement of meaningful and constructive dialogue and to try to find consensus.

As the Federal Court of Appeal observed: "The inadequacies of the consultation process flowed from the limited execution of the mandate of the Crown consultation team. Missing was someone representing Canada who could engage interactively. Someone with the confidence of Cabinet who could discuss, at least in principle, required accommodation measures, possible flaws in the Board's process, findings, and recommendations and how those flaws could be addressed."[21]

Frank Iacobucci was that person. Trudeau and his government drew on Frank's proven record and trustworthiness to counter growing frustration among First Nations communities and, more broadly, on the part of both proponents and detractors of the Trans Mountain Pipeline. The concerns presented to the Federal Court of Appeal by the Tsleil-Waututh Nation emphasized the risk of oil spills and their anticipated widespread impact on habitat and species, as well as on First Nations title, interests, and economies. Other communities in the path of the proposed pipeline also wanted their say, whether to reiterate those concerns, add others to the list, or indeed to consider potential benefits.

Frank could be counted on to listen, translate, and ensure the broad and concrete consultation mandated by the court of which he had once been chief justice. He was familiar with both the language of the Indigenous participants, and the language of a corporate entity like Trans Mountain. He understood the features of meaningful process or encounter in this kind of context, including the Crown's fiduciary duty and the active engagement of administrative bodies such as the National Energy Board and the British Columbia Environmental Assessment Office. Finally, he appreciated the tensions associated with federalism on this file: the provincial governments of Alberta and British Columbia were at loggerheads, while the federal government had purchased the pipeline from Kinder Morgan with the intention of getting it built. Consultations with First Nations could not resolve those conflicts but would take place against the backdrop they characterized. "Fragile" and "fragmented" were potential adjectives for Canadian federalism with which Frank was familiar, long before the results of the 2019 federal election strikingly reminded all Canadians of their continued presence.

I turn again to John Terry, from his vantage point as Frank's colleague, to conclude this description of Frank's cathedral building:

"I have been privileged to work with Frank as he has turned the focus of the last stage of his long career to working on complex Aboriginal issues ... It seems to me that Indigenous issues involve him on multiple levels – as a lawyer, public policy maker, and compassionate individual – in ways that other files do not. And it is that fact that makes him so uniquely effective in resolving these complex Indigenous issues. ... While Frank on the court had many opportunities to engage intellectually on complex Indigenous rights issues, the Residential Schools settlement brought him into a direct process of conversation and collaboration with Indigenous peoples and their leaders. And while Indigenous issues may have previously engaged his mind, they now engage his heart."

Earlier, in introducing Frank's appointment as federal representative, I borrowed from John Terry some of the reasons for which Frank was "uniquely effective": he was a scholar and judge, someone with unique stature and a gift for finding the right words. To that list, Terry adds Frank's generous heart.

"Last but most important of all is Frank's humanity and compassion. Frank was moved to tears more than once during the Residential Schools negotiations. His wearying winter journeys on small planes never dampen the enthusiasm for meeting with Indigenous peoples in their home communities. When I think of the respect and empathy Frank brings to Indigenous issues I think of a photograph included in a report we did for the Ontario Government on the underrepresentation of Indigenous peoples on Ontario juries. Frank had visited the home of an elder for an afternoon get-together. They had spoken for a while and then posed for a photograph. The photograph shows the two of them, arm-in-arm, each with broad, loving smiles." (John Terry)

The speaker in Rita Joe's poem, "I Lost my Talk," holds out her hand and the promise to teach:

> I lost my talk
> The talk you took away.
> When I was a little girl
> At Shubenacadie school.
> You snatched it away:
> ...
> So gently I offer my hand and ask,
> Let me find my talk
> So I can teach you about me.[22]

Poetry, music, and storytelling are all modes of learning and reconciliation that can feel more powerful than law. But jurists can be understood to share the work of poets in finding words, in re-forging relationships, in imagining where real talk might lead. To be clear, Frank Iacobucci would never characterize himself as a poet. In accepting the F.R. Scott Award from McGill's Faculty of Law in 2006, an award in the name of a poet-lawyer-Law dean, he laughed at my suggestion that there might be poems hidden away somewhere in his files. But if Frank's work in building the cathedral provokes others to pick up the necessary tools, or to accept an offered hand, then it belongs alongside creative modes of memory and inspiration.

4

Cathedral as Congregation – Mentorship and the Extended Family

If my epitaph is: "He remained the same person in the values that he rep-resented, or the beliefs that defined him as a human being," that wouldn't be bad.

In 2009, when Frank Iacobucci spoke with alumni celebrating 30 years since graduation from law school, he reported being happy with their perception that he was still the teacher they remembered. As I have suggested, his involvement in reconciliation projects, both before and after that particular class reunion, underscores some of the features of legal education that shape the cathedral building capacities of jurists. On a more personal level, the skills associated with good teaching – acute ability to listen, heightened sensitivity, and commitment to knowledge-building and meaningful exchange – are precisely the skills necessary for Indigenous and non-Indigenous participation in constructive and ongoing conversations.

In accepting as a compliment his past student's observation that he hadn't changed, Frank conveys the fairly simple message that being a good person is more important than a list of achievements. It might seem a little disingenuous for a retired Supreme Court justice to expect people not to focus on the positions he has held and the successes he has enjoyed. And yet maybe a class reunion context is exactly where it would feel strange for participants to focus primarily on accomplishments or titles. Indeed, this is a moment in which we count on past classmates to have realized along the way how important it is to sustain decency and kindness along with success and even fame, and to weave values and beliefs into professional roles and the realization of projects. The alumni at the reunion knew very well that Iacobucci had transformed from "professor" to "the Honourable," but he was still importantly "Iac."

I was part of their journey to where they are going in life … I take pride in being a supporter and participant in the journey that others have had. There's no static or rigid definition of success.

As a complement to his emphasis on the importance of nourishing and sustaining personal integrity throughout a career, Frank's pride in providing support for others introduces another dimension to thinking about achievement and impact as a jurist.

It is easy to understand the pride and acknowledgement that teachers express in playing some role in the varied life journeys of their students. Like anyone for whom teaching is a vocation, Frank treasured his impact as significant supporter of the individuals briefly in his care. I want to dissect his words a little bit further, however, to make a connection between *participation in the journey that others have had* and the rejection of any *static or rigid definition of success.* While Frank probably meant to underscore the fact that successful journeys on the part of his past students came in all shapes and sizes, his words could also indicate awareness of the fluid and dynamic character of his own success. Perhaps filling the role of supporter and participant is precisely what Frank did best.

Again, teachers would not find this idea particularly surprising. It resonates with the insight that the best teachers teach students rather than stuff; they offer learning and knowledge rather than impart expertise and information. Against the backdrop of Frank's many ways of making $5 a day, the idea invites us to look for cathedral building not in the shape of the projects but in the shape of the people in the picture. The building of the Sagrada Familia in Barcelona, for example, is handed down from generation to generation of workers, each teaching and taking pride in the next. Cathedral building in this sense is all about the sustainability and evolution of institutions like the University of Toronto or the Department of Justice. In each one, Frank worked with people, listened to people, liked people, supported them, counted on them, celebrated them, and took pride in them. They became members of the team. He needed them and they could count on him.

The Supreme Court of Canada, or at least the collection of Iacobucci-signed judgments, would appear to be the leading contender for the label of Frank's most significant cathedral. Instead of taking that approach, however, I have looked beyond the court to Frank's work on residential schools compensation and reconciliation as one form of his cathedral building. Now, I return to the court and characterize it as the most striking of Frank's workplaces in which to consider the creation of human networks as cathedral construction. That is, his work in mentoring the people around him – his law clerks – is what counts in the words of the third worker. The clerks themselves constitute the cathedral. Frank's support and participation in their journeys constitute its building.

Frank's Law Clerks

Like students, law clerks retain their identity for a finite period: they arrive at the Supreme Court one fall and move back out the next. They have a very particular role to play within the relationships they have with the judges they call their own. The judge intensely relies on them for one year. They intensely focus on the research, analysis, writing, and recommendations required by the judge. At the end of the year they get replaced, and new interpersonal relationships between the judge and the next batch of clerks are forged.

We have already heard from numerous past law clerks to Justice Frank Iacobucci as they comment on his substantive engagement with challenging questions for law and society. Here, I turn to some of them for insights into what it is Supreme Court clerks do, how judges can act as mentors in important ways, and how that mentoring can have an impact on future leaders, teachers, and mentors for the next generation.

Law clerks are selected from applicants from across Canada's Faculties of Law. Rather than applying directly to the Supreme Court, students prepare their application materials and forward them to their deans who, in turn, send on a package of dossiers with a supportive cover letter introducing the individual students to the judges. The deans highlight the academic achievements of the candidates, their writing abilities, their experiences and activities, and their backgrounds. In choosing their clerks, judges pay attention to where they grew up and where they studied, how they present themselves and express their desire to contribute to the work of the court, and the areas and issues of law that seem to have attracted their energies and passion.

Every year a handful of students asks me to write reference letters in support of their applications. The conclusion to one of those letters, written for a student who had taken two courses with me and written an essay under my supervision, indicates both the kind of job the clerkship represents and the kind of person who can do that job well:

"I know from my own experience as a Supreme Court clerk that a law clerk should be ready for intellectual challenge, exacting and demanding work, and engagement with some of the most significant and difficult issues of our time. I have no doubt that this student would be a greatly valued contributor to the work of the justices of the court. I have watched this person develop and flourish as a young jurist and have been constantly struck by her integrity and complete dedication to all her projects. It has been a joy to teach her, and I know she will continue to learn, write, teach, and lead others."

When Frank was at the court, there were three clerks in each chambers. That is, each justice was supported by three recent law graduates, all of whom had excelled in their studies and were keen to delve into difficult legal issues. The clerkship is typically the first "$5 a day" job these law graduates hold, and the competition for the position is overwhelming. It is an honour just to get an interview.

Matthew Milne-Smith describes that experience: "The most striking thing about Frank Iacobucci is his ability to connect with people. I learned this from the very first time I met him, in our interview. The clerk interview is a very intimidating experience. You travel to Ottawa and meet consecutively with whichever justices had offered you an interview. One judge asked me about recent decisions. Another was famous for testing Anglophones' fluency in French. It's enough to put most candidates into a cold sweat.

"Most of the justices were kind and did their best to put the nervous law students before them at ease, but I can't remember a single clerk who didn't say that their best interview was with Justice Iacobucci. He has an uncanny knack for finding common ground and putting people at ease despite the natural intimidation factor associated with being one of the nine most senior jurists in the country. I think the reason he is so good at it is that he honestly, legitimately cares about each and every person he meets. It's not an act. It is simply who he is." (Matthew Milne-Smith)

What is it that law clerks do for the justices of the Supreme Court? The simple answer is that they review all the documents submitted to the court prior to the hearing of the appeal, and then help prepare their judge for listening to oral arguments and participating in decision-making. Indeed, clerks typically divide up the cases on which their judge will sit, and then each reads the written arguments provided by the lawyers for the two sides. Sometimes there are additional arguments to read in the form of factums filed by intervenors invited to provide a fuller picture of the issues at stake. The clerk writes a "bench memo" for the judge, indicating the questions to be decided, summarizing and assessing the relevant arguments and sources, and making a recommendation as to whether the appeal should be allowed or dismissed. Bench memo in hand, the judge is ready to hear oral arguments, ask questions, figure out how to respond to the issues, and, if asked to do so by the chief justice, to draft a judgment. The law clerk may be tasked with further research as the judge fills out written reasons.

While it gives a basic picture of the job, this description is limited and somewhat superficial. It doesn't capture the special relationship that can develop between judge and clerk, and the reasons for which the job lasts only one year and is reserved for people recently in intensive learning mode. Clerks bring enthusiasm for ideas and for addressing tough questions that don't have obvious answers. They carry with them recent memories of conversations in the classroom that pushed them to explore the justifications for rules, and to consider the possibilities of reform. They haven't yet developed particular areas of expertise or been immersed in particular areas of practice; they bring to the chambers the curiosity and openness that got them through their formal legal education and that continue to drive their approach to the spectrum of problems with which the Supreme Court is confronted every year.

All of this means that the clerks are more than research assistants. They are not simple providers of summaries and sources. Instead, they are co-creators; they are trusted and relied upon over the year they spend with their judges. While they retain their unique backgrounds and knowledge and abilities – those are, after all, what got them the job – they also incorporate the judge's voice and perspective into their thinking. They can work in more than one register: the direct voice that enters into energetic conversation with their judge and co-clerks, and the vicarious voice they adopt as they contribute to drafting a judgment. In response to the question of whether clerks "write" judgments (a question that often takes the form of easy assertion or indignant critique), I usually answer that only judges sign judgments. That signature signals the judge as author; the words are the judge's words even if first drafted by a clerk; the judge takes responsibility for substance and form. That takes nothing away from the fact that the work that precedes the signature is always and crucially shared.

Brian Beck offers a picture of one piece of the work experience: "It is 1995, the court is in session, and Mr. Justice Frank Iacobucci is seated together with (depending on the day and case) four, six, or eight other justices at the bench. It doesn't matter which case was being heard. What matters is that I was seated at the clerks' table along the side of the courtroom, to the left of the bench as the justices face the courtroom. Justice Iacobucci catches my eye and scribbles a private note, which the court attendant, the military and commanding Mr. Plourde, brings to me. I reply. The highly paid career lawyers making submissions cast nervous glances. Justice Iacobucci does this all the time, this public sharing of thoughts and intimacies with his clerks. And he does not need to do it. Certainly, he did not need my contributions while seated at the bench as often as he invited them. He did it to share the moment. I was part of his team, for a short while. It was a *big* team, one that obviously and most importantly included his fellow judges. But it was a team nonetheless, in his eyes. I feel that he made a special point of sharing his incredible experience and good fortune at every chance. It is hard for me now to find the right words: there was a feeling of immense privilege, as I sat there in the courtroom, passing notes with Justice Iacobucci. The helper always credits the team." (Brian Beck)

What is it that Supreme Court justices do vis-à-vis their law clerks? They demand their loyalty, their integrity, and their honesty. They count on their clerks to do the difficult work of reviewing and offering evaluation of the arguments put forward by the lawyers for the parties in each case. They require clear, well-justified analysis grounded in a solid understanding of the sources, the vocabulary and method of the legal tradition in which the issues are to be addressed, and the connections between resolution of this appeal and consequences for related issues and developments in law and society. They expect compelling justifications, in written and oral form, for the positions argued by the clerks, even if – and perhaps especially when – they disagree.

Beyond what justices count on their clerks to do for them, the justices can play a significant role in the trajectories of these young people. Without the formal title of teacher, the judges are constantly teaching their clerks how to ask questions, how to consider and weigh possible answers, and how to act as leaders and mentors to the people around them. All clerks get to know their judges in a unique and intense way, and they all learn from watching, listening to, and engaging with, the person with whom they are matched for twelve months. The nature of the experience varies of course across clerks, judges, and years. But the following account of working for Frank illustrates the potential that exists in the judge-clerk relationship for learning about the value of mentoring and the characteristics of good leadership.

"Ideally, being a great leader also includes being a great mentor. I do not believe that great leaders lead alone. Rather, they do two strategic, and inclusive, things particularly well. One: they build great teams. Implicit in this is the ability to instinctively recognize talent in others, no matter how non-traditional, or unconventional, the candidate might be perceived to be by others. Two: great leaders bring people along in such a way that they too become poised to lead. Not only does such mentorship guarantee one's commitments and passions will continue, insofar as mentees have been well-positioned to carry on the work, and, hopefully, build upon the legacy of the mentor, but the great mentors, like Justice Iacobucci, champion their mentees, and provide needed experiential counsel from a place of insight and expertise.

"[T]wo very important things happen when you are privileged enough to work with someone like Justice Iacobucci – both temporal. First, the mentor ensures that the work at hand is indeed accomplished, and the substantive and procedural work is impeccably done; this is in the immediate frame. Second, the mentor also casts his, or her, gaze into the future, grooming, guiding, enhancing, and cultivating in order to plant seeds of possibility in, and for, the mentee.

"I believe that exceptional mentors, like Justice Iacobucci, take seriously the task of producing future leaders, *and* future mentors … Implicit in this concept of mentorship is the recognition that part of the job of leadership is to make space at the table for others with divergent experiences, talents, insight, or interests that contribute to, and thereby further, the conversation towards the most informed decisions and ends. Unfortunately, many people prefer self-replication and ultimately choose a cookie-cutter approach to team-building, and therefore to mentorship.

"Not so with Justice Iacobucci. I know that his intellectual curiosity, love of life, and genuine interest in people led him to construct one of the most diverse chambers, intellectually, linguistically, ethically, racially, and in terms of class, gender, and sexual orientation – he did this intuitively, and instinctively as a great mentor would." (Camille Nelson)

For Camille Nelson, the first Black Canadian woman to clerk at the Supreme Court of Canada and later a Law dean, Frank's instincts and intuitions were worth watching, absorbing, and emulating as much as possible. It seems strange to say that instinct and intuition, by definition personal and unique, are things to be shared or taught. But the ability to work with the judge's voice in your head – something that law clerks are expected to do as they consider substantive arguments and possible directions for the law – is perhaps the same ability that allows you to appreciate the connections between the judge's instincts and actions, intuitions and leadership. That appreciation might not happen on the job. It may only be after the clerkship year is well over and past clerks lend support to the next generation that they notice how their mentors took on the tasks of, in Camille Nelson's words, "grooming, guiding, enhancing, and cultivating in order to plant seeds of possibility in, and for, the mentee."

Another one of Frank's clerks, Angela Campbell, connects the dots between delving into the substantive work before the court, incorporating the lessons her judge offered as a role model and guide, and taking on responsibility vis-à-vis young people in the context of university campus life:

"For twelve months, August 1999 to August 2000, I experienced my own intellectual and personal evolution, growing up as a jurist under the guidance of a man who for me, like many others, has modelled a life in the law committed to humanism, integrity, service and justice.

"My year within the Iacobucci chambers was one of enormous learning. Like other clerks, I had occasion to gain greater insights into certain areas of the law, and into the arts of appellate litigation. More importantly, however, working alongside Justice Iacobucci I learned about three core principles – relationships, responsibility, and respect – that have become central to my own work in law, higher education, and institutional administration. I will refer to these principles as 'Frank's three Rs.' This strikes me as apt since, like the three Rs central to basic education, Frank's three Rs have been foundational to a juridical career that seeks critical self-reflection and substantive fairness."

Between the R of relationship and the R of respect, Angela Campbell fills out Frank's R of responsibility:

"The Second R: Responsibility:

> Strip searches are thus inherently humiliating and degrading for detainees regardless of the manner in which they are carried out and for this reason they cannot be carried out simply as a matter of routine policy. The adjectives used by individuals to describe their experience of being strip searched give some sense of how a strip search, even one that is carried out in a reasonable manner, can affect detainees: 'humiliating,' 'degrading,' 'demeaning,' 'upsetting,' and 'devastating.' Some commentators have gone as far as to describe strip searches as 'visual rape.' Women and minorities in particular may have a real fear of strip searches and may experience such a search as equivalent to a sexual assault. The psychological effects of strip searches may also be particularly traumatic for individuals who have previously been subject to abuse. Routine strip searches may also be distasteful and difficult for the police officers conducting them.[23]

"In *R v Golden*, the court contemplated the scope and legality of police powers to conduct a strip search as an incident of their arrest power. Frank's majority judgment, coauthored with Louise Arbour, undertook a careful analysis of whether and when the common law of search incident to arrest may be unconstitutional.

"In discussions about cases like *Golden*, Frank urged his clerks to reflect on the vulnerabilities of individuals enmeshed in our criminal justice system. He further invited us to consider how these vulnerabilities impose acute responsibilities on those charged with administering that system.

"While my own career has had little to do with the administration of criminal justice, I have had occasion to think about administrative responsibility within the university. These contexts (criminal justice and universities) are distinct. But Frank's lessons about institutional authority and responsibility have provided an important touchstone when confronted with tough decisions.

"These lessons resonated, for example, in the spring of 2016 when a group of McGill students sought to convince me and others of our university's need for a sexual assault policy. I disagreed. I was skeptical about a university policy's ability to deal with campus sexual violence. I made the mistake of telling the students as much, bluntly and with little in the way of reasons, and did not listen to them as well as I should have.

"It did not take long for these students to communicate, vigorously and publicly, their displeasure with my stance. They made sure that I listened. Once I engaged with these students, remembering Frank's insights about institutional responsibilities, it became clear that addressing the issue of campus sexual violence required reflection on institutional accountability. The students made plain that universities have a responsibility to acknowledge campus sexual violence as a real challenge that confronts many students. Additionally, the burden of developing fair and effective processes for confronting this challenge cannot rest solely on the shoulders of individual students, especially those who may have experienced assault. That responsibility instead had to lie with the institution and those charged with administering it. The experience was humbling, but enriching, reminding me of the singular importance of institutional responsibility and accountability over individual views, particularly where there are evident social vulnerabilities and exposures." (Angela Campbell)

From putting candidates at ease in their interviews, to solidifying the sense of teamwork through the passing of individual notes, to ensuring and relying on a diversity of backgrounds, experience, and perspective, to passing on valuable leadership lessons to young jurists eagerly looking for them, Frank rolled teaching, motivating, and mentoring into his persona as Supreme Court justice. He seemed to do it effortlessly and intuitively, drawing on his years of experience with young people whether in classrooms, on committees, or in public service.

I cannot assert unanimity of Frank's law clerks on the kind of relationship they enjoyed with their judge; neither do I want to fill out an argument that positive mentoring capacity is a requirement of being a good member of the Supreme Court. Instead, I want to underscore the ways in which it is possible to combine the work of judging with the work of nurturing and modelling and guiding. The structure of the chambers – one senior justice with a small group of young jurists – gives rise to the marked potential for intensive learning about what it means to build trust, shape constructive interactions with people, and provide support for others as they develop their voices and figure out their pathways.

Raji Mangat reflects on her judge's place in the voyage she made from Vancouver to Ottawa and back:

"I was surprised and delighted when I received a call offering me the job. My excitement was not at all tempered by my father, who didn't think that a job as a 'clerk' would impress anyone, and wondered if I wouldn't rather be an 'associate' at a law firm. To him, law clerk sounded like someone who sat in a filing room filled with cobwebs and unfulfilled potential. I enthusiastically took the job.

"I entered the legal profession with some trepidation. While I did choose a career in law, early on I didn't have any sense that law would choose me. I started law school with some insecurity. Shortly after being accepted, my father told me that he thought my success in law might be stymied by my lack of connections. He seemed sad that he couldn't offer me an 'in' with the legal world and advised me that I should be prepared for the possibility that merit alone may not be enough.

"But that is not how things worked out for me. In many ways, I see myself reflected in Frank Iacobucci's journey. I relate to how he came to the law as an outsider of sorts; I relate to how he found his footing, and then stood his ground even when his parents' lack of formal education, or blue-collar vocations, were regarded as impediments to his advancement. My law school class had heaps more diversity than his, but I see that the legal profession, despite having made much progress, is still working out access and equity.

"The year I spent as one of Justice Iacobucci's law clerks was an incredibly rich one, and one that went by far too quickly. When discussing cases before the court during that time, Justice Iacobucci and I had many moments of agreement, and possibly even more of disagreement. Working with him was intellectually challenging: I frequently rushed back to my desk to research just one or two (or four) additional points to bolster my interpretation or rebut some nuance he picked up on in the case that totally escaped my attention. Justice Iacobucci's door was always open, and I grew confident in voicing my views on what the law is and what it ought to be.

"I have come to value those exchanges with Frank Iacobucci more and more over the years because they made me see so clearly that in a profession marked by tradition, strict adherence to procedure, and *stare decisis*, the best legal minds are those – like Justice Iacobucci – who are willing to revisit their conclusions, revise their viewpoints, and question their assumptions. I also learned from watching Justice Iacobucci at work that a true justice is one who engages both his mind and his heart, and has the courage to face the implications of his decisions long after the court file is closed. Justice Iacobucci's commitment to fairness, substantive equality, and his ability to truly engage with views that differ from his own are all traits that I share and try to embody in my work every day.

"My path in the law has been a winding one. It has taken me from Wall Street to The Hague, from securities class actions to social justice. The common thread has been a commitment to be true to myself – to retain my voice in a profession that typically speaks for others. This is a gift that I trace back to Justice Iacobucci's influence. I am confident that the lawyer I am today is not the lawyer I would have become without Justice Iacobucci's mentorship. He helped me find a home in the law. That might sound hyperbolic, but it isn't." (Raji Mangat)

Mentoring successive generations of lawyers, three law clerks at a time, might seem to be something particularly personal or private, something small in scope and important primarily on an individual level. It is all of those things, of course. But it can also be understood as big, even limitless, and all about investment in society and evolution of our world. Law clerks at the Supreme Court sometimes joke that their careers start at the top, so it's all downhill from there. We could say that their first job out of law school demands their explicit participation in building the cathedral. During their year as clerks, they delve into areas of law they will never forget, and they participate in the complexities of judicial decision-making. They learn to listen, to lead, and – as Frank's clerks suggest – how to act as mentors to the young people at their sides. While very few find themselves back at the court decades later, this time dressed in judicial robes, all of them might remain in cathedral-building mode through their responsibilities vis-à-vis others in their careers and lives.

What do *past* law clerks do? Who are they working with, and what difference are they making? Frank's clerks provide a good illustration of the range, and of the ripple effect of the one year of mentoring they received at the court. Some are teaching law students, others are running universities. Some are engaged in social justice advocacy, others are focused on Indigenous rights and reconciliation. Some write litigation documents, others write law journal articles. Some serve clients, others suggest policy directions.

The first time I taught law students, I handed out questionnaires at the end of the term in order to find out how I had done as a teacher. I was a doctoral candidate at Columbia Law School, responsible for three small groups of first-year students in their Legal Research and Advocacy course.

Some of the comments were extremely enthusiastic, some were engaged, detailed, and constructive, and some were highly critical and even mean-spirited. I went to see Arthur Murphy, a senior law professor who had been teaching first-year law students at Columbia for decades to think through how to respond to the feedback. Specifically, I needed to figure out how to avoid complete despair over the negative evaluations. He offered expected advice about how to put things in perspective and how to focus on the positive more than the negative. And then he offered counsel I have never forgotten and have always followed. Once you have tenure, he said, never bother to read formal student evaluations. Get your feedback elsewhere. Figure out whether you're doing a good job in other ways. How do the students improve in making arguments over their year with you? Do they ask better questions? Do they listen more carefully to their colleagues in your class? More generally, do they connect what and how they learned from you to what they go on to do? If so, then you're doing OK.

If this is a good approach for a teacher, it seems to be the obvious one for a mentor. Apart from the fact that there aren't usually formal evaluation forms to be filled out and read after the semester is over, the impact of mentoring can't be precisely assessed at a given moment. The mentor can never claim full credit or responsibility for the pathways, actions, and successes of others. But if those others identify a connection between their actions and their experience of being mentored, then it's there. The mentor did OK. The wide-ranging contributions made by his law clerks fall into the sphere of Frank's influence. That isn't to say that they followed precisely in his footsteps; unlike the stonecutter, Frank didn't simply train apprentices. Instead, he seemed to invite them to join him in the grander project of supporting each new layer of stone in an ever-expanding structure.

There is something else that Frank's clerks have done, something that goes beyond the list of their $5 a day jobs as jurists. Like the Supreme Court judge for whom they worked for a year, many of them have raised children, the young people whom Frank refers to as his "grand-clerks." Mentoring, after all, shares characteristics not only with teaching but with parenting. The clerks, and their children, have become part of the Iacobucci family.

This "intergenerational wing" of the cathedral is perhaps the clue to the mystery Aharon Barak was so keen to solve. Why did Frank leave the Supreme Court? It's true that the official answer – to spend more time with his family – didn't sound so convincing at the time, and doesn't seem to line up with Frank's relentless work schedule in the years after his retirement as a judge.

But maybe, in retrospect, the answer makes perfect sense if the term "family" is given the kind of broad and purposive interpretation that the Supreme Court is expected to give to constitutional frameworks. If, as a judge, he was building an intergenerational cathedral (by mentoring, teaching, counselling, and acting as role model for his law clerks), then after he finished being a judge, he seemed to take on that building role in a more and more explicit way. One could say he spent all his time with an ever-expanding family, day after day, constantly in cathedral-building mode.

Frank's "Family"

"It's about keeping people – families – together. That's where true happiness lies." –Alanis Obomsawin[24]

A focus on family is one way of understanding Frank's particular contribution to repair and reconciliation as a response to residential schools. We have already seen how that contribution belongs in general in the category of Frank's post-Supreme Court cathedral construction. Marked by Frank's intense appreciation of the significance of family and instinctive grasp of the tragic consequences of destroying family ties, it also belongs in the category of support for intergenerational renewal.

This intergenerational or "expanding family" character of Frank's work – symbolized by the mentoring of his law clerks while at the court – can be identified in other spheres of his post-court life. His first stop after leaving Ottawa was a university campus, the setting in which he had developed his talents in supporting students, colleagues, and leaders in education. The journey continued through a range of projects characterized by the construction and generation-to-generation maintenance of the "Canadian" cathedral. In all of these contexts, I suggest that mentoring people has been as or more important than the more visible or concrete reports, agreements, or even celebrated achievements.

First, then, as we have already seen, he went back to the university fully focused, as U of T president, on the mission of post-secondary education to engage generation after generation of young people. A successful university leader keeps front and centre the precious nature of close interaction with students, something that would have been easy for Frank given his experience in the classroom, at the Department of Justice, and in his chambers at the Supreme Court.

One of Frank's junior colleagues at Torys LLP, the law firm to which Frank "retired," remembers his experience as a student of first meeting Frank at the pan-Canadian Wilson Moot competition in 1995. David Outerbridge was a member of McGill's team of young pleaders, arguing a fictional case based on Justice Iacobucci's own Supreme Court judgment on equality law. Frank had agreed to act as justice of the tribunal that would hear the students and grill them with questions in the final round of the pleading.

In a very literal way, the running of the event was all in the family: Frank's daughter-in-law at the time, Melanie Aitken, was the chief organizer and director of the competition; his son, Andrew, volunteered for the day as a timekeeper. David drily recounts that, while "Frank heard the case in his usual thoughtful, reasonable way, Andrew sat below the dais, doing a very effective job, I thought, of holding up the time cards that told the mooters they had 5 minutes left, 1 minute, no minutes." It was after the intense day of pleading was over that David discovered what it felt like to be brought into the broader Iacobucci clan:

"It is not Frank's deliberative skills at the moot that I remember. It is his kindness and his humour, both on the bench that day and at the dinner that followed. As Frank stood with a group of law students, overlooking the U of T law school of which he had previously been dean, he interacted with the students in a way that made them feel as though he considered them just as important as his colleagues on the Supreme Court of Canada bench. Because he did. Frank treats people – all people – the way everyone wants to be treated – with kindness, friendship, respect, empathy, and understanding. Frank's wonderful wife, Nancy, and their children are the same, so welcoming, kind, down to earth, and engaging. What a great gift." (David Outerbridge)

This is the story of one student, someone for whom meeting Frank Iacobucci on a special occasion served as precursor to a life path intertwined with Frank and the Iacobucci family. As president of U of T, Frank could not possibly meet all the students for whom he was ultimately responsible. What he could do, however, is model constantly the key elements of the vocation of the university. If the people around him felt like they were part of his family, and at the same time got some sense of how important family was for him, then they might pass that on in their own leadership or teaching or mentoring.

Janice Gross Stein, one of University of Toronto's most well-known and respected professors and scholars, explicitly identifies mentorship as core to Frank's reach as university leader:

"I was never a student of Frank Iacobucci. Nor was I a colleague at the Faculty of Law, nor even at the University of Toronto when he was provost. I came to the University after his time, when he had already left academia to become deputy minister of Justice and deputy attorney general of Canada. I knew of him only by reputation, by the respectful tone my colleagues used when they talked about him. There was a noticeable absence of academic whine when they spoke about him. That absence stood out; it was exceptional.

"I first met Justice Iacobucci at a University of Toronto event. I was a new, if no longer young faculty member, and it was a large event. But somehow Frank found me, and I had my first encounter with the indescribable Iacobucci warmth, which envelops and charms. The twinkle in the eye says it all ...

"Frank became a mentor, a source of wisdom when decisions were difficult. When I struggled, unsure of what to do or which way to go, I would ask Frank if I could come and talk to him, for just a few minutes. He always made time. Not surprisingly, he is what today we call an 'active listener,' not only attentive to content but to tone and nuance, and, most impressive, always fully present. There were other pressing demands, deadlines to meet, decisions to be made, but in the time Frank gave me, he was completely focused on the conversation of that moment. It hardly needs saying, in the age of the smartphone, what a rare and unusual quality that is. We choose our mentors, and how smart was I to choose Frank. But the mentor has to agree, and how blindingly lucky was I that he did. To this day, when I worry that my moral compass is off course, I go and talk to Frank. I always come away wiser, more reflective, and humbled." (Janice Stein)

Beyond the university, there were other, less visible contexts in which Frank's special mentoring capacity was appreciated. According to John Butler, past general counsel of the Canada Pension Plan Investment Board (CPPIB), "few people know the story" of Frank as Conduct Review Advisor to a Board that oversees a national pension plan supporting roughly 20 million Canadians. In October of 2005, as a new school year started after Frank's term as interim university president had come to an end, the Canada Pension Plan Investment Board invited him to take on a recently created position.

Heather Munroe-Blum, past chair of the Canada Pension Plan Investment Board as well as past principal of McGill University, puts that invitation in context:

"To my knowledge, CPPIB is the only organization to engage an external conduct review adviser, a role that is more expansive than that of traditional ombudsman. Frank's warmth and compassion, powerful moral compass, and brilliant legal mind made him ideal for the position. CPPIB as an organization, and its employees and stakeholders – the working people of Canada – have been exceptionally well served by Frank Iacobucci." (Heather Munroe-Blum)

As general counsel of the board when Frank became adviser, John Butler explains the significance of the adviser's role and reflects on Frank's impact in that position:

"The conduct review adviser was intended to be an individual from outside the organization appointed by the board under the Code, who would serve as a confidential source of advice, guidance, and counsel to directors, employees, and persons outside CPPIB with respect to Code issues … This was a quite substantial and somewhat gnarly role, and it required a singular set of skills. The conduct review adviser had to have a reputation for gravitas, wisdom, trustworthiness, and approachability, such that individuals would feel confident in approaching him or her, but at the same time had to walk a fine line in appropriately interacting with CPPIB itself to ensure that its views on its own ethical standards were being respected and that non-Code issues were identified and directed appropriately.

"From October 2005 until I retired in December 2014, I had the immense pleasure and honour of working closely with Frank. Having mentioned how difficult and challenging the role is, I can say quite simply that Frank filled it every day with passion, enthusiasm, unerring judgment, and practical effectiveness. There is in my view no one more astute on ethical issues or better in coming efficiently and elegantly to the right answer than Frank. Our Code of Conduct issues intensified and grew more complex as the organization grew to over 1200 employees, several international offices (including London, Hong Kong, New York, and São Paulo) and in excess of $250 billion of assets … The CEO and I met with new employees every month for a 90-minute session designed to emphasize the importance of the Code of Conduct.

At the end of the meeting, we showed a five-minute video clip of Frank from one of his semi-annual employee sessions and, as we looked at the rapt attention being paid by our new employees to Frank's thoughtful and inspirational words, we often wondered why we had bothered with the prior 85 minutes.

"On a personal level, what a true joy it was for me to be engaged with Frank often during that nine year period. His intelligence, humility, clarity of thought, and warmth are attributes from which I learned volumes and which I will always treasure ... 'What would Frank say?' remains central to my thinking on an ongoing basis." (John Butler)

In yet another context, Frank turned his attention to long term investment, but this time not in the form of advising on the ethical contours of pension plan investments, recommending the establishment of a process of Truth and Reconciliation, running a university, or guiding young jurists. In 2006, it was the Higher Education Quality Council of Ontario that was looking for an inaugural holder of its chair, someone well suited to issues related to the design, sustainability, and development of institutions dedicated to high quality, accessible education.

In his message from the chair that introduced the first annual report of the Council, Frank used his storytelling skills to describe the path to ensuring excellent higher education in Canadian society:

There's a story of a tourist in Ireland searching for a certain stately home. Exhausted after getting lost trekking across the countryside, he asks a local farmer for directions. The farmer takes him to the beginning of a long, winding road at the far end of which, barely visible, stands the stately home. The tourist says, "That's still a long road," to which the farmer replies with a twinkle, "Sure then, 'tis a long road, but if't were any shorter it wouldn't reach the house, now would it?" The road to an excellent higher education system is very long, one with no proper end. There are, however, places along the way where a society can stop and check direction, take stock of provisions, and replenish its resolve to reach the goal.

Norie Campbell, who met Frank through serving on the Board of the Higher Education Quality Council, offers the following reflections in a tone that should seem familiar by now:

"Frank's passion for building a better education system – and through it a better Canada – is something I can personally relate to. I grew up on a farm in Southwestern Ontario and was in the first generation in my family to graduate from university; yet the opportunity I had to achieve a post-secondary education meant that I could still become part of the senior executive team at a major bank ...

"I believe the single greatest gift a career can bring is the chance to learn from seeing superb leaders in action ... One of the most important lessons I have drawn from Frank is how judiciously but generously he would use his good name and reputation to stand behind decisions. A blessing from Frank carries much weight, a responsibility he takes very seriously. Yet, he understands the importance of consensus-building and always puts in the effort to solicit other points of view before reaching his well-reasoned conclusions. Most importantly, he leads by example – always sharing his reasoning with others, in particular those whose opinions may have differed from his.

"To say that Frank makes the world a better place would be an understatement. And he brings out in others the desire and the confidence to do the same." (Norie Campbell)

Lance Finch, past chief justice of British Columbia and Frank's classmate from the UBC Law Class of 1962, captures the repeated essence of these personal reflections: "I have many times asked myself what special qualities Frank possesses that light up a room when he walks in and, without words, makes us all feel better about ourselves and our world. I do not know the answer to that question." (Lance Finch)

The individuals I have quoted all try to provide answers to the question. They describe Frank's impact through his concrete contributions, his approach to leadership, and his careful attention to building connections of trust and support. Most of all, they try to point to his special qualities, to articulate how Frank made them feel better about themselves and the world. Of course, there is a profound circularity that has to be acknowledged: the very people quoted are the ones suggested by Frank himself when asked to provide names of individuals with whom he had worked and interacted in a range of contexts. Given that closeness, it is perhaps not surprising that the accounts are uniformly positive. What is striking, however, is the emphasis on articulating the significance and impact of Frank as a mentor, and the sense of closeness in each of the mentoring relationships. As Janice Stein puts it, each of these mentees chose Frank. In each case, and over and over, Frank agreed to the task.

When we talk of Frank in cathedral-building mode, there is a good reason that his own voice is submerged, taken over almost completely by the voices and projects of others. In considering his impact as a justice of the Supreme Court through his law clerks, we pay attention primarily to their words and actions. In identifying his contribution to the long and perhaps never-ending path to reconciliation between Indigenous peoples and their non-Indigenous neighbours who share this land, we are invited to look not only at a nation-wide settlement but to ongoing lessons for learning and listening. In pointing to his impact on investments in Canada's future, we listen to narratives of individuals committed to sustaining those investments whether in the form of healthy pension funds or high-quality university education.

In all of these contexts, there is listening, trust, care-giving, and the explicit acknowledgment that important projects don't have an endpoint. There is no fixing or finishing; instead, our attention is turned to the importance of giving, building, and sustaining. I have tried to suggest that the congregation under construction *is* the cathedral. Frank's extended "family" is what he has built, one relationship at a time. The members of that family are handed tools to keep building: to teach in formal and informal settings, to translate in the sense of facilitating dialogue and mutual understanding, and to take on trusteeship of precious collective projects.

Frank's children tell the following two stories, among many others, about growing up in the Iacobucci family. They recount how Frank volunteered as a hockey coach without knowing how to play hockey: if his kids were going to play the sport, then Frank was going to be involved even if he had never even owned skates. And they recall with amusement how Frank turned to duct tape to hold the rusting family car together – an effective and fairly sustainable way to deal with the problem of rain water coming through holes in the roof. The stories reveal pretty simple insights. First, you can build a cathedral by encouraging others to do things that you never actually do yourself. Second, you can maintain it with very humble tools.

Frank's Partner

Even if we can say in retrospect that Frank retired from the court to spend more time with family, very broadly defined, that doesn't mean he stayed home. Neither does it mean that he ever challenged Nancy's position as director of Iacobucci family matters. Frank has said with strong conviction, to me and no doubt to others, that the most important thing that matters must be family. The prioritizing of family is probably the most significant shared value for Nancy and Frank. It is also the thing most explicitly guaranteed by Nancy's role in the partnership.

Turning to Nancy, however, is not solely about underscoring the allocation of responsibility and leadership vis-à-vis their own children and grandchildren. Nancy also played a crucial role in supporting the extended or ever-expanding family. For Frank, answering like the third worker always required a partnership: "*We* are building a cathedral" was the more precise response. As a team of two, Frank and Nancy were checking the scaffolding, recruiting members of the building team, and often directing the work. Her own version of cathedral building as a jurist underscores the idea that the "cathedral" is designed by, held up by, and made up of people.

The fact that Nancy was based at home meant that she was easy to find. When Frank and Nancy moved to Ottawa, they had bought a house in the west end where I had grown up. Their daughter, Catherine, was in high school with my younger brother. It wasn't hard to look up their address. And so, determined to introduce myself to the woman I had heard so much about from Frank as he gave me advice about applying to law school and for a clerkship at the Supreme Court, I turned up at their house one day, uninvited and unannounced.

I rang the doorbell and there was Nancy. I introduced myself. I am sure I was far from unique as a young woman student inspired by Frank. But I don't know how many others ever decided that it was time to meet his better half one-on-one. Nancy invited me in for coffee. She knew exactly who I was, and I found in her a new model and mentor – a generous, confident, interested, and brilliant mother of three. At that point, we shared the experience of being women in law. I had no idea then that I too would become a mother of three, figuring out how to combine a career as a lawyer, a life partnership with a peer whom I met just before my 25th birthday, and shared parenting of always challenging children.

For each of my three boys, Nancy sent a gift of a baby calendar to record day-to-day details of the first twelve months. It was a perfect present from one lawyer with a background in life sciences to another. The mix of zoological classification and legal categorization in our backgrounds naturally leads to the careful writing down of events and accomplishments on a regular basis in order to capture the development of a new little person. Even after going back to work as a full-time law professor after six months at home with each baby, I managed to fill out the calendar.

But sustaining a career isn't so compatible with keeping up that kind of minute attention to all of the needs and achievements of children. I try to remind my own law students, who may contemplate becoming parents in the future, or, in some cases, come to law school with young children, that it's not possible to balance absolute dedication to family with total perfection in a career. But it is possible to be dedicated to parenting on one hand and to excellence at paid work on the other as long as you reach out to, and lean on, and share with, others. That is a message that wouldn't have been heard in the 1960s, and it is a message that remains challenging to put into practice.

Nancy has always overseen family matters without the pull of an out-of-home office. One of the roles that Nancy plays is that of archivist and genealogist, something that goes way beyond the level of baby calendar. She likes to think about where people fit in. One of the projects she has directed is that of exploring the family's Italian roots: she has filled in much of Frank's mother's family tree, while information and names are still missing on his father's side, but not for lack of trying. On the Eastham side, there have been regular family reunions in Silver Bay on the Northeast Atlantic coast. And there are the annual Christmas letters, updating friends on the children and grandchildren. In those letters, Nancy puts particular emphasis on the work done as mothers by her daughter and daughters-in-law. The sons' careers are mentioned; in a family of two boys and one girl, only their daughter didn't follow Frank and Nancy to law school. But it's the raising of children, clearly the domain of the women, that gets the most attention.

All of this seems to sit somewhat awkwardly with Frank's enthusiastic support for women law students, clerks, and colleagues in their careers. It is complicated for Frank and Nancy to serve as role models to individuals who try their best to care about career ambitions at the same time as they care for kids. But there is no set recipe for getting that mix right. And indeed, Frank and Nancy *combined* show remarkable ambition in terms of both work and parenting, and a willingness to join complementary talents and strengths. Together they demonstrate what it is to be content with trying your best, muddling along, figuring it out, and celebrating success and the successes of others. Spouses, co-parents, partners, and closest companions, they structure each other's lives, day after day.

The intertwined paths taken by Frank and Nancy force us to take seriously the idea that supporting the people around us is the fundamental work of someone with a law degree. Law students might hear this message when they start their studies and again as they graduate. But it might only be much later that they start to connect the dots between studying law, the stops along their multi-faceted trajectories, and the value or impact of what they have spent time doing and being.

My perfect day begins with a cup of coffee with Nancy and ends with a couple of glasses of wine with Nancy.

5

Cathedral as Identity – Community and Belonging

Where We Come from

On a very hot Saturday afternoon in July of 2020, I walked out to check on my hanging baskets of flowers. Cheskie, the Hasidic Jewish baker of my neighbourhood, and his wife, Malkie, were paying a Shabbat visit next door. When Malkie saw me, she turned to her son and told him to "listen to the neighbour." He says he wants to be a lawyer, she told me. So you should talk to him. Understandably, the boy looked embarrassed. On top of having his mother talk about him to someone he didn't know, I wasn't the kind of person he would feel comfortable talking to. He could barely look up the front stairs at me – a woman in a sleeveless top and shorts, head uncovered, whose only connection to his own community seemed to be the mezuzah affixed to the front door frame.

I asked him how old he was. His mother answered. He's 12, she said, almost a bar mitzvah. I wished him luck, and congratulations in advance. And then I said that I was writing about someone else who decided he wanted to be a lawyer at the age of 12. This other boy, I said, was the youngest of four children; his parents, who came to Canada from Italy, didn't have any books in their house. That caught this kid's attention. Can you imagine, no books? I knew there would be books at Cheskie's house – mostly in Hebrew and Yiddish – and I also knew that this boy had lots of older siblings, none of whom would have gone to university let alone law school. Not only that, I continued, this other boy named Frank was told even when he got a little older that he shouldn't become a lawyer, that he didn't have the right kind of name. But he didn't listen to other people. He knew what he wanted to do and he stuck with it.

Odds are that a 12-year-old Hasidic boy growing up in Outremont, the neighbourhood of Montreal where 25 per cent of the population lives a strictly orthodox life governed by religious norms, won't become a lawyer. On one hand, his parents seem supportive of the possibility. Their bakery – Cheskie's – is famous in Montreal both for delicious bread and for its spirit of openness and positive neighbourly relations. On the other hand, his school and synagogue spheres make little space for figuring out how to grow up to be both a good community member and someone prepared for university education or a career in the legal profession. There are daunting, even if metaphysical, walls around the community. But the walls are indeed necessarily permeable in an urban setting in twenty-first-century Canada. The extent of that permeability will depend on this boy and others in his generation.

What I could do is share Frank's story. What might stay in this young man's head is the idea that someone who was told he had the wrong name, that he couldn't pursue his dreams, grew up to do what he said he would. I didn't emphasize the part about Frank becoming famous, I didn't list his accomplishments, I didn't tell this family about what it means to become a justice of the Supreme Court of Canada. But I did tell them Frank's last name. This young boy might never write it down, and if he does, he probably won't spell it right. But I have a feeling that he will remember what it sounds like. Regardless of whether he goes on to study law, that name might end up meaning something important in his life.

As one of the people mentored by Frank, I can trace his influence in my teaching, my approach to my students, my relationships with colleagues, and my commitment to the university. But I think Frank would like the fact that I referred to him in reaching out to someone decades younger, that I could share his story with a young person for whom that story would feel unfamiliar, unusual, and even a little exciting. There is a tangible and undeniable ripple effect, reaching individuals and communities not directly situated along Frank's path. They too might be included in the family. Strange to say about a young Hasidic Jew and his parents, they too might be part of the cathedral. After all, if the term "cathedral" can refer to people rather than to an actual building, it can also refer to the synagogue down the street.

This brings us to a final way of exploring the image of cathedral building, this time through the lens of identity and community. The people who do the literal work of building are often unseen, undocumented, uncounted. They have to rely on each other; they keep going in the hope that their children will live easier lives. Despite their contributions, they may not feel fully welcome in the cathedral once built. All of this resonates with Frank's own Italian-Canadian community, but also, in innumerable variations, with other communities in Canada each with their own histories and timelines.

Like the young would-be lawyer outside my front door, Frank grew up surrounded by lots of people with families just like his, interspersed with lots of people with very different backstories. On Commercial Drive, an Italian flag marks the Vancouver neighbourhood; as you look towards the ocean along the wide avenue lined with little stores and cafés, you see the mountains behind green, red, and white banners announcing Little Italy. It is a concrete reminder of this site of Italian-Canadian community, although the Italian character of Commercial Drive, almost a century after Frank's parents settled here, is sustained primarily through imagination and memory.

At the Peter A. Allard School of Law at UBC, an exhibit of images taken by Fred Herzog in the mid-twentieth century includes a photo of the houses called "Vancouver specials" that still fill the Commercial Drive neighbourhood. According to the descriptive text that accompanies the collection, Herzog, professionally a medical photographer with the Department of Biomedical Communications at UBC, was interested in capturing moments in time of ordinary people and their connections to the city around them. In the early 1950s, when he started walking around Vancouver and taking photos, Fred Herzog might well have crossed paths with a teenaged Frank Iacobucci heading home from Britannia High School with a group of friends whose shared identity came from living in Vancouver specials rather than from their parents' countries of origin.

Frank would have been one of the ordinary people of the neighbourhood, living in one of the ordinary houses captured by Fred Herzog's camera. His family would have fit the Little Italy designation of this corner of Vancouver. But a few years later, as we know, Frank wasn't walking those sidewalks anymore. Once he left Vancouver, he never lived in a home belonging to a space that could be marked by the Italian flag.

At the opening of the Frank Iacobucci Centre for Italian Canadian Studies at the University of Toronto, Frank referred to where he came from with his typical humour:

I wish my parents had been alive to see the Iacobucci name associated with a Centre. My father would have asked, "What did you do to deserve this?" And my mother would have added, "Why did it take so long to get some recognition?" This Centre serves as a constant reminder of the good fortune to be born of Italian parents – hard-working, honest, and insistent on values and the importance of education.

A 12-year-old who knows nothing but his neighbourhood and community and families just like his might find it incomprehensible that he would have to leave in order to pursue his dream of becoming a lawyer. The choice might not be quite so stark. After all, while Frank didn't stay in one place, he carried his Italian heritage with him. His example does suggest, however, that there is a necessary move to make in order to live as a jurist. Even if, unlike him, you return to the neighbourhood you come from, your participation in community life necessarily changes. You become an active re-imaginer of the space and the relationships and the possibilities around you. You notice the co-existence of communities even if you feel like you belong to only one.

Heather Munroe-Blum, past Principal of McGill University, captures the complexity of identity – both for Frank and conveyed by Frank's own path – with the following reflection:

"Over the years, I have participated in awarding hundreds of honours to distinguished people from all walks of life. Yet hosting Frank during his McGill honorary degree celebration was different. On the day his family, friends, peers, and academic community had gathered to celebrate his accomplishments, Frank gave me two gifts that I treasure. Now, you can imagine that it is unusual for the recipient of an honorary degree to offer a gift to those awarding the degree. It is akin to someone giving *you* a gift on *their* birthday.

"The first gift I received from Frank was a book entitled *The Kidnapping of Edgardo Mortara*. It is the true story of a Bolognese Jewish infant who, in the 1850s, had been secretly baptized by his Italian nanny and then kidnapped by agents of the Vatican on the pretext that no Christian child, by prevailing statute, could be raised by Jewish parents. This case became an international legal *cause célèbre* at the time, and the outcry contributed to Italy's transition from a state dominated by the Catholic Church to a modern, secular society.

"The book made me profoundly aware of the importance of identity and the indelible injustice that is perpetrated when one's identity and culture are taken from a person or community against their will … Yet it is the second gift I received – the gift of his friendship – that I cherish most." (Heather Munroe-Blum)

The two gifts, handed from one university leader to another, illustrate the significance of community belonging intertwined with the value of sharing across identity-delineated boundaries. It is unjust and painful to deny an individual's connection to community. But limiting an individual's interactions and friendships based on a restricted notion of community can be equally unfair and sad.

The pride felt by Frank for his Italo-Canadian heritage is mutual. Celebrated by the Italian-Canadian community in many ways, Frank's achievements as a cathedral builder can be counted and documented. As a Supreme Court justice in particular, he is one of the individual members of that community who has filled an important position of responsibility and leadership.

Marc Caira, whose family immigrated to Canada in 1960 and who later became the CEO of Tim Horton's, talks about how he first heard of Frank:

"Growing up in Little Italy in the St Clair and Dufferin area of Toronto, my family would sometimes hear of successful Canadians of Italian origin in the media, such as the Italian weekly, *Corrierre Canadese*, or perhaps the multicultural CHIN radio, but more often from other Canadian Italians in the neighbourhood or on the bocce courts. People enjoyed talking and reflecting on the achievements of individuals whose roots originated in the 'old country.' It created a sense of pride and hope for one's own family and future.

"Frank Iacobucci was a name that became deeply respected in our community. ... Although my family and I had never met Frank, he became a role model for many of us and the subject of discussion around our family dinner table of what you could accomplish in this country by working hard." (Marc Caira)

That doesn't mean that Frank's is a household name throughout the numerous Little Italy neighbourhoods of this country. Even the job of serving on the Supreme Court of Canada was not the kind of visible role that made it regularly to the front pages of national newspapers or of *Corrierre Canadese*.

In August 2019, the Honourable David Lametti invited me to walk with him through Montreal's Little Italy for the annual Italian Week festivities.

I was interested in talking with people about whether they were familiar with Frank Iacobucci's name. I noticed that everyone seemed to know David Lametti, federal minister of Justice at the time and a Member of Parliament for a Montreal riding. He in turn seemed either to know everyone he encountered, or to be ready to shake hands with people keen to introduce themselves. Before working together as McGill law professors, David and I had served as law clerks together thirty years earlier – me for Chief Justice Dickson, and him for Justice Cory, well before that judge became one of Frank's close colleagues on the bench.

As a politician, David necessarily counts on attention and public recognition. The Lametti name, at least during Justin Trudeau's time as prime minister, has become well known as that of a pretty famous Italian Canadian. With David at my side, generously introducing me to individuals and community leaders at the pavilions lining St. Laurent Boulevard from rue Saint Zotique up to Jean Talon, I ask whether people know the name "Frank Iacobucci." I am not so surprised when young adults shake their heads. I try a couple in their 50s, and am more surprised when they say no and, somewhat apologetically, ask whether they should. I have more luck when I speak with a community organizer in his late 60s who not only knows Frank but is happy to claim substantial credit for getting David into the cabinet. I get a confident "of course" when I ask a group of young lawyers whether they know the Iacobucci name.

All Italian-Canadian law students, they tell me, are proud of Justice Iacobucci. He is their judge with a vowel at the end of his name: their "Cardozo" but, unlike the judge that Frank had identified with as a student, firmly situated in the history of their own community in this country. They joke that if you don't know Iacobucci, you can't pass the Bar. One of them says Iacobucci was her favourite judge because of his simple, structured, easy-to-understand way of writing. Another says he has a photo of himself with Justice Iacobucci, taken at the University of Ottawa graduation ceremony in 2000, and remembers him as nice and soft-spoken. Yet another says that, for Italian-Canadian jurists, "it's a must" to have heard of Frank Iacobucci, while "it's maybe not the same for monsieur or madame tout le monde."

Before heading home from the Italian Week festivities, I hear an important message from both David Lametti and Tony Sciascia, a lawyer who works with the National Congress of Italian Canadians (for which, it turns out, Frank served as vice-president in the 1980s). You can't assume one monolithic Italian-Canadian community, they tell me. There are three major centres and foundations – in Toronto, Montreal, and Vancouver – and each is distinct. In general, there are complex relationships among the national level and the regions and districts. This is a community of communities, characterized by a variety of voices, interests, and leaders. As is the case for other identity-based communities in Canada, internal complexity might not be easily apparent from the outside. But that doesn't mean it isn't there, or that it doesn't contribute to the similarly complicated relationship of individual community members to their shared identity.

The fascination for me is "Where do I come from?"

In the summer of 2013, well after Frank's retirement from the court, the entire Iacobucci family set off for a trip to Italy. Sixteen people headed to Calabria, the region Frank refers to as his "mother's territory": all of them tracing this one path, inevitably merged with others, in their backgrounds and lives. By then, Frank had been made an honorary citizen of both Cepagatti in Pescara (2001) and Mangone in Cosenza (1996), and his name had been included on Toronto's Italian Walk of Fame (2010). Frank was impressed with the fact that his kids had taken Italian courses at university. He was grateful for Chief Justice Lamer's words of welcome in Italian at the time of his swearing-in – video-recorded for the benefit of Frank's father who wasn't well enough to make the trip to Ottawa and who told the chief justice that he had a better accent in Italian than his own son. In 2013, it felt important to share his fascination with where he came from with his grandchildren.

Frank's recognition of his roots comes along with fierce resistance to a unidimensional understanding of identity. *Notice the contradictions associated with Italy and Italians,* Frank tells me. *Creativity, imagination, and humanity – all juxtaposed with ruthlessness and real inhumanity. But then most countries are contradictions. It's interesting that the Italian diaspora tends to be much more unified than the "homeland."*

Frank continues: *What I don't like about the Italian presence in Canada is the initiative of Italo-Canadians voting in Italian elections. I also don't like pandering to the ethnic vote. And I'm not keen on what I would call soft multiculturalism or a sop to the "ethnic voice." We need to talk about real issues with integrity.* For Frank, any politicization vis-à-vis identity-based communities in Canada is problematic. *When I was with the National Congress of Italo-Canadians, asking for help from Canada in the wake of the earthquake in the Naples region, I asked why there couldn't be an "all-party" committee. I got no response.*

Frank's friendship with Aharon Barak illustrates how identity for him is about interaction, co-existence, points of connection, and unexpected discoveries. Both retired Supreme Court judges have told me how they have fun claiming each other, sharing and borrowing in equal measure. Frank jokes that Aharon must be Italian, with parents who struggled and worked hard to make sure their son excelled at school. Aharon in turn refers to Frank's sensitive soul as that of a fellow Jew. Indeed, Iacobucci could be a Jewish name given its reference to Jacob, son of Abraham. Frank is happy to consider the possibility of his unproven Jewish heritage; Aharon easily understands the hardships of immigrating to a new country, building from nothing, and retaining a sense of humour.

After spending time at the Barak apartment in 2016, I joined colleagues from the law faculty at Tel Aviv for dinner. I recounted to them how Justice Barak considered Frank Iacobucci to be a "Jewish judge," wondering whether they would find the notion either amusing or interesting to analyze. Every one of them was horrified by the label. There is no such thing, they insisted. What does it mean, a "Jewish judge"? Let's not even start to go there. All Jewish jurists, they refused the risk of any simplistic definition. Maybe it sounds nice to say that there is something intangibly Jewish about Frank's "soul" as a judge, but a positive stereotype is a dangerous stereotype, nonetheless.

Frank would understand. The humorous back-and-forth with Aharon Barak is a way to share vulnerability intertwined with confidence; the mixing up of identities underscores the possibility of cross-cultural trust, understanding, and friendship. Neither one subscribes to a simplistic picture of members of any group, especially the ones to which they belong. Instead, they enjoy the feeling of multidimensional overlap, of similarities across what might appear to be very different backgrounds. In particular, the Jewish-Italian exchange reflects the fact that members of both communities know what it feels like to blend in in some ways while remaining the "other" in others.[25]

Frank has always laughed at the inter-identity confusion and messiness that his "funny sounding" name produces. The confusion has accompanied him forever. In March of 2019, Frank's name was in the news as counsel to SNC-Lavalin, the corporation at the centre of a political crisis over alleged improper interference by the prime minister. The Iacobucci name –well known as that of a retired justice of Supreme Court of Canada – was presumably the reason for which SNC-Lavalin had turned to Frank for advice. Keen to negotiate a deferred prosecution agreement, SNC-Lavalin officials had met in the fall of 2018 with the clerk of the Privy Council. Ironically, the handwritten notes from that meeting, reproduced in *The Globe and Mail* at the time of hearings before the House of Commons Justice Committee, refer to "Yakabuchi"![26]

The repeated mix-up of the actual Italian and the hypothetical Japanese versions of Frank's last name is recounted with humour, time after time. We can recall how Frank's law clerk Raji Mangat was sure for a long time as a law student that Frank was the first Asian Canadian to sit on the Supreme Court of Canada. Like her judge, she laughs at how she discovered her mistake. It is important, however, to note the bittersweet character of the mix-up. After all, it is not so amusing to realize that no one with a name like Yakabuchi had made it to the court. Raji, like all of us, was still waiting. Not until 2021, with the appointment of the Honourable Mahmud Jamal, had there been a Supreme Court of Canada justice with an Asian-Canadian name of any kind.

Not so Funny Names

The less amusing consequences of funny-sounding names were something of which Frank was well aware. He understood that the seeming lightness of celebrating and sharing identity does not detract from serious considerations of how to acknowledge and sustain human diversity within law and in Canadian society. Names, backgrounds, countries of origin, community membership can too easily signal susceptibility to harm.

In the fall of 2008, Frank released the public report of the Internal Inquiry into the Actions of Canadian Officials in Relation to Abdullah Almalki, Ahmad Abou-Elmaati, and Muayyed Nureddin.[27] As the commissioner appointed by Order in Council to conduct the Inquiry, Frank examined the actions of Canadians working with the Department of Foreign and International Trade (DFAIT) and the Canadian Security Intelligence Service (CSIS) vis-à-vis these three individuals. Mr. Almalki, Mr. Abou-Elmaati and Mr. Nureddin, all Canadians with dual citizenship (Egyptian, Syrian, Iraqi respectively), had been detained in Syria and (in the case of Mr. Almalki) in Egypt. The Inquiry's task was to determine whether, and to what extent, Canadian officials had played some role in their mistreatment during detention.

The report is long, dense, and painstakingly detailed. The names and stories of the three detainees never became widely known throughout Canada, largely due to the internal and thus quiet nature of the Inquiry's process. But people working in this country's foreign and intelligence services were presented with a careful and thorough assessment of their words, actions, and omissions.

In the commissioner's statement that precedes the 500-page text of the report, Frank put the work into broader perspective:

"At its core, this Inquiry involves the appropriate response of our democracy in Canada to the pernicious phenomenon of terrorism, and ensuring that, in protecting the security of our country, we respect the human rights and freedoms that so many have fought to achieve. [...] Canada must choose means to deal with terrorism that are governed by the rule of law and respect for our cherished values of freedom and due process. This is a balance that is easy to describe but difficult to attain. However, difficulty of achievement cannot be an excuse for not trying to achieve that equilibrium."[28]

Frank made findings in all three cases that the mistreatment in detention had amounted to torture, something that the individuals and their families knew, but that it took the report to confirm. Further, he found that some of the actions of Canadian officials – for example, failure to act promptly and failure to make effective representations to Syria in the case of Mr. Almalki - had indeed been deficient in the circumstances and had resulted indirectly in the mistreatment suffered. In one section of the report, entitled "The Submission that 'More Would Have Made No Difference,'" Frank wrote: *"More strenuous efforts by DFAIT to secure access to Mr. Almalki would have at least sent Syria the message that the Canadian government was concerned about his well-being. Instead, DFAIT's failure to make such efforts [...] can reasonably be regarded as suggesting to Syria that Canada did not want Mr. Almalki back in Canada [...]."*[29]

John B. Laskin, invited by Frank to act as lead counsel to the Inquiry, suggests that Frank was asked by governments and government agencies to take on assignments like this because of the "attributes that he can bring to the resolution of difficult issues of public law and policy":

"[The Internal Inquiry's] mandate was to determine whether there were any links between the actions of Canadian officials (particularly in relation to the sharing of information with foreign countries) and the detention and any mistreatment of the three men; whether, if so, these actions were deficient in the circumstances; and whether there were any deficiencies in the provision of consular services to the three men while they were in detention. This mandate was to be carried out through a private but fair inquiry using means that would not involve the time, cost, and complexities associated with a full public inquiry.

"As Frank stated in his report, there was no template for conducting an inquiry of this kind. It was therefore necessary to design a process that would permit a private but thorough investigation while allowing all Inquiry participants, including the three men, to have input into the fact-finding process.

"Working with Frank and other Inquiry counsel to design and implement a process that would serve these objectives was both a challenging and a satisfying exercise. I am constrained in the details that I can provide. But I can say that Frank's conduct of the Inquiry consistently motivated us to do our best to fulfill his vision of a fair and thorough process – one that was acutely sensitive to all of the human dimensions of the events that we were examining." (John Laskin)

Frank's cover page statement as commissioner concludes with a reminder of the importance of combining the guarantee of individual rights with the assurance of collective security:

"Conducting the Inquiry has reinforced my conviction that we can and must continue to do everything possible to protect our country, and to do so with genuine respect for the fundamental rights and freedoms of Canadian citizens." [30]

As noted in the supplement to the public report,[31] released in 2010, it is troubling to confront evidence of compartmentalization of human rights concerns across Canadian government agencies such that concern for the human rights of a Canadian detainee falls under Foreign Affairs jurisdiction while excluded from that of Intelligence. By the time the supplement came out, Frank could acknowledge with approval improved consultation and collaboration between the agencies. The result of that collaboration should be a diminished possibility of stories like those of the three detainees who shared their names with that of the Inquiry.

John Terry, Frank's colleague who had worked with him on the Residential Schools settlement, was also a member of the Inquiry team. We heard from him earlier with respect to Frank's experiences that made him well suited for conversation with members of communities indigenous to this territory; here, I reproduce his reflections on Frank's particular attributes as a first generation Canadian:

"Anyone will tell you that when it comes to negotiating with Indigenous communities, the first thing is to establish a relationship based on respect. But it is one thing to say the word 'respect,' and another to convey that respect in every word, gesture, and action. With Frank, communicating that respect comes easily and naturally. One of the reasons for that – I think – is Frank's experience as an outsider/insider – a son of Italian immigrants who has been immensely successful while remaining acutely aware of his roots. People meeting Frank for the first time constantly remark on how comfortable they feel in his company, his self-deprecating humour, and his ability to relate to them." (John Terry)

The complexities of identity and loyalty, of trust and distrust, and of belonging and exclusion: all are woven into Frank's attention to the minute details as well as to the big picture. The strength of community, whether Indigenous or immigrant, nation-based or attached to the neighbourhood, always combines with its fragility. The histories told are plural, and so are the futures imagined.

In the introduction to Part III – Building a Cathedral: Called to Action – the third worker's words invited us to think about cathedral building in fresh or unexpected ways. The image of the Sagrada Familia in Barcelona reminded us of the unfinished, generation after generation continuity of the task. That of Notre Dame de Paris reminded us of vulnerability even of structures thought to be invincible. As Part III draws to a close, with a discussion of identity, diversity, and community, the Hagia Sophia in Istanbul might serve as a strong metaphor. In 2020, this cathedral building, having served as church, mosque, and museum over its 1500-year history, was re-converted to a mosque by the Turkish president.[32] There exists a wide array of responses to that dictate and change – some enthusiastic, others profoundly distressed. But, considered in the best possible light, the transformation might be said to underscore the fluidity of identity, the commensurability of communities, the evolving contours of heritage, and the co-existence of perspectives and opinions.

If a cathedral can be at the same time a mosque, then it can be a shrine or a temple, a chapel or a longhouse. It need not serve a faith-based group at all; instead, it can be a community centre or the campus meeting room for a student group. Frank would probably be ready to lend a hand to build any one. In doing so, he would be happy to celebrate along with the congregation; as we have seen, he might even incorporate members of that congregation into his ever-expanding family. As long as the doors to any cathedral are open, then the sharing, visiting, and mixing essential to real diversity, and evident in Frank's relationship to identity, are possible.

6

Individuals and the Cathedral – The Maker's Mark

In this last section on building a cathedral, we return to the stonecutters through history whose careful work was crucial to the slowly rising structure. These people were typically unsung and unknown, aware of how small they were in comparison to the huge cathedral under construction, and often keen to share in the grand aspirations of their communities. Most builders of great cathedrals never lived to see the finished product. They were necessarily part of a process larger than they were.

The humility that infused the job didn't mean cathedral builders weren't aware of their individual value in a collective and ambitious project. Skilled stonecutters would carve their mark on every stone they cut. At first, this was simply a method to keep a running calculation of how much they were owed – we might say a way of ensuring they received their $5 a day. As these maker's marks became more elaborate, they transformed into a sign of pride and a way to ensure an everlasting signature.[33] They are a reminder of the creativity and commitment of people: a reminder without which it might be possible to confuse the building itself with the social structure that holds it up.

The story of someone who builds a cathedral, a story traced by maker's mark, is thus both mundane and special, potentially invisible but very visible if you know where to look. Frank Iacobucci's story is the same. He is both ordinary and extraordinary, sometimes noticed and sometimes behind the scene. Stonecutter, wage earner, and cathedral builder combined, Frank has carved his signature on a wide range of stones and in an equally wide range of styles. Some stand out in the design of the finished building, others form the base hidden from view.

Also like the stonecutters of past centuries, Frank has never accepted true retirement and the accompanying and expected transformation from builder to observer. His good friend and long-time U of T colleague Michael Trebilcock asks rhetorically and with a good dose of humour, "What has Frank *not* done?" He then answers his own question with another: "Does he play violin?!" While Frank may never have learned to play the violin, that doesn't mean he wouldn't add it to his list of things to do.

There are real risks to accepting work beyond the age of 80, to keep adding stones each individually marked; indeed, there are good reasons to shift responsibility to less senior co-workers and even apprentices. Frank's modus vivendi, however, is to stick with the team and continue to pull his weight. As long as the building is incomplete, Frank keeps adding to it. Rather than trying to identify the cathedrals themselves in Frank Iacobucci's life, perhaps the greater challenge is in figuring out how to identify his signature on the stones.

What words can we find to capture Frank's own maker's mark?

Even if not framed in this way, this was the precise question addressed by participants in the "To Be Frank" colloquium organized at the time of Frank's 80th birthday. By structuring the discussion around two general themes central to legal education in twenty-first-century Canada – first, Diversity and Inclusivity in Canadian Institutions and Society and, second, Ethical Practice in Leadership, Governance and Law – I invited attempts to trace Frank's mark and its impact on his fellow makers. These are open-textured themes that pose hard challenges and demand constant conversations; indeed, they might constitute the conceptual cathedrals for which jurist-cut stones are a substantial component.

In his response to the question, Bob Rae – jurist, political leader, diplomat, and University of Toronto alumnus – invited us to look far and wide: "Frank Iacobucci continues to leave a deep imprint on our legal system, our courts, and our way of treating each other. The political and jurisprudential world in which we all work is profoundly different from what it was when he entered it as a young man in the 1960s, and for that he can claim some real responsibility. A deeply intelligent and decent man, whose good works will continue – 'if you seek his monument look around you.'" (Bob Rae)

Janice Stein, University of Toronto colleague and a non-jurist, pointed to Frank's pursuit of justice as a Canadian, and for Canadians: "Frank Iacobucci has contributed a sense of justice to what it means to be Canadian: a sense of justice that is deep, inclusive, complex, and balanced, leavened with a sensibility of what it means to be human and flawed ...

"Frank Iacobucci's leadership in all that he has done has always reflected that rich sense of justice. Every institution that he has touched within Canada is the better for it. Every person that he has touched in his many roles, at home and abroad, is the better for it. Justice Iacobucci has expanded our sense of what citizenship means. He has pushed the boundaries so that our understanding of citizenship is richer and more capacious. ... Were I to be asked whom I admired most as a Canadian, who best represented Canada to me, I would answer in a nanosecond: Frank Iacobucci." (Janice Stein)

These are striking testaments to Frank's contributions as jurist, in the name of justice, and for his country. They capture the diffuse and ubiquitous impact of Frank's work and leadership. They insist on the presence of his mark on our political and jurisprudential world, and on the quality and consequences of belonging to Canada.

But there is another way of describing Frank's maker's mark, a way that avoids trying to describe the cathedral or monument or legacy, and instead looks carefully at the underside of every stone. After describing Frank's achievements and contributions as a Canadian, Janice Stein turns to the one word that, for her, captures the person: "In my tradition, we have an untranslatable word to describe the kind of person that Frank Iacobucci is. He is quite simply, a 'mensch.' My tradition also tells us that being a 'mensch' is not simple at all." (Janice Stein)

John B. Laskin, Frank's one-time student and later colleague, turns to the same word: "I am told based on what these days passes for good authority – a Google search on the internet – that the Yiddish word 'mensch' has no precise Italian equivalent. The internet is not infallible. I say there is an equivalent: 'Frank Iacobucci.'" (John B. Laskin)

Being referred to as a mensch – a person who acts with integrity, decency, and kindness – is an honour not tied up in lists of achievements or completed projects. Frank would get that it is no less complimentary. He would no doubt like the fact that it comes from a tradition other than his own, a tradition referred to with pride and readily shared by Jewish friends and colleagues. And he would appreciate that this is a label particularly hard to earn. Mensch is a word that conveys, with deep respect and appreciation, the mark maker's unique impression. It may be exactly what Bob Rae is getting at when he points to Frank's imprint on how we treat each other.

Another set of words, from yet another tradition, seems to be a particularly good fit for Frank. These are terms used for people who make individual marks as they build something much bigger than they are; they are labels that depend on what others see in you and how they count on you; they are names for individuals who continue to learn with humility. They are the words found in Anishinaabe tradition for elders.

"In the Ojibwe languages, a number of terms apply to elders. The primary one is *gichi anishinaabe* ('great person'), nothing short of the paragon of humanity, a Mensch."[34] These are the opening sentences of the book, *Honoring Elders*, by Michael D. McNally. The word "mensch," it turns out, does have its equivalent in other idioms.

The introduction by McNally continues: "An 'old man' is an *akiwenzii*, glossed by one Ojibwe source as 'long dweller on earth'; to call a woman 'an old woman,' *mindimooyenh*, is a huge compliment. An elder is also known as a *gichi-aya'aa* ('a great/old being there' or 's/he that is greater'), a term that can also be applied to impressive or aged animals, trees, and plants. Even the verb denoting the plain fact of being aged, *gikaa-*, can be closely related by Native speakers to the root term for understanding or wisdom, *gikendam-*."[35]

All these words refer to elders – the people or even non-human living beings honoured in such a distinctive and significant way that they deserve to be called grandmother or grandfather. As McNally points out, "respect your elders" or "honour your elders" may be a central maxim throughout what he refers to as "Indian country," but the concrete meaning of that maxim depends on practices associated with specific cultural contexts. "No simple straightforward concept this"[36], respect for elders within Anishinaabe tradition rests on demonstrated community recognition and deference. It demands hard work both on the part of those who do the honouring and on the part of the elders themselves, "committed to the calling of learning."[37]

While aging is indeed associated with approaching the lifelong goal of becoming human, becoming an elder is not simply a consequence of adding years to one's life. In the Anishinaabe scheme – and Michael McNally underscores the sharing of many features with other religious traditions across time and space – the elder woman or man, a *gichi anishinaabe*, is "the ethical paragon ... and practitioner of proper relations."[38] Wisdom or sagacity is thus a practice on the part of the elders: "a performance whose worth may be judged by the community but is also a product of the mastery of gestures, postures, and ways of speaking that bespeak and perform wisdom."[39]

If we mix together the image of the cathedral with these insights on wisdom and respect, the elders can be seen as both the building and the builders. As individuals, they are themselves under constant construction: never finished, always evolving, increasingly awe-inspiring. That is why they are the most valued workers: leading by example, offering guidance to the next generations, welcoming young learners at their sides. They are the grandmothers and grandfathers upon whom the past, present, and future of their families and communities depend.

This appears to be a particularly promising and appropriate way to trace Frank's maker's mark through various permutations of building a cathedral. He listened to elders, learned from elders, and was welcomed by elders in his contributions to responding to the legacy of residential schools; one might say he joined the circle of grandfathers and grandmothers dedicated to the processes of reconciliation. Within the multi-dimensional Italian-Canadian community, he has been honoured as an elder, a leader, and a role model. At the court, and before and after, he mentored the young people around him; in the case of his law clerks, he accepted with real pleasure a grandfather-like role vis-à-vis his "grandclerks." Throughout, Frank's gestures, postures, and ways of speaking arguably have become part of the never-ending practice of sagacity necessary on the part of an elder.

If he *is* an elder, Frank would by definition have to deny the title. As McNally points out in his study, deep modesty and humility are characteristic of true elders. To be an elder is to be acutely aware of the limits of one's knowledge and wisdom. "This kind of humility is so deeply engrained in contemporary practices of eldership that its violation is a keen measure of imposture."[40] Elders are moral exemplars, indeed life exemplars, but they cannot acknowledge that stature. At most, they can situate themselves on the path to becoming an elder, always reaching for wisdom rather than claiming they have it.

At the close of the "To Be Frank" colloquium, the conversation turned specifically to finding an image that resonated with the example set by Frank. One participant suggested the character in Jewish mysticism of the *lamed vavnik*. "*Lamed*" and "*vav*" are letters in the Hebrew alphabet the numerical values of which add up to 36. At any given time in the world, there are exactly 36 *lamed vavniks* or 36 "righteous ones." There are so few that they are very special. Exactly as in the case of an elder, modesty and humility are crucial characteristics of any one of the 36. They are hidden and anonymous. No one knows who they are. They cannot fulfill the role if they think they are doing so.

Also like elders, each *lamed vavnik* lives day-to-day doing the right thing, setting a moral example, guiding and supporting others, continuing to learn, reaching for wisdom. The word in Hebrew for righteous ones is *tzadikim*, and so the full term for what are referred to in shorthand as the *lamed vavniks* is *tzadikim lamed vav*: 36 righteous ones. The word *tzedek*, the root of *tzadikim*, means "justice." To be righteous is to pursue justice; conversely, the pursuit of justice is the essence of righteousness. Carolyn Tuohy, a University of Toronto colleague and one of the people who repeats Frank's "three workers story," refers to Frank's contribution as "laying a cornerstone of empathy in the cathedral of justice." But this description seems too grand for the contributions made by *lamed vavniks*. They simply do justice – and empathy is always fundamental to the task.

This is not to say that the 36 righteous individuals are recognized jurists. That would confuse vocation with profession. Nor is it to assert openly that Frank just might be one of them. No one at the colloquium could quite do that – especially since to do so might erase the possibility! But it is to suggest that the mythical and mystical image of the *lamed vavnik* is an ideal to strive for. And I do mean to add that any jurist, whether recognized or not by name or deed, can be inspired by the intertwining of justice and righteousness.

The myth of the *lamed vavniks* goes further. The world depends on them. At any moment, these 36 are necessary to the functioning of humanity. To explore the connection between some of the things we can learn from Frank's example and the concrete sustenance of communities and the people within them, I turn to John Helliwell, a friend of Frank's going back to their shared Vancouver days. He finds in Frank's work what he sees as "impressively strong threads of civility and humility," and more specifically traces those threads, often left unrecognized, through shared discussions on principles, rights and responsibilities, trust, and collective confidence:

"One thing Frank has always stressed to me – whether discussing residential schools, immigration ... or the relations between people and police – is the importance of looking ahead, of learning from history rather than dwelling on past wrongs. Seen from this perspective, the most important of rights may be the opportunity to make a fresh start, where all parties can collaborate on building a shared future. I have seen both the importance and the promise of this approach in studies of human happiness. To dwell on past wrongs makes all parties think worse of themselves and others, and less likely to reach out to help others in the future. People are happiest living in an environment of mutual regard and shared values." (John Helliwell)

John Helliwell focuses in particular on the "strength of existing and emerging leadership and innovation within Canada's Indigenous populations"; he also insists on the possibility of a fresh start with respect to models of policing and incarceration. "In these examples," he says, "communities and institutions inspired by trust and opportunities show what can be done. But for these examples to become normal requires renewed reliance on principles and social norms, abandoning opportunity-killing risk management strategies, and recognizing that humans are essentially social, with inherent desires to work and play together in unselfish ways. And to laugh together, as Frank knows better than us all. In life, as in humour, he would remind us, the secret is timing."

These words underline not just the importance of Frank himself as jurist aware of the power of social trust and the possibilities for positive change, but the importance of people in general. People have the ability to work together to articulate and live by governing principles; they have the capacity to collaborate, to hold out a hand, to share knowledge, to imagine a future of wellbeing. In this vein, it is striking that the individuals who know Frank well emphasize the special ways in which he works with people, listens to them, likes them, connects to them, supports them, counts on them, celebrates with them, borrows from them, accompanies them, and takes pride in them.

It would be difficult, of course, for any individual to describe their own maker's mark. The attempts of others to describe Frank's seem to produce a multi-faceted picture: a mensch with a good sense of humour, a generous and wise elder, maybe even a righteous one participating in the pursuit of justice. Any of these images supports Frank's often-repeated emphasis on what he calls the *psychic returns* of any job, inevitably tied to its human dimensions. It helps to show how and why cutting stone both deserves concrete recognition in the form of daily wages and produces symbolic satisfaction in the shape of contributing to the cathedral.

Throughout the "To Be Frank" colloquium in 2017, law students in their 20s paid careful attention to the conversations among Frank's contemporaries, colleagues, law clerks, and family members. Particularly for them, the shift to critical scrutiny of Frank Iacobucci as mensch or elder signals a transformative notion of participation in society as a jurist. Instead of focusing solely or even primarily on Frank's accomplishments as Supreme Court justice (the title law students knew best), they were invited to shift gears: to think about interpersonal relations, social values, community construction, and the contributions anyone concerned with justice can make. Ideally, they found themselves thinking about their legal education, and trying to articulate the ways in which they were preparing to enrich the world around them through law.

In his famous essay "The Path of the Law," written in 1897, Oliver Wendell Holmes Jr. challenged the usual way of thinking about legal education, albeit from a different angle:

"I have been talking about the study of law, and I have said next to nothing of what commonly is talked about in that connection – text-books and the case system, and all the machinery with which a student comes most immediately in contact. Nor shall I say anything about them. Theory is my subject, not practical details."[41]

He went on to suggest a focus in thinking about the learning of law that intersects with the lessons gleaned from Frank's story:

"[W]e all want happiness. And happiness, I am sure from having known many successful men, cannot be won simply by being counsel for great corporations and having an income of fifty thousand dollars. An intellect great enough to win the prize needs other food besides success. The remoter and more general aspects of the law are those which give it universal interest. It is through them that you not only become a great master in your calling but connect your subject with the universe and catch an echo of the infinite, a glimpse of its unfathomable process, a hint of the universal law."[42]

Holmes, in emphasizing theoretical or intellectual engagement with law, underscored the connection he saw to happiness or human fulfilment. The study of law is not rewarding because of its path to success and salary; instead, if students focus on what Holmes refers to as the law's "general aspects," they just might catch an echo of the infinite. Iacobucci's example adds another element. If the students focus at the same time on people and their stories, they just might catch the promise of justice. That too is what makes us happy.

This combination of theory (the "why") and narrative (the "who"), more important than the implementation or even creation of rules (the "what"), points to the dynamic and ever-changing rhythm of learning law and of acting as a jurist. Argumentation and analysis in law is all about why and how to behave in certain ways. It is always about general principles, and at the same time always about real people. And it is always pedagogical, caught in an endless cycle of teaching and learning. Law students in this sense never come to an end of their legal education, even as they gradually take on the responsibility of teaching those who come along behind them.

Neither Oliver Wendell Holmes Jr. nor Frank Iacobucci might articulate these ideas in exactly this way, even though both of them would probably agree with the message. The American jurist who preceded Frank by a century would likely be surprised, however, in a way his Canadian counterpart might not, by the resonance of these ideas in feminist legal theory and Indigenous ethics.

When I think about my own experience as a law student, it seems to me that the combined attention to theory and narrative was a central feature of feminist legal theory, emerging and developing in North American legal education in the 1980's. A focus on women in law offered constructive critique and insights regarding the contours of care and responsibility, the potential and perils of relationships and community, and the necessary messiness of autonomy. Demonstrated by my feminist law professors[43] at the University of Toronto in their teaching, supervising, and mentoring, this sensibility shaped the varied paths as practitioners of law of all their students.

Three decades later, when I think about the experience of my own law students, some of whom I introduced to Frank at McGill in 2017, it seems to me that the exploration of Indigenous ethics has become a particularly fruitful terrain for combining the why and who in the study of law. In his book *Law's Indigenous Ethics*, John Borrows addresses the intertwined theoretical and pragmatic nature of the challenge of organizing the teaching of Indigenous people's laws.[44] As he shares the aspects of that challenge specific to Indigenous systems and communities, Borrows notes that in every legal tradition, the more general challenge is that "our knowledge and experience fall short of our actual needs."[45] "I believe that this challenge is experienced in every legal tradition, by every legislator, judge, lawyer, law professor, elder, chief, council member, clan mother, and Indigenous law keeper – even if they do not admit it [...]. Therefore, we need one another when we teach and practise law."[46]

John Borrows and others engaged in the teaching of Indigenous law know that the "what" and "how" deserve much careful attention. But the "why" is always and infinitely necessary, and the "who" – the actual people who build knowledge and pursue wisdom through learning and teaching – is foundational. This brings us back full circle to the importance of honouring elders, and of recognizing them as teachers both of and within their traditions.

Meaningful comparison of legal traditions never lies in lining up precise equivalents of concepts or terms embedded within the histories and frameworks of those traditions.[47] That does not preclude John Borrows, however, from tracing a challenge shared by individuals in respected positions across tradition-delineated borders. Similarly, we can undertake productive comparison by noting the common central importance of teaching across legal systems and traditions. Scholars, judges, leaders of religious communities, Indigenous elders: all are teachers. All give law its pedagogical character, its back-and-forth of questions and answers and arguments. As teachers, they are the principal stewards of their respective legal traditions.

This leads to a final observation as to the quality of the maker's mark left by Frank. Perhaps, in the end, we could say that Frank's mark, his distinctive signature as a jurist, was one of a teacher. Over and over, in every $5 a day job and beyond, Frank taught. Not just as a law professor, and indeed, as we have seen, his time as "just a law professor" was short. Maybe the stones he cut all have a teacher's signature carved into them. Maybe that is exactly what turns stonecutting *as a jurist* into building a cathedral *as a jurist*.

James Boyd White, in a convocation address to the law class of 2004 at the University of Michigan, told the graduating law students: "You will become an educator; this may in fact be your most important and meaningful role ... Having been taught, you will teach; this is a life full of promise, uncertainty, hope, and challenge."[48]

If a life as a jurist may be most importantly a life of teaching, then we might just have found the key to what matters most at a law class reunion. It would be strange for members of a past law class to get up and talk about how they have contributed to building cathedrals in their lives as lawyers. Among other things, the lack of humility would be striking. But they could, and perhaps should, report on how well they have taught, whom they have taught, what they have learned, and what they still hope to learn. From the perspective of elders in Ojibwe tradition, such an accounting of learning and teaching and striving would lead to, and justify, practices of respect and honour.

Perhaps the nicest aspect of turning to the role and importance of an elder is that the words for old man and old woman are equally complimentary.

This is also a nice observation relevant to considering feminist theory and Indigenous ethics together as sources helpful for rethinking the teaching and practice of law. Both a grandmother and a grandfather can hold the wisdom associated with being an elder; both can lead lives in which they are constantly learning to become more human and to nurture good relations with others. Both are teachers, taking on responsibility for educating young people, generation after generation.

If, as in the case of Frank and Nancy, both grandmother and grandfather are also jurists, then the different paths they take in law merge through this vocation as teachers. Interestingly the educator mode of being a jurist may be easier to see and cherish when the individual, like Nancy, has not also ticked all the boxes of successful lawyerly achievement. It is certainly the case that leading a public life in law can also invite the respect and honour given to an elder, but never simply because of impressive job titles or honorifics. Instead, only if done as a true seeker of knowledge and a sharer of wisdom, might that life in law earn Frank the label of *akiwenzii* or "old man."

It's not clear whether either Frank or Nancy could be considered an elder. What is clear is that Frank as grandfather co-exists with Nancy as grandmother. Each relies on the other. Perhaps only together might they be recognized as elders constantly practising what it means to be wise, what it means to teach and guide and support others, and what it takes to be honoured. It would not be surprising to discover that their individual maker's marks on the stones they cut as jurists are strikingly similar.

This brings us to the end of exploring what building a cathedral might mean for Frank Iacobucci, and what Frank can show others about building a cathedral. As Frank's story of the workers told us all along, the third worker simply articulates what all three are doing, but does so in a way both aspirational and humble, that incorporates acute awareness of the awe-inspiring dimensions and the potential infinite impact of the collective project. In this context, it is not so strange to think about an epitaph, as Frank did, at an event like a class reunion. In addition to prompting a search for words that might convey something of one's essence, a reunion can invite reflection about who will remember us and how.

In my tradition, something I only discovered when confronted with the imminent passing of my father, people say "May he reach 120 years" at the same time that they draw up contracts for the services of the Jewish burial society and for a plot in the Jewish cemetery. Between now and when he turns 120, Frank will likely keep taking on projects, and following and supporting the projects of others. There is much work left to do. Accompanied by an enthusiastic "May he live to 120," it is permitted, however, to imagine the remarkable range of languages and communities and creeds in which Frank will be honoured, by people with all kinds of names.

They will talk about how he did OK; they will retell his stories. They will remember lessons learned, advice given, and ideas suggested. For the people who never met him, they will learn about him from others. His projects will roll into new projects; his contributions to never ending conversations will flow into those made by new interlocutors. There will be many people, whether lawyers or potential law students or people who don't consider themselves within the sphere of law at all, who will not even realize how something he did had some impact on their world.

There will be thank-yous – *grazie mille, miigwech, merci mille fois.* There will be tears. Frank Iacobucci would insist that there also be a whole lot of laughter.

Epilogue – Foot Fragments: The Work of Building and the Journey of Justice

I wrote this epilogue in the summer of 2020. Fifteen years earlier, I first mentioned the idea of this book to Frank. A year later, I committed to the project, and he agreed to sit down and talk with me. I had no real idea about writing a book. Law professors mostly write articles; even at their longest, they are nowhere as large. A doctoral thesis might be similar in scope and length, but I wrote my own dissertation as three connected law journal articles – a format that Columbia Law School allowed and I greatly appreciated. Perhaps it is the fact that I am the daughter of journalists that explains why I have always enjoyed writing short pieces and why a sustained book was such a challenge. Whenever I sit down to write an essay, book chapter, or article, I typically have the whole thing already completed in my head. A few hours or days, or at the longest, weeks, of intensive typing brings me to the end of the document, and a little bit of rereading and editing brings me to its final form.

A month before he died, my father talked with me about the painful process of bringing a book to completion. It was November 2019, and he had been in long-term care for three years already. I told him that I was still working away on my Iacobucci project, and I asked him for advice on getting it finished. He knew Frank – through me, but also through shared conversations at the Ottawa barber shop they both went to. As I grew up, he had always been in "writing a book" mode – in between teaching journalism students and constantly producing newspaper articles and opinion pieces – and he managed to publish two books while leaving a third in the form of piles of typewritten manuscript in his home office. He told me, "If you want to do it, you just have to keep going." No point in regretting how much time it was taking, or that I had promised myself that I would finish by the age of 50 and here I was heading for 55. No point in going backwards in reflection on what stages the book had gone through and why. I just had to keep deciding that I wanted to write and then do so.

In the end, it seems that the summer of 2020 was exactly the right time to get to the end of this book. This was the summer of the Covid-19 pandemic and of related confinement, uncertainty, and shifting notions of time and space. It was a summer in which people were staying at home – with all of the complications that come with isolation and loneliness, or with the intense closeness of family members, or with the structural and social inequities that affect the security that home can offer. It was a summer in which people were protesting – against ongoing racist violence, against the slow pace of moving forward on meaningful equality, against the failure to confront painful histories and to construct progressive futures. This was a summer in which the Olympic Games were cancelled, soccer teams played in empty stadiums, and children's playgrounds made a slow transition to full accessibility.

Within this context, there are some obvious insights embedded in a book focused on Frank Iacobucci. First, individuals who thrive on human contact, who like people, who enjoy playing on a team, have a particularly hard time when they shift into remote or virtual mode. Like Frank, people value connection in face-to-face format; they need feedback in the form of real smiles and nods and confirmation that they are doing OK. Second, shared space and real proximity are conducive to the meaningful interactions foundational to learning, whether formal or informal. A pandemic that favours remote engagement and risk avoidance serves as reminder of the precious nature of the closeness associated with classrooms, corridors, and common rooms. Third, effective responses to existing inequalities, vulnerabilities, and systemic injustices in our world depend on ongoing learning and relearning, reaching out to rebuild, and immersion in the intensive processes of listening and reimagining.

In many ways, the pandemic simply underscored what we already knew: uncertainty is always present, change is always possible, justice is always crucial, and education is always central. These may seem like very broad observations or assertions, dissociated from the particular parameters of this project. But if we return to the foot fragments sculpted by Rodin, the image found in the prologue, we see how the placing together of small pieces can reflect a larger, if incomplete, whole. The fragments are not even full footprints. Instead, they form a collage, traces of paths walked with others: a collage that invites readers to consider their own stories and their own foot fragments, a collage that just might inspire ongoing conversations about uncertainty, change, justice, and education.

There is another, more personal, way in which it was the right moment to come to the end of the writing of this book. As the author, I had a lot of growing up to do between conceiving the project and bringing it to completion. That time has been filled with work as a law professor, work in which I have the incredible honour and responsibility of teaching and guiding young people around me. It has sharpened my appreciation of the impact of Frank as a mentor to my younger self as well as my more general appreciation of the importance of people and the nurturing of relationships.

With time, I realized that Frank's stories were best shared by others: a conviction that shaped the form and feel of the book, and invited the imagined interactions of Frank's voice (through interviews, speeches, judgments or publications) and the voices of those who know him in a broad range of ways. My own words turned into something like the glue holding the pieces of the collage together in juxtaposition. All I have done is make choices about how to place those pieces on the background paper – with attention to the diversity of colours, patterns, and textures that contribute to the overall effect.

Of course, the notion that we understand someone best by listening to others is not particular to Frank Iacobucci; the paths and projects and contributions of individuals in our spheres of influence are good reflectors of who we are and what we accomplish. But it may be especially true of teachers. Whether or not they hold onto that official title throughout their lives, teachers understand that their impact and their success are illustrated by tracing the directions taken by their students. In the time since I started thinking about this project, I have lost individuals important in my life, including senior colleagues in law teaching. I have paid careful attention to how their legacy is best assessed not so much by lists of their achievements but by the circles of their students, and the ways in which they were respected and honoured. They serve as reminder of the ripple effect of human impact.

From the vantage point of teaching law students for three decades, I think of my own teachers as the individuals from whom I learned to cut stone, whose academic mode of making $5 a day I followed, and whose congregation I joined. As a law professor, I support future jurists as they learn how to ask hard questions, grapple with principles, situate sources of law in social context, and appreciate the impact of rules and decisions on real people. It is my job to support them as they connect the before, during, and after of their formal legal education. It is my job to encourage them to find ways to build a cathedral.

In reflecting on the roles and responsibilities of law teachers, I have previously written the following: "We teach our students to re-tell well-known stories, to feel the weight that goes with the exercise of judgment and to participate in the constant reshaping of projects ... As law teachers with the obligation to teach our students how to know and do, we share stories of, and faith in, the actors and ideas and practices that have shaped law in the past. And, as our students develop their capacities crucial to their roles as jurists, we try to trigger their imaginations for the future."[1]

In early March of 2020, I had the opportunity to speak to colleagues at the University of British Columbia about the conversational feel of Frank's contributions within the sphere of Canadian constitutional law and beyond. It was particularly fitting to share my ideas in Vancouver, where I could visit Britannia High School and imagine Frank as a child, cross the UBC campus and imagine him as a university student, and walk past the Little Sisters bookshop and imagine him as a judge. After the workshop, I received a message from Hoi Kong, a past McGill student and now a colleague at UBC's Peter Allard School of Law, in which he shared an excerpt of a recent essay by James Boyd White that he thought I would appreciate. Given the way in which White uncovers a link between Saint Augustine and legal education – a link particularly apt given the cathedral imagery that frames this book – I share it here:

> It is possible to hope to have, as a lawyer, an educative transformation of another sort, leading to something like what Augustine comes to attain for himself: that is, an awareness of the evanescence of all things; of the unreliability of memory and intellect; of the essential emptiness of most goals of ambition or competition; of the springs of life and strength within oneself, upon which one may rely; of the hope of speaking always to another as that person is, in that situation at that moment, out of the center of oneself and of one's mind; of the openness of our texts and practices of authority to multiple readings and uses; and ultimately of the power each of us might hope to have of speaking in ways that are true and alive – for only through such speech is justice possible.[2]

Frank Iacobucci's trajectory shows us that studying law can lead in many different directions. It demonstrates the kinds of problems central to the study and practice of law, and provides insight into what exactly it is that lawyers think about and do. In offering advice to law students beginning law school at a pandemic-required distance, Frank reflected on the signifi-cance of legal education: *For me, it was the beginning of a journey that is ongoing. Even for an old guy like me, I haven't stopped learning about the law and about justice. It's a lifelong experience.*

Of course, most readers are not and will never be law professors, university provosts or Supreme Court justices; indeed, many or most readers will never go to law school. Even for those who never study law in a formal setting, the fact that they too can appreciate, through Frank's stories, the responsibilities and reach of jurists serves to remind us of how law shapes the world in which we live.[3] They will recognize the transformative potential that comes with lawyering: the importance of what James Boyd White refers to as "speaking to another as that person is" and engaging with the "multiple readings and uses" of our texts and institutions.

Among all of the people from whom we have heard in this book, I am the only one who went to law school specifically on Frank's recommendation. In an important way, he played a central role in literally shaping my own world. When he spoke to me back in 1986 about how much power lawyers have, he may not have had in mind the power to inspire combined with the responsibility to take care of the people around us. He was surely not thinking specifically of what White refers to as the "power each of us might hope to have of speaking in ways that are true and alive." But it is that picture of power that has emerged for me as I have thought about the ways in which individuals and their ideas and practices are central to the study and practice of law.

As I come to the end of the book, I share two final observations about Frank, both of which offer lessons for readers in the form of potential models for our personal practices. One of the things that Frank does is send handwritten notes to people: notes of appreciation or congratulations, condolence or simple connection. Each of those notes underscores a special relationship between sender and recipient. I have a small collection of those precious notes and the tiny pieces of text they contain. So do many other people. My guess is that the recipients of those notes have become senders of our own notes. If we imagine all those little notes, all those miniscule foot fragments, they add up to a remarkable testament to the importance of personal connections, the reach of individual influence, and the impact of people on the unfolding of our paths.

The other thing that Frank does is ask, of everyone he meets, "What's your name? Where do you come from?" People sometimes associate such questions with an attempt to exclude or an attitude of suspicion or disdain. But Frank's own answers show us how asking those questions is fundamental to making connections, to appreciating the complex and always-dynamic identities of human beings in our lives. How do we refer to ourselves? What's in a name? How do we spell it and pronounce it? And where do we come from? What paths have we travelled in getting to where we are? Whose families do we belong to? Of what communities are we members? Most importantly, what are the stories we tell and re-tell, listen to and share – as individuals, as workers, as parents and children, as neighbours and as entire societies?

Perhaps in the end, this book can be read as a compilation of little notes, and a collection of never-ending questions: a composite of one person and, at the same time, a collage in time and space that reaches out to countless others.

Appendix – Selected Sources by and about Frank Iacobucci

Materials by Frank Iacobucci

Journal Articles

Frank Iacobucci, "The Exercise of Directors' Powers: The Battle of Afton Mines" (1973) 11:3 Osgoode Hall LJ 353.

– "Planning and Implementing Defences to Take-Over Bids: The Directors' Role" (1980) 5:2 Can Bus LJ 131.

– "Recent Developments in Legal Education at the University of Toronto" (1982) 7:2 Dalhousie LJ 400.

– "Commissions of Inquiry and Public Policy in Canada" (1990) 12:3 Dalhousie LJ 21.

– "The Practice of Law: Business and Professionalism" (1991) 49:6 Advocate 859.

– "The Evolution of Constitutional Rights and Corresponding Duties: The Leon Ladner Lecture" (1992) 26 UBC L Rev 1.

– "Recent Developments Concerning Freedom of Speech and Privacy in the Context of Global Communications Technology" (1999) 48 UNB LJ 189.

– "Articulating a Rational Standard of Review Doctrine: A Tribute to John Willis" (2002) 27:1 Queen's LJ 859.

– "The Charter: Twenty Years Later" (2002) 21 Windsor YB Access Just 3.

– "The Supreme Court of Canada: Its History, Powers and Responsibilities" (2002) 4:1 J App Pr & Pro 27.

– "'Reconciling Rights.' The Supreme Court of Canada's Approach to Competing Charter Rights" (2003) 20 SCLR: Osgoode's Annual Constitutional Cases Conference 137.

– "A Tribute to My Friend, Professor Robert A. Burt" (2016) 125:4 Yale LJ 831.

Books

Robert A Burt, *Justice and Empathy. Toward a Constitutional Ideal*, ed by Frank Iacobucci, (New Haven: Yale University Press, 2017).

Frank Iacobucci, Marilyn Pilkington & Robert Prichard, *Canadian Business Corporations: An Analysis of Recent Legislative Developments* (Toronto: Canada Law Book, 1977).

Frank Iacobucci & Carolyn Tuohy, eds, *Taking Public Universities Seriously* (Toronto: University of Toronto Press, 2005).

Edited Course Materials

Frank Iacobucci, Stanley M Beck, Leon Getz & David L Johnston, eds, *Business Associations Casebook* (Richard De Boo Ltd., 1979).

Frank Iacobucci, Stanley M Beck, David L Johnston, & JS Ziegel, eds, *Cases and Materials Relating to Partnerships and Canadian Business Corporations* (Carswell Co. Ltd 1983).

Frank Iacobucci & Warren Grover, eds, *Materials on Canadian Income Tax* (Richard De Boo Ltd., 1973, 1974, 1976, 1980, 1983, 1985, supplements 1977 & 1979).

Reports

First Nations Representation on Ontario Juries. Report of the Independent Review Conducted by the Honourable Frank Iacobucci (2013).

Internal Inquiry into the Actions of Canadian Officials in Relation to Abdullah Almalki, Ahmad Abou-Elmaati and Muayyed Nureddin (Ottawa: Minister of Public Works and Government Services, 2008).

Police Encounters with People in Crisis: An Independent Review (Toronto, prepared for Police Service, 2015).

Selected Topics in Canadian Company Law Reform (Alberta, prepared for Consumer Affairs Department, 1975) (with J.R.S. Prichard & M.L. Pilkington).

Conference Papers (Published)

Frank Iacobucci, "Striking a Balance: Trying to Find the Happy and Good Life Within and Beyond the Legal Profession" (1992) 25:3 L Soc'y Gaz 205.

– "The Need for and in Praise of the Federal Court" (Remarks at the 25th Anniversary Celebration of the Federal Court of Canada) (1996) 10:8 Monde Jur 14.

– "Remarks in Tribute to the Honourable Peter de Carteret Cory on His Being Awarded the G. Arthur Martin Criminal Justice Award" (1999) 20:6 Criminal Lawyers' Assoc. Newsletter 45.

– "Droits, devoirs et communauté" (2021) 26:3 Lex Electronica 1.

About Frank Iacobucci

University of Toronto Law Journal Special Issue: "Education, Administration, and Justice: Essays in Honour of Frank Iacobucci" (2007) 57(2) UTLJ 154–368.

- Choudhry, Sujit et al, "Editors' Note" (2007) 57:2 UTLJ 129.
- Weinrib, Ernest Joseph, "The Teacher" (2007) 57:2 UTLJ 131.
- Beatty, David M, "Dean of Law" (2007) 57:2 UTLJ 145.
- Friedland, Martin L, "Frank Iacobucci and the University of Toronto" (2007) 57:2 UTLJ 155.
- Choudhry, Sujit & Jean-François Gaudreault-DesBiens, "Frank Iacobucci as Constitution Maker: From the Quebec Veto Reference to the Meech Lake Accord and the Quebec Secession Reference" (2007) 57:2 UTLJ 165.
- Alarie, Benjamin RD, "The Reasonable Justice: An Empirical Analysis of Frank Iacobucci's Career on the Supreme Court of Canada" (2007) 57:2 UTLJ 195.
- Duggan, Anthony & Jacob S Ziegel, "Justice Iacobucci and the Canadian Law of Deemed Trusts and Chattel Security" (2007) 57:2 UTLJ 227.
- Iacobucci, Edward, "Directors and Corporate Control Contests: Reconciling Frank Iacobucci's Views from the Academy and the Bench" (2007) 57:2 UTLJ 251.
- Trebilock, MJ, "The Doctrine of Privity of Contract: Judicial Activism in the Supreme Court of Canada" (2007) 57:2 UTLJ 269.
- Anand, Anita, "Carving the Public Interest Jurisdiction in Securities Regulation: Contributions of Justice Iacobucci" (2007) 57:2 UTLJ 293.
- Chapman, Bruce, "Allocating the Risk of Subjectivity: Intention, Consent, and Insurance" (2007) 57:2 UTLJ 315.
- Waddams, SM, "'Modern Notions of Commercial Reality and Justice': Justice Iacobucci and Contract Law" (2007) 57:2 UTLJ 331.
- Langille, Brian & Patrick Macklem, "The Political Economy of Fairness: Frank Iacobucci's Labour Law Jurisprudence" (2007) 57:2 UTLJ 343.
- Barak, Aharon, "Proportional Effect: The Israeli Experience" (2007) 57:2 UTLJ 369.
- Grimm, Dieter, "Proportionality in Canadian and German Constitutional Jurisprudence" (2007) 57:2 UTLJ 383.
- Weinrib, Lorraine E, "'This New Democracy …': Justice Iacobucci and Canada's Rights Revolution" (2007) 57:2 UTLJ 399.
- Moreau, Sophia, "The Promise of Law v Canada" (2007) 57:2 UTLJ 415.
- Cossman, Brenda & David Schneiderman, "Beyond Intersecting Rights: The Constitutional Judge as 'Complex Self'" (2007) 57:2 UTLJ 431.
- Roach, Kent, "A Dialogue About Principle and a Principled Dialogue: Justice Iacobucci's Substantive Approach to Dialogue" (2007) 57:2 UTLJ 449.

- Maxwell-Stewart, Hamish, "Justice Frank Iacobucci and the Revolution in the Common Law of Evidence" (2007) 57:2 UTLJ 479.
- Austin, Lisa M, "Information Sharing and the 'Reasonable' Ambiguities of Section 8 of the Charter" (2007) 57:2 UTLJ 499.
- Duff, David, "Justice Iacobucci and the 'Golden and Straight Metwand' of Canadian Tax Law" (2007) 57:2 UTLJ 525.
- Sossin, Lorne & Colleen M Flood, "The Contextual Turn: Iacobucci's Legacy and the Standard of Review in Administrative Law" (2007) 57:2 UTLJ 581.

Acknowledgments

As this project winds down over the 2020–1 academic year, there are many tangible pieces testifying to the space it has occupied in my life. There are index cards to stack and wrap together with rubber bands, file folders to refill with student memos and copies of speeches, reports, and journal articles, and binders in which to gather presentations and evolving versions of text. Three years ago, I installed a home desk solely dedicated to book writing in the front window of our living room. It is time to clear it off, to make room for new directions, and to store all the precious documents that have supported my work.

In the end, of course, it is people – rather than pieces of paper – that have provided true and meaningful support. From the moment I had the initial idea for this project, I tried to keep track of all the people who have contributed encouragement, hard work, and good ideas. As the book took up more and more time and space in my life, the list got longer and longer. It included not only individuals but groups, collectives, and places. Naming each individual became an impossible task. Rather than try to do so, I offer instead a picture of circles: circles of relationships and communities within which my thinking and writing and the building of this book have evolved.

The story started at the University of Toronto. More specifically, it began at University College where, as an undergraduate student leader, I met Frank Iacobucci during orientation week of 1984. My warmest thanks go to Frank and Nancy, for their constant kindness, hospitality, and wisdom. U of T is where I went on to study law, taught in my first year by Ted Alexander, Alan Mewett, Denise Réaume, Bob Sharpe, Stephen Waddams, and Arnie Weinrib – all dedicated, thought-provoking, and generous professors who guided us through the foundations of a legal education. The fact that University of Toronto Press has been so positive and supportive through the publishing process marks a lovely and appropriate return to my alma mater, and I am particularly grateful to Daniel Quinlan at UTP for his insight, optimism, and accompaniment.

Since 1993, the Faculty of Law at McGill University in Montreal has constituted the exceptional and inspiring community in which I have grown and flourished as a legal scholar and university teacher. As the content and form of this book illustrate, a law faculty encompasses many, always intersecting, individuals and groups: leaders, colleagues, administrative staff, and students. I am extraordinarily fortunate to have had support from all.

Over my time at McGill, the wellbeing of our Law Faculty has been in the hands of remarkable deans: Yves-Marie Morissette, Stephen Toope, Peter Leuprecht, Nicholas Kasirer, Daniel Jutras, and Robert Leckey. In their capacity as leaders, they have all offered support to colleagues and our projects. I thank Nicholas, Daniel, and Robert in particular – McGill Law deans over the timeline of this book – for their confidence in my scholarly contributions, their constructive comments, and their willingness to distribute faculty research funds in my direction. Associate deans of research at McGill have also played a significant role in supporting my research and writing, from inviting me to share early ideas in the context of a 2009 faculty seminar to encouraging the organization of a book-related colloquium in 2017.

Deans and associate deans, colleagues who take on governance responsibilities for a limited time over their career, remind us that collective participation and contributions are what keep universities going. In this vein,

I refrain from naming every one of my past and current colleagues and instead thank them all – for their friendship, their integrity, their dedication, and their constant presence in my life and the life of our shared academic community. For taking on the role of trusted readers of the entire manuscript, Angela Campbell and Stephen Smith receive especially warm recognition. My thanks and appreciation extend beyond McGill to colleagues at other Canadian faculties of law – in particular those I have worked with and learned from through the Canadian Association of Law Teachers, l'Association des professeur(e)s de droit du Québec, and research networks (Regroupement droit, changements et gouvernance, Centre de recherche en droit public) based at l'Université de Montréal.

Individuals who provide administrative assistance are often referred to as members of the "support team." That label is exactly right, and it invites us to highlight and underscore the crucial quality of the foundational support they provide. At McGill, my deep gratitude goes to the entire team over the years, with special thanks to Julie Fontaine, Michelle Sarrazin, and Maria Marcheschi for their work on the "To Be Frank" colloquium, and to Pina Ricco for repeated check-ups on my progress. Sharon Fitchett at Torys LLP in Toronto deserves special mention for her efficient, warm, and always positive assistance in responding to requests for documents and facilitating meetings with Frank over many years.

Students constitute the final, most dynamic and energy-producing, circle in a law school community. The McGill law students who started in September 2018 will graduate at about the same time that the book comes out, and I thank them in particular for their enthusiastic engagement with the book's themes and directions shared in a lecture I gave in the winter of their first year. A wonderful group of students actively participated in the "To Be Frank" colloquium in June 2017, and I hope the inspiration they felt that day continues to motivate them. In particular, a team of law students ensured the smooth running of the colloquium, and members of that team deserve special thanks: Emilie de Haas and Marie-Laure Saliah-Linteau (coordination), Meghan Pearson (media/design), and Ana Lucia Lobos (photography).

Finally, McGill law students offered significant support between 2006 and 2021 in the form of research assistance. They made my thinking and writing possible, and they all contributed creativity, excitement, and real passion for the project. It is an honour to name my "Iacobucci project assistants" in chronological order: Joydeep Sengupta, Joyce Tam, Thomas Lipton, Seo Yun Yang, Anthea Vogl, Katherine Webber, Miriam Clouthier, Nick Kennedy, Christophe Cinqmars-Viau, Alec Angle, and Maria Ceballos-Bedoya. My deep gratitude also goes to my research assistants on other projects over those years; I think of all of you as contributors to the book. Particular appreciation for student support goes to the Social Sciences and Humanities Council of Canada, funder of a team project, « Gouvernance pédagogique dans l'enseignement du droit au Canada », directed by Université de Montréal colleague Pierre Noreau.

While McGill has always been home base, I have reached well beyond its borders to develop this project. In organizing and hosting the "To Be Frank" colloquium (graciously co-sponsored by the McGill Institute for the Study of Canada and Torys LLP), I invited visitors from across Canada as well as across Frank's life and multifaceted career. Their generosity in covering their own individual travel costs, contributing written reflections, and participating in colloquium conversations was obviously crucial to the form and content of the book. In addition to bringing people together in Montreal, I have taken the project on the road. Invitations to share my project at different stages at Sciences Po (Paris), City University (London), the Halbert Centre for Canadian Studies at Hebrew University (Jerusalem), and the Peter A. Allard Faculty of Law at the University of British Columbia (Vancouver) connected me to ever-expanding circles of people who have enriched my thinking and writing. Like the insightful and constructive anonymous colleagues who reviewed my manuscript for UTP, the students, scholars, and teachers who listened and asked questions in varied venues all improved the final version.

The list of places associated with work on the book – places in which I have participated in thought-provoking conversations or written pieces of text – extends beyond the cities listed above. It includes Buenos Aires and Barcelona, Singapore and Jaffna, New York and Washington, Pine Point and Austin, and, closer to home, Toronto and Ottawa. What makes all of these places special are the people: good friends, valued colleagues, new acquaintances, and close family members, all of whom I am so happy to acknowledge and thank for sharing precious time and space. I always return to Montreal. This is where I count on individuals for the day-to-day support necessary for sustaining this project over the years. For those of you reading this, you know who you are – and I thank you for listening and caring.

I have written much of the text of this book at La Croissanterie Figaro, a café at the corner of Fairmount and Hutchison that serves as an inspiring spot for creative thinking and hard work. Situated a half hour walk from the McGill classrooms where I teach, and two blocks from the home I share with René Provost and our three sons, it is a good spot for reflecting on the smallest circle. Thank you to my mom, Patricia Bell, for believing in the project, spending time in both Regina and Montreal with our family, and sharing your talents as a brilliant journalist by reading my words and offering editorial feedback. Thank you to Daniel, Micah, and Ari for constantly offering important lessons in life, and for all your critical insights and hard questions. I love you, and I wish you many special projects of your own. Finally, merci à René – my closest colleague, best friend, constant partner, and fellow traveller. Writing, and everything else in life, is always better with you at my side.

Notes

Prologue

1 Shauna Van Praagh, ed, *To Be Frank. Colloquium Contributions* (Montreal: McGill Faculty of Law, 2017). All written contributions by participants are on file with the author.
2 "'Jurist' is a broad term referring to a thoughtful or learned person whose main subject, field or profession is Law, and who reflects about it strategically or in relatively abstract ways." William Twining, *Jurist in Context: A Memoir* (Cambridge: Cambridge University Press, 2019) at xiv.
3 Italics are used throughout the book to indicate the words of Frank Iacobucci. All the quoted excerpts from individuals whose names are identified in the text in parentheses come from the written contributions by participants in the "To Be Frank" colloquium.

Part I. Cutting Stone – Welcome to Law

1 JK Rowling, *Harry Potter and the Deathly Hallows* (New York: Arthur A. Levine Books, 2007) at 123–4.
2 Tom Watt, *A Beautiful Game: The World's Greatest Players and How Soccer Changed Their Lives* (San Francisco: Harper One, 2010).
3 *Ibid* at 7.
4 *Ibid* at 16.
5 *Ibid* at 91–2.
6 *Ibid* at 205.
7 Takashima, *A Child in Prison Camp* (Toronto: Tundra Books, 1971) at 46.
8 See generally Ken Adachi, *The Enemy That Never Was: A History of the Japanese Canadians* (Toronto: McClelland and Stewart, 1976).
9 See Peter A. Allard School of Law, "Allard School of Law History Project," online: *Allard School Law History Project* <https://historyproject.allard.ubc.ca/>.

10 Hunter McEwan, "Narrative Reflection in the Philosophy of Teaching: Genealogies and Portraits" (2011) 45:1 J of Philosophy of Education 125.

11 See Wesley Pue, *A History of British Columbia Legal Education* (University of British Columbia Legal History Working Paper, 2000) at 232–5.

12 Benjamin Cardozo, "The Game of the Law and Its Prizes" in *Law and Literature and Other Essays and Addresses* (New York: Harcourt, Brace and Co, 1931) 160 at 166.

13 Franz Kafka, "Before the Law" in *The Basic Kafka* (New York: Pocket Books, 1979) 174; a classic reading in first year (at McGill, in Foundations of Canadian Law).

14 William Cronon, "A Place for Stories: Nature, History, and Narrative" (1992) 78:4 J of American History 1347.

15 *Ibid* at 1376.

16 Greg Gilhooly, *I Am Nobody. Confronting the Sexually Abusive Coach Who Stole My Life* (Vancouver: Greystone Books, 2018).

17 *Ibid* at 120.

18 *Ibid* at 132.

19 Frank Iacobucci, 'Some Personal Reflections on the Legal Profession: Past, Present and Future' (Remarks to 1st Year Students, Faculty of Law, University of Toronto, September 5, 2003), on file with the author.

20 The approach referred to as "critical legal pluralism" and notably developed by Roderick Macdonald, professor and dean of law at McGill, incorporates this picture of the relationship between individuals and law in their lives. See Richard Janda, Rosalie Jukier & Daniel Jutras, eds., *The Unbounded Level of the Mind. Rod Macdonald's Legal Imagination* (Montreal: McGill-Queen's University Press, 2015).

21 Thomas King, *The Truth about Stories: A Native Narrative* (Toronto: Anansi, 2003).

22 Shauna Van Praagh, "Stories in Law School: An Essay on Language, Participation, and the Power of Legal Education" (1992) 2 Colum J Gender & L 111 at 122.

23 *Waldick v Malcolm* [1991] 2 SCR 456 [*Waldick*].

Part II. $5 a Day – Lawyering in the World

1 Martti Koskenniemi, Convocation address (Honorary Doctorate Recipient, McGill University Convocation, 2015), online: *McGill Graduation and Convocation* https://www.mcgill.ca/graduation/convocation/history.

2 James Boyd White, *Justice as Translation: An Essay in Cultural and Legal Criticism* (Chicago: University of Chicago Press, 1990) at 16.

3 Martha Minow, Convocation address (Honorary Doctorate Recipient, McGill University Convocation, 2011), online: *McGill Graduation and* Convocation https://www.mcgill.ca/graduation/convocation/history.

4 Brenda Cossman & David Schneiderman, "Beyond Intersecting Rights: The Constitutional Judge as 'Complex Self'"" (2007) 57:2 UTLJ J 431.

5 Frank Iacobucci, Convocation address (Honorary Doctorate Recipient, delivered at McGill University Convocation, 2003), on file with the author.

6 Frank Iacobucci, "Recent Developments in Legal Education at the University of Toronto" (1982) 7:2 Dal LJ 400 at 403–4.

7 *Ibid* at 405.

8 Frank Iacobucci, "Shareholders under the Draft Canada Business Corporations Act" (1973) 19:2 McGill LJ 246.

9 Ernest J Weinrib, "The Teacher" (2007) 57:2 UTLJ 131.

10 Frank Iacobucci, "Planning and Implementing Defences to Take-Over Bids: The Directors' Role" (1980) 5:2 Can Bus LJ 131 at 134.

11 Frank Iacobucci, "The Exercise of Directors' Powers: The Battle of Afton Mines" (1973) 11:3 Osgoode Hall LJ 353.

12 *Blair v Consolidated Enfield Corp,* [1995] 4 SCR 5.

13 *London Drugs Ltd v Kuehne & Nagel International,* [1992] 3 SCR 299 at 452.

14 David G Duff, "Justice Iacobucci and the 'Golden and Straight Metwand' of Canadian Tax Law" (2007) 57:2 UTLJ 525 at 579.

15 *Ibid* at 568.

16 *Ibid* at 578.

17 Frank Iacobucci, "The Practice of Law: Business and Professionalism" (1991) 49:6 Advocate 859 at 864.

18 Frank Iacobucci, "Message from the Chairman" in 2006 Annual Report (Torstar, 2006) 3 at 3.

19 See, e.g., Harry W Arthurs, "The Future of Legal Education: Three Visions and a Prediction" (2014) 51 Alta L Rev 705; Susan B Boyd, "Corporatism and Legal Education in Canada" (2005) 14:2 Soc & Leg Stud 287–97; W Wesley Pue, "Legal Education's Mission" (2008) 3:42 The Law Teacher 270; David Sandomierski, *Aspiration and Reality in Legal Education* (Toronto: University of Toronto Press, 2020).

20 Ross H Paul, *Leadership under Fire: The Challenging Role of the Canadian University President* (Montreal: McGill-Queen's University Press, 2015) at 81.

21 See, e.g., Charles Taylor, *Reconciling the Solitudes: Essays on Canadian Federalism and Nationalism* (Montréal: McGill-Queen's University Press, 2014), and Jeremy Webber, *Reimagining Canada: Language, Culture, Community, and the Canadian Constitution* (Montreal: McGill-Queen's University Press, 1994).

22 L Ian MacDonald, *From Bourassa to Bourassa: Wilderness to Restoration.* (Montreal: McGill-Queen's University Press, 2014) at 278.

23 Frank Iacobucci, *The Quebec Secession Reference: Law, Politics and Nationhood* (2009) [unpublished, on file with the author].

24 See Yves-Marie Morissette, *Le renvoi sur la sécession du Québec* (Montréal: Les éditions Varia, 2001).

25 Iacobucci, *supra* note 23.

26 Interview of Chief Justice Frank Iacobucci for the Osgoode Law Society (November 17, 1992).

27 *Ibid.* Drawn from pages 55–9.

28 *Ibid.* Drawn from pages 82 and 53.

29 See, on the risk of hagiography, Richard A Posner, "Judicial Biography" (1995) 70:3 NYU L Rev 502.

30 Roderick A Macdonald, "Still 'Law' and Still 'Learning'?" (2003) 18: Part 1 CJLS 5–32; Roderick A Macdonald, *Lessons of Everyday Law* (Montreal: McGill-Queen's University Press, 2002); Roderick A Macdonald and David Sandomierski, "Against Nomopolies" (2006) 57(4) N. Ireland L.Q. 610.

31 Shauna Van Praagh, "Seduction of a Law Professor. Review of Allan C. Hutchinson, *Laughing at the Gods: Great Judges and How They Made the Common Law*" (2013) 59:1 McGill LJ 211.

32 Benjamin Cardozo, *The Nature of the Judicial Process* (New York: Yale University Press, 1921) at 178–9.

33 Shauna Van Praagh, "Identity's Importance: Reflections of - and on - Diversity" (2001) 80: Issues 1–2 Can Bar Rev 605 at 617.

34 Cardozo, *supra* note 32 at 12.

35 Allan M Linden, "Custom in Negligence Law" (1968) 11 Can Bar J 151 at 153, cited in *Waldick v Malcolm* [1991] 2 SCR 456 at 473–4.

36 *Roberge v Bolduc*, [1991] 1 SCR. 374.

37 Paul W Kahn, *Making the Case: The Art of the Judicial Opinion* (New Haven and London: Yale University Press, 2016).

38 Cardozo, *supra* note 32 at 9.

39 Robert J Sharpe, *Good Judgment. Making Judicial Decisions* (Toronto: University of Toronto Press, 2018).

40 *Ibid* at 273.

41 See Robert A Burt, *Justice and Empathy. Toward a Constitutional Ideal*, Frank Iacobucci, ed (New Haven: Yale University Press, 2017). In the foreword, at vii–viii, Robert C Post explains that Burt "argued that constitutional decision makers should not imagine themselves as settling disputes, as creating clear-cut rules that would control the actions of rational actors. Constitutional jurists should instead understand their role as dynamically shaping with the complex psychosocial forces that cause and characterize intergroup conflict. When Bo [Robert Burt] died, he left a nearly finished manuscript that directly and beautifully addresses these issues and that has been brought to completion by Bo's dear friend Frank Iacobucci […]".

42 Aharon Barak, *Human Dignity. The Constitutional Value and the Constitutional Right* (Cambridge: CUP, 2015).

43 Cossman & Schneiderman, *supra* note 4 at 433.

44 Written contributions, on file with the author, by McGill law student participants [Brian Bird, Sophie Doyle, Aliah El-houni, Trevor May] in the 2017 "To Be Frank" colloquium, who responded to an invitation to submit brief reflections on Frank Iacobucci.

45 Karen Crawley & Shauna Van Praagh, "'Academic Concerns' - Caring about Conversation in Canadian Common Law" (2011) 34:2 Dal LJ 405 at 429, 432 and 442.

46 James Boyd White, *Heracles' Bow: Essays on the Rhetoric and Poetics of the Law* (Madison: University of Wisconsin Press, 1985) at 35.

47 Lorne Sossin & Colleen Flood, "The Contextual Turn: Iacobucci's Legacy and the Standard of Review in Administrative Law" (2007) 57 UTLJ 581.

48 Grade Review Policy, Faculty of Law, McGill University.

49 *Canada (Director of Investigation and Research) v Southam Inc.*, [1997] 1 SCR 748 [*Southam*].

50 *Ibid* at para 61.

51 *Law Society of New Brunswick v Ryan*, 2003 SCC 20 [*Ryan*].

52 *Southam, supra* note 49 at para 56.

53 *Ibid* at para 62.

54 *Ryan, supra* note 51 at para 51.

55 *Southam, supra* note 49 at para 57.

56 *Ryan, supra* note 51 at para 46.

57 *Southam, supra* note 49 at para 51.

58 *Ryan, supra* note 51 at para 44.

59 Sossin & Flood, *supra* note 47.

60 *Dunsmuir v New Brunswick*, [2008] SCC 9.

61 Sheila Wildeman, "Pas de Deux: Deference and Non-Deference in Action" in Colleen M Flood & Lorne Sossin, eds, *Administrative Law in Context* (Toronto: Emond Montgomery Publications Limited, 2018) 342 at 350.

62 See, e.g., Margaret Davies, "The Ethos of Pluralism" (2005) 27:1 Syd Law Rev 87; Sally Engle Merry, "McGill Convocation Address: Legal Pluralism in Practice" (2013) 59:1 McGill LJ 1; John Griffiths, "What is Legal Pluralism?" (1986) 24 J Leg Pluralism 1; Roderick A Macdonald, "The Swiss Army Knife of Governance" in Pearl Eliadis, Margaret M Hill & Michael Howlett, eds, *Designing Government: From Instruments to Governance* (Montreal: McGill-Queens, 2005) 203; Brian Z Tamanaha, "Understanding Legal Pluralism: Past to Present, Local to Global" (2008) 30 Syd L Rev 375.

63 *Delisle v Canada (Deputy Attorney General)*, [1999] 2 SCR 989 at para 62 [*Delisle*].

64 *Ibid* at para 48.

65 For a window into the liberal-communitarian back-and-forth, see Elizabeth Frazer & Nicola Lacey, *The Politics of Community: A Feminist Critique of the Liberal-Communitarian Debate* (Toronto: University of Toronto Press, 1993); Michael J Sandel, ed, *Liberalism and Its Critics* (New York: New York University Press, 1984).

66 Brian Langille & Patrick Macklem, "The Political Economy of Fairness: Frank Iacobucci's Labour Law Jurisprudence" (2007) 57:2 UTLJ 343 at 357.

67 *Delisle, supra* note 63 at para 68.

68 *Berry v Pulley*, 2002 SCC 40.

69 *Ibid* at para 48.

70 *Ibid* at para 50.

71 David M Beatty, "Dean of Law" (2007) 57:2 UTLJ 145 at 152.

72 *R v Gladue*, [1999] 1 SCR 688.

73 *Ibid* at para 68.

74 *Ibid* at para 37.

75 *Ibid* at para 61.

76 *Ibid* at para 70, 71.

77 *Ibid* at para 66.

78 *Ibid* at para 76.

79 *Ibid* at para 65.

80 *Ibid* at para 71.

81 Independent Review Conducted by the Honourable Frank Iacobucci, *First Nations Representation on Ontario Juries* (Ontario: Ministry of Attorney General, February 2013).

82 *Ibid* at 19, para 71.

83 *Ibid* at 85, para 355.

84 *M v H*, [1999] 2 SCR 3.

85 *Vriend v Alberta*, [1998] 1 SCR 493.

86 *Ibid* at para 139.

87 *M v H, supra* note 84 at para 106.

88 *Ibid* at para 91.

89 *Ibid* at para 97.

90 Robert Leckey, "Private Law as Constitutional Context for Same-Sex Marriage" (2007) 2 J Comparative L 172.

91 *Little Sisters Book and Art Emporium v Canada (Minister of Justice)*, 2000 SCC 69.

92 *Law v Canada (Minister of Employment and Immigration)*, [1999] 1 SCR 497 [*Law*].

93 *Andrews v Law Society of British Columbia*, [1989] 1 SCR 143.

94 *Law, supra* note 92 at para 51.

95 *Ibid* at para 53.

96 See inter alia: Peter Hogg, "What Is Equality?: The Winding Course of Judicial Interpretation" (2005) 29:1 SCLR (2d) 39; Christopher Bredt & Adam M Dodek, "Breaking the Law's Grip on Equality: A New Paradigm for Section 15" (2003),

20 SCLR (2d) 33; Bruce Ryder, Cidalia Faria & Emily Lawrence, "What's *Law* Good For? An Empirical Overview of Charter Equality Rights Decisions" (2004) 24 SCLR (2d) 103; Sheila McIntyre, "The Supreme Court and Section 15: A Thin and Impoverished Notion of Judicial Review" (2005) 31 Queen's LJ 731.

97 *R. v Oakes*, [1986] 1 SCR 103.

98 *R. v Sparrow*, [1990] 1 SCR 1075.

99 See Cass R Sunstein, "On Analogical Reasoning" (1993) 106:3 Harv L Rev 741; Emily Sherwin, "A Defense of Analogical Reasoning in Law" (1999) 66:4 U Chicago L Rev 1179.

100 *Henderson v Merrett Syndicates Ltd*, [1995] 2 AC 145, [1994] UKHL 5 at 20.

101 Hogg, *supra* note 96 especially 47–57.

102 *Law, supra* note 92 at para 62–75.

103 *R. v Kapp*, [2008] SCC 41.

104 *Ibid* at paras 21–4.

105 Denise Réaume, "Law v Canada (Minister of Employment and Immigration)" (2006) 18:1 CJWL 143.

106 Robert M. Cover, "Violence and the Word" (1986) 95:8 Yale LJ 1601 at 1601.

107 *Law, supra* note 92 at para 99.

108 *Lovelace v Ontario*, 2000 SCC 37.

109 *Ibid* at para 58.

110 *Ibid* at para 82.

111 *Ibid* at para 75.

112 Frank Iacobucci, "Legal Frameworks for Reconciliation" (conference delivered at the Pathways to Reconciliation Conference, University of Winnipeg, 17 June 2016), [unpublished].

113 Frank Iacobucci, "The Evolution of Constitutional Rights and Corresponding Duties: The Leon Ladner Lecture" (1992) 26:1 UBC L Rev 1 at 19.

114 Frank Iacobucci, "Recent Developments Concerning Freedom of Speech and Privacy in the Context of Global Communications Technology" (1999) 48 UNBLJ 189 at 190.

115 *R. v Keegstra*, [1990] 3 SCR 697 [*Keegstra*].

116 *R. v Zundel*, [1992] 2 SCR 731 [*Zundel*].

117 *Figueroa v Canada (Attorney General)*, 2003 SCC 37 [*Figueroa*].

118 *Ibid* at para 28.

119 *Ibid* at paras 28–9.

120 *Haig v Canada (Chief Electoral Office)*, [1993] 2 SCR 995.

121 Claire L'Heureux-Dubé, "The Dissenting Opinion: Voice of the Future?" (2000) 38 Osgoode Hall LJ 495; Ruth Bader Ginsburg, "The Role of Dissenting Opinions" (2010) 95 Minn L Rev 1.

122 Frank Iacobucci, *The Mapping Conference and Academic Freedom: A Report to President Mamdouh Shoukri from the Honourable Frank Iacobucci* (York University, 2010) at 1, online: http://www.yorku.ca/acreview/iacobucci_report.pdf.

123 *Ibid* at 35–6, citing Dr. James Downey, *The Consent University and Dissenting Academy* (Association of Universities and Colleges of Canada, 9 April 2003).

124 Iacobucci, *supra* note 122 at 40.

125 *Ibid* at p 53.

126 *Zundel, supra* note 116 at para 169.

127 *Ibid* at para 174.

128 Iacobucci, *supra* note 114 at 190.

129 *Syndicat Northcrest v Amselem*, 2004 SCC 47 [*Amselem*].

130 *Ibid* at para 87.
131 *Ibid* at para 39.
132 *Ibid* at para 46.
133 *B. (R.) v Children's Aid Society of Metropolitan Toronto*, [1995] 1 SCR 315.
134 *R. v N.S.*, 2012 SCC 72.
135 See, for example, contributions to these book collections: Richard Moon, ed, *Law and Religious Pluralism in Canada* (Vancouver: UBC Press, 2008); J-F Gaudreault-DesBiens, ed, *La religion, le droit et le "raisonnable"* (Montreal: Éditions Thémis, 2009); René Provost, ed, *Mapping the Legal Boundaries of Belonging: Religion and Multiculturalism from Israel to Canada* (Oxford: Oxford University Press, 2014); Benjamin L Berger & Richard Moon, eds, *Religion and the Exercise of Public Authority* (Oxford: Hart Publishing, 2016); Dwight Newman, ed, *Religious Freedom and Communities* (Toronto, Ontario: LexisNexis, 2016).
136 "Emerging Issues: Judging in the Context of Diverse Faiths and Cultures" (seminar hosted by the National Judicial Institute – Court of Appeal of New Brunswick and Supreme Court of Prince Edward Island Education Programme, St. Andrews-by-the-Sea, October 2007).
137 Benjamin L Berger, *Law's Religion: Religious Difference and the Claims of Constitutionalism* (Toronto: University of Toronto Press, 2015) at 87.
138 See the collected papers in Newman, *supra* note 135.
139 *Minister of Home Affairs & Another v Fourie & Doctors for Life International & Other; Lesbian and Gay Equality Project & Others v Minister of Home Affairs* 2006 1 SA 524 [CC], paras. 90–3 & 98) judgment by Sachs J., cited by Newman, *supra* note 135 at 8–9.
140 *Adler v Ontario*, [1996] 3 SCR 609 [*Adler*].
141 *Trinity Western University v British Columbia College of Teachers*, 2001 SCC 31 [*TWU*].
142 *Adler, supra* note 140 at para 35.
143 *TWU, supra* note 141 at para 36.
144 *Ibid* at para 34.
145 *Law Society of British Columbia v Trinity Western University*, 2018 SCC 32.
146 *Amselem, supra* note 129 at para 50.
147 Shauna Van Praagh, "Welcome to the Neighbourhood: Religion, Law and Living Together" in Newman, *supra* note 135 at 65.
148 See Pierre Anctil & Ira Robinson, eds, *Les juifs hassidiques de Montréal* (Montréal: Presses de l'Université de Montréal, 2019).
149 Shauna Van Praagh, "The Chutzpah of Chasidism" (1996) 11:2 CJLS 193; Shauna Van Praagh, "View from the Succah: Religion and Neighbourly Relations" in Richard Moon, *supra* note 135, 20; Shauna Van Praagh, "Quelques leçons des enfants hassidiques pour le droit" in Pierre Anctil & Ira Robinson, *supra* note 148.
150 Cardozo, *supra* note 32 at 12.
151 Frank Iacobucci, *The Law in My Life – Some Reflections*, presented to The Canadian Bar Association, British Columbia Branch at the San Diego Conference (2013).
152 See Consultative Group on Research and Education in Law, *Law and Learning – Report to the Social Sciences and Humanities Research Council of Canada* (Canada, 1983) (Chair: Harry W. Arthurs) – known as the "Arthurs Report."
153 Sabine Barles, "History of Waste Management and the Social and Cultural Representations of Waste" in Mauro Agnoletti & S Neri Serneri, eds, *Basic Environmental History* (Geneva: Spring International Publishing, 2014) 199.
154 Iacobucci, *supra* note 151.
155 Macdonald, *Lessons of Everyday Law, supra* note 30.

Part III. Building a Cathedral – Called to Action

1 John Green, *Cathedrals of the World Coloring Book* (New York: Dover Publications, 1994).
2 See Alice Woolley & Adam Dodek, *In Search of the Ethical Lawyer: Stories from the Canadian Legal Profession* (Vancouver: UBC Press, 2016).
3 *Indian Residential Schools Settlement Agreement* (8 May 2006), online: https://www
.residentialschoolsettlement.ca/IRS%20Settlement%20Agreement-%20ENGLISH.pdf.
4 *Class Actions and IRS Settlement*, by Frank Iacobucci (Cambridge: The Cambridge Lectures – Fitzpatrick Hall, Queens' College, 2007) at 2.
5 Cited in the introduction of Truth and Reconciliation Commission of Canada, *Honouring the Truth, Reconciling for the Future. Summary of the Final Report of the Truth and Reconciliation Commission of Canada* (Canada: Truth and Reconciliation Commission, 2015) at 2.
6 *Report of the Royal Commission on Aboriginal People* (Ottawa: Supply and Services Canada, 1996).
7 Truth and Reconciliation Commission of Canada, *Canada's Residential Schools: The History, 1939 to 2000, The Final Report of the Truth and Reconciliation Commission of Canada,* part 2, vol 1 (Canada: Truth and Reconciliation Commission, 2015) at 572.
8 *Quatell v Canada*, 2006 BCSC 1840 at para 9.
9 Law Commission of Canada, *Restoring Dignity: Responding to Child Abuse in Canadian Institutions* (Ottawa: Law Commission of Canada, 2000).
10 Prime Minister Stephen Harper, *Statement of Apology to Former Students of Indian Residential Schools* (Government of Canada, 2008).
11 All taken from Truth and Reconciliation Commission of Canada, *They Came for the Children: Canada, Aboriginal Peoples and the Residential Schools* (Canada: Truth and Reconciliation Commission, 2012).
12 Quoted in Truth and Reconciliation Commission of Canada, *Summary of the Final Report,* *supra* note 5 at 9–10.
13 Truth and Reconciliation Commission of Canada, *Truth and Reconciliation Commission of Canada: Calls to Action* (Canada: Truth and Reconciliation Commission, 2015) at 3.
14 Gerald Torres & Kathryn Milun, "Stories and Standing: The Legal Meaning of Identity" in Dan Danielsen & Karen Engle, eds, *After Identity: A Reader in Law and Culture* (New York: Routledge, 1995) 129 at 136.
15 Macdonald, *supra* note 30; Martha Nussbaum, "Cultivating Humanity in Legal Education" (2003) 70:1 U Chic L Rev 265.
16 James Boyd White, *From Expectation to Experience: Essays on Law and Legal Education* (Ann Arbor: University of Michigan Press, 1999) at 11.
17 On the importance of ongoing learning within a reconciliation framework, see, e.g., Harold Cardinal & Walter Hildebrand, *Treaty Elders of Saskatchewan: Our Dream Is That Our Peoples Will One Day Be Clearly Recognized as Nations* (Calgary: University of Calgary Press, 2000); Lance SG Finch, *The Duty to Learn: Taking Account of Indigenous Legal Orders in Practice* (Vancouver: Continuing Legal Education Society, 2012).
18 First Nations Representation on Ontario Juries – Report of the Independent Review Conducted by the Honourable Frank Iacobucci. (Ontario: February 2013).
19 Following the 17 Recommendations, set out in the Introduction. *Ibid* at 11.
20 *Tsleil-Waututh Nation v Canada (Attorney General)*, 2018 FCA 153.
21 *Ibid* at para 759.
22 Rita Joe, "I Lost My Talk" reproduced in Patricia A Monture & Patricia D McGuire, eds, *First Voices – An Aboriginal Women's Reader* (Toronto: Inanna Publications and Education, 2009) 129.

23 *R v Golden*, 2001 SCC 83 at para 90.
24 From Alanis Obomsawin, *Our People Will Be Healed* (National Film Board, 2017).
25 Robert A Burt, *Two Jewish Justices. Outcasts in the Promised Land* (Berkeley: University of California Press, 1988).
26 *The Globe and Mail*, "Wernick urged SNC chief to ask for a deal directly," *The Globe and Mail* (9 March 2019) A12: reproduction of handwritten notes taken at the meeting of 18 September 2018, by Catrina Tapley, deputy-secretary of the Cabinet for operations.
27 Frank Iacobucci, *Internal Inquiry into the Actions of Canadian Officials in Relation to Abdullah Almalki, Ahmad Abou-Elmaati and Muayyed Nureddin* (Ottawa: Minister of Public Works and Government Services, 2008).
28 *Ibid* at 5.
29 *Ibid* at 430–1, para 116.
30 *Ibid* at 5.
31 Frank Iacobucci, *Internal Inquiry into the Actions of Canadian Officials in Relation to Abdullah Almalki, Ahmad Abou-Elmaati and Muayyed Nureddin. Supplement to Public Report* (Ottawa: Minister of Public Works and Government Services, 2010).
32 Michael Goodyear, "Heaven or Earth: The Hagia Sophia Re-conversion, Turkish and International Law, and Universal Religious Sites" (2020) UCLA Journal of Islamic and Near Eastern Law.
33 Jean Gimpel, *The Cathedral Builders* (New York: Grove Press, 1961) at 86–7.
34 Michael D. McNally, *Honoring Elders. Aging, Authority and Ojibwe Religion* (New York: Columbia University Press, 2009) at 1.
35 *Ibid* at 1.
36 *Ibid* at 25.
37 *Ibid* at 291.
38 *Ibid* at 48.
39 *Ibid* at 282.
40 *Ibid* at 292.
41 Oliver W Holmes, "The Path of the Law" (1897) 10 Harv L Rev 457 at 477.
42 *Ibid* at 478.
43 Jennifer Nedelsky, Denise Réaume, Carol Rogerson, Kathy Swinton, Lorraine Weinrib were all professors at the University of Toronto Faculty of Law when I was a student (1986–1989). Influential feminist scholars at other law schools to whom my classmates and I were introduced through their work include Martha Minow, Lucinda Finley, Toni Pickard, and Carrie Menkel-Meadow.
44 John Borrows, *Law's Indigenous Ethics* (Toronto: University of Toronto Press, 2020), especially Chapter 6 (Honesty: Legal Education and Heroes, Tricksters, Monsters, and Caretakers).
45 *Ibid* at 183.
46 *Ibid* at 184.
47 Patrick Glenn, *Legal Traditions of the World* (Oxford: Oxford University Press, 2010).
48 James Boyd White, "Schooling Expectations" (2004) 54:4 J Leg Educ 499 at 502–3.

Epilogue

1 Shauna Van Praagh, "Teaching Law: 'Historian and Prophet All in One'" in Helge Dedek & Shauna Van Praagh, eds, *Stateless Law: Evolving Boundaries of a Discipline* (Farnham, Surrey: Ashgate, 2015) 23 at 30.

2 James Boyd White, "Augustine's 'Confessions' as Read by a Modern Law Teacher" (2014) 29:2 JL & Religion 330 at 335.
3 "[L]aw becomes not merely a system of rules to be observed, but a world in which we live." Robert M Cover, "The Supreme Court, 1982 Term. Foreword: Nomos and Narrative" (1983) 97:4 Harv L Rev 4 at 5.

Index